INDIAN SILVER JEWELRY OF THE SOUTHWEST

1868-1930

Overleaf:

A striking group of Navajo women are assembled at Fort Defiance, Arizona, in 1912. They are wearing their best finery, including trade blankets (and what seems to be a Plains Indian–influenced blanket, upper right), for this occasion. Several of the squash blossom necklaces are fine examples, and the dark blouses worn by most of the women are closed by a row of shiny silver buttons. These women proudly display their jewelry for all to admire; such adornments were considered by them to be an essential part of everyday living. Courtesy Southwest Museum, Los Angeles.

INDIAN SILVER JEWELRY OF THE SOUTHWEST

1868-1930

LARRY FRANK

with the assistance of Millard J. Holbrook II

NEW YORK GRAPHIC SOCIETY BOSTON

First Edition

Designed by Susan Windheim

LIBRARY OF CONGRESS CATALOGING IN PUBLICATION DATA
Frank, Lawrence Phillip.
    Indian silver jewelry of the Southwest, 1868–
1930.
    Bibliography: p.
    Includes index.
    1. Navaho Indians-Costume and adornment.
2. Indians of North America-Southwest, New–
Costume and adornment.   3. Jewelry-Southwest, New.
I. Holbrook, Millard J., joint author.   II. Title.
E99.N3F82   739.27'0979   78-7071
ISBN 0-8212-0740-7

New York Graphic Society books are published by Little, Brown and Company.
Published simultaneously in Canada by Little, Brown and Company (Canada) Limited.
Printed in the United States of America

Green turquoise in a dry, yellow land;
Green and blue lost in a giant's space;
Green fertility woven into myth;
Green, soft stone the reincarnation of a dead bloom;
Green reflecting the sky's underwater flow;
Green-blue stone on a somber, dark-earthed Navajo,
Green thoughts withered on the land of his face;
Green tipped and blue bodied run the rare storm drops;
Green turquoise in a dry, yellow land.

LARRY FRANK

✧ Acknowledgments

I would like to express my gratitude to Millard (Skip) Holbrook, whose indispensable contribution in writing the chapter "Techniques and History," the Chronology of Techniques, and the Glossary helped make this book possible. Also special thanks to Larry Klein of the Field Museum of Natural History, who gained for me access to the Field Museum's jewelry collection; Joe Ben Wheat, who opened up new avenues of important information; and Ross Frank, who rendered me invaluable assistance in compiling this book.

Additional color photographs for this book were made possible by a grant from the Graham Foundation for Advanced Studies in the Fine Arts.

⟡ Contents

INDIAN SILVER JEWELRY OF THE SOUTHWEST

1868-1930

1. This photograph of the 1890s shows a young Navajo woman with a horse outfitted with a Navajo silver bridle. Even by that relatively late date a bridle such as this one could only evoke esteem and pride for its owner for possessing such a valu- able item. Horses were considered worthy recipients of adornment of such quality. Courtesy Southwest Museum, Los Angeles. Photographed by George Wharton James and given to the museum in 1901.

CERTAINLY this book is a salute to the intrepid Navajo people, who have added much color, verve, and beauty to North American Indian art. "Beauty" is a quality the Navajos particularly appreciate; it is a repeated theme in their songs and chants and it is manifested directly in their weaving and jewelry. The same intensely felt appreciation for beauty is shared by the Pueblo Indians who live their lives in ceremonial splendor (of which jewelry plays an important part).

Set in a dry and austere environment where food and water are scarce, the seminomadic Navajos are all the more remarkable for their artistic accomplishments. They directed their creative energies toward blankets; sand paintings of great beauty, which were immediately erasable; and items of personal adornment that they could easily take with them since they were constantly on the move. They hardly ventured into pottery, which their sedentary Pueblo Indian neighbors made, because it was next to impossible to transport.

When the horse was introduced to the Navajos in the 1700s by the Spanish, it gave the Navajos mobility to raid and travel with their flocks of sheep. As with the Plains Indians, much of Navajo life became centered upon this animal. By the 1850s the Navajos used silver work and colorful blankets to adorn their horses, much as the Plains Indians bestowed feathers and bead-and-quill work upon them.

The life-style and arts of the Navajos paralleled those of another seminomadic, horse-oriented culture, Arab tribes living in the desert. Like the Arabs, the Navajos excelled in weaving and jewelry-making and functioned as a loose federation of tribes, each governed by its own chief or leader.

The Navajos are of Athapaskan stock and speak Athapaskan. Compared to the prehistoric entrance into the Southwest of the Pueblo Indians they came rather late, sometime in the sixteenth century. According to the most recent theory, they came essentially as raiders, not as farmers or food gatherers, and after crossing the land route into the Athapaskan areas of Alaska and Canada, they eventually descended into the Southwest region that is now New Mexico and Arizona. As raiders they struck terror into the hearts of the Pueblo Indians and, later, the Spanish settlers. The Navajo raised a few crops — corn, squash, beans — as well as some scraggly bands of sheep and goats, but mainly they plundered their Spanish and Pueblo Indian neighbors. Like the Plains Indians, their full strength and mobility were realized when they stole horses from the Spaniards.

Each clan or family lived in simple, mound-shaped shelters made of tamped earth reinforced with brush and wood, called hogans. These were sporadically scattered over the desert (like Arab tents); there existed no central community in the sense of the sophisticated Pueblo Indians with their adobe complexes and solidified social structure. Each Navajo family abandoned its hogan when necessary to seek food or water, which was quite often the case, due to frequent environmental disasters.

But when the call to arms came, given by some local clan leader commanding his own band, suddenly the desert came alive with thundering horsemen, hailing from separate hogans but threading together into a formidable, collective raiding force. The Pueblo Indians were generally overwhelmed, the Spanish held their own; and it took a concerted effort by United States government troops to convert the Navajos from raiding to a life of sheep raising and marginal farming.

Although jewelry-making and blanket-weaving were not native to the Navajos, they were quick to learn these crafts from their neighbors, through conflict, social contact, and assimilation. Both the Navajos and Spanish made raids upon each other and took captives. The Navajos grasped new concepts and adapted easily to new situations, abilities in which they have always excelled. Whatever fields they entered, they literally took over and became undisputed masters. In the domains of jewelry and textiles the Pueblo Indians made significant contributions, but the Navajos focused on these arts with such bursts of energy that they made them their own.

The emergence of Southwest silver jewelry took a long and diffuse course. From 1821 to 1846 the Spanish and Mexicans were the main sources of trade items into the Southwest. Trade fairs in Pueblo centers such as Taos and Pecos, New Mexico, flourished. Silver crosses, brass and copper ornaments, even European glass beads and other objects came tortuously up from Mexico and were traded to the peaceful Pueblo Indians who lived under the domain of the Spanish and then the Mexican governments. The Navajos not only raided the Spanish in New Mexico; they traded with them as well. At the Indian trade fairs they traded with the Pueblo tribes who assembled together for such important occasions; these gatherings also attracted the Apaches, Utes, Comanches, Plains Apaches, and other Plains tribes.

In 1846 Mexico lost its sovereignty over New Mexico, which became a territorial possession of the United States. Outwardly the daily life of the New Mexican and Indian populace remained relatively unchanged, but the supply routes from Mexico to El Paso to Santa Fe and points leading into Navajo land began to shrivel as the bustling settlers from the expanding United States choked off Mexican trade avenues by supplying goods from Missouri and the East.

During the decline of the Spanish Empire in this period, the Plains Indian nations were on the rise. They began to make coveted silver and metal ornaments, based on European prototypes traded to Eastern and Woodland Indians in the seventeenth and eighteenth centuries. By the early 1860s an enormous amount of handsome silver and German silver (a nickel alloy) jewelry decorated the Plains people, who had evolved their own individual style of silver concha-like hair plates and belts, pectoral ornaments, and bridles with crescent pendants, bracelets, and rings. The Plains Indians were at their greatest strength then and, coincidentally, the Navajos were enjoying their strongest raiding days before the United States Army abruptly ended them.

There were many opportunities for the Navajos to win Plains Indian booty. Both the Plains tribes and the Navajos raided into Southern Plains areas on the borders of New Mexico. Throughout the eighteenth and nineteenth centuries the Comanches, who were devoted traders, brought goods of all kinds to trade with the Spanish and the Navajos and other Indians at the Taos Pueblo trade fairs. Furthermore, the Spanish and the Pueblo Indians made extensive journeys into Comanche territory to conduct trade (called the Comanchero trade), and much material, such as imported cloth and metal items, fell into the hands of the raiding Navajos. The Utes and Apaches who traded with the Plains people also raided in New Mexico, and tro-

2. This Navajo "warshirt," circa 1840–1850, is illustrated here to show the diverse influences upon the Navajos, through trade materials and trade routes, during the period before they were making silver jewelry.

The "warshirt" appears to be a locally made copy of a Spanish military jacket made of standard trade items with the addition of certain pure Indian elements. During this period it was common practice for the Spanish to give Indian head men, whose favor they wished to cultivate, fancy military dress uniforms with brass buttons and heavy wool cloth. After the United States took over New Mexico in 1846 this practice continued, and other goods were given, such as the cloth called stroud list cloth, in the Plains regions and bayeta in the Southwest.

Half of this jacket is made of blue list cloth and half of red list cloth. On the red side is a small rectangular flap of blue list cloth ornamented with flat brass buttons (also called Ute buttons). The buttons were trade items throughout the Southwest and Southern Plains area during this period. On the blue side there is a similar flap made of red cloth also ornamented with brass buttons. These flaps were made to simulate the pocket flaps of a military jacket. Sometime after aniline dye was introduced into the Southwest (after 1865), the red

side of the shirt was repaired leaving the earlier cochineal dyed list cloth exposed only across the bottom. Buckskin panels of early design and with early style pony beads were sewn onto the sleeves and across the shoulders of the shirt. As beadwork developed across the Plains territory in the early 1800s it also developed to some extent among the Navajos, much as the use of silver ornaments spread from the Plains Indians to the Navajos in the 1860s and 1870s. As soon as the Navajos began making silver jewelry for ornamentation they stopped producing beadwork. The beaded designs used by the Navajos, heavy triangular elements and blocky bands and rectangles, were the same designs then in use by the Southern Plains Indians and the Apaches. The beaded panels here are edged with long, finely cut buckskin fringes, characteristically a Plains Indian trait.

The shirt was collected from a Navajo "chief" around 1850 by a Pueblo Indian who accompanied one of the United States punitive expeditions against the Navajos. Both the pony beads and that particular type of brass button went out of use by 1850. The shirt was used in the ceremonial dances of one of the Rio Grande pueblos until about 1970. Courtesy University of Colorado, Boulder.

phies of valuable jewelry became the property of each warrior camp. The Navajos received Plains booty and, impressed with the Plains forms and techniques, were inspired to try to re-create them. Most of the Plains Indian ornaments are rocker-engraved or filed, both on silver and on the relatively newly arrived German silver. The thin and delicately tight designs on Plains Indian rocker-engraved jewelry hark back to a European tradition of penmanship and lettering. These designs could have come from the British and French through the eastern colonists or from the Spanish in the Southwest. The Navajos made their own renditions. This influence of Plains Indian prototypes on Navajo jewelry, which has been largely ignored, will be shown in the illustrations and discussed in the captions.

In 1863 the Navajos were defeated by United States government soldiers and herded into a camp for confinement. There they wasted away for five years before they were released and allowed to walk back to their homelands. At Bosque Redondo they had proven that they were not farmers and did not want to farm extensively. By this time all shreds and roots of their former mode of living had been completely shattered and they had to begin all over again. Their meager, hard-earned crops and carefully planted peach trees had been destroyed; their hogans were in disarray; their religious shrines unused and abandoned. They had been forced to leave their homelands where their gods dwelled, and to live an existence totally alien to their very being. But somehow they managed to avoid a cultural holocaust that would have eliminated them as a people. They overcame a disaster of incomparable suffering; they kept their holy land of myths and reversed the relentless historical fate that had ruined so many Indian tribes. They went home. That year, 1868, marks the beginning of what we call the first phase of Southwest Indian jewelry.

Just before their internment at Bosque Redondo, the Navajos had some exposure to iron metalworking. Spanish blacksmiths had shown this craft to at least one early Navajo smith, who made iron buckles, bits, and horse trappings with elementary tooled designs. Cheaper metals such as brass and copper were also used to produce some of the earliest bracelets. During the intern-

3. The photograph, circa 1880s, is labeled "Tom Torleno, Navajo boy, as he came to Carlisle." Before Tom was made to conform to the White Man's image of a gentleman, he wore long hair, a headband, a pair of old silver loop earrings, a Pueblo-style double-barred silver cross necklace with many small crosses and an odd-shaped silver cross which resembles a German silver example in the Lynn D. Trusdell Collection (Figure 174). One wonders whether he was allowed to keep his possessions after completely changing his dress and life-style at the school which was his destination. Courtesy Smithsonian Institution, National Anthropological Archives.

ment some Navajos already wore simple silver items, mostly of Ute and Plains origin, and some may have tentatively tried working with silver. When the Navajos were released and established again in their homeland, the blacksmiths, now turned novice silversmiths, resumed their training. Using makeshift tools of castoff broken pieces from metalworking trades, the Navajos changed gradually from working with iron to working with silver.

In much the same way that symbols of status

4. An old-style, flat silver naja with knoblike terminals is shown on this Hopi man from Mishongovi village. The early necklaces had no squash blossoms strung between silver beads, only a naja. Photograph taken between 1903 and 1911. Courtesy Field Museum of Natural History, Chicago.

and wealth were the principal concerns of the Northwest Coast Indians, jewelry came to fill a similar role for the Navajo. A rich man might own a good many sheep but he and his family would also be the proud possessors of a large quantity of silver jewelry, which would proclaim for them a certain rank and respect. In the 1870s only the relatively wealthy who were friends of a silversmith could own jewelry, since the metal was quite difficult to obtain and very costly. There was great pestige in being a silversmith; he was almost a priest at his craft, and his knowledge and output were in great demand among the Navajos.

The production of silver jewelry accelerated at the end of the 1870s. The desire for silver ornaments spread rapidly throughout the Southwest; these ornaments found their way into the Pueblo villages such as Laguna and Acoma, where the Pueblo Indians started to learn the craft themselves. Jewelry-making techniques were steadily refined. In the 1890s turquoise began to be set in silver — a natural and inspired marriage which, in retrospect, ensured the popularity of Indian jewelry.

After the turn of the century the Navajos were renowned as silversmiths, and the Fred Harvey hotel chain began to promote the manufacture and sale of Indian jewelry to tourists (a development that took twenty years to be widespread). To meet this demand a craft industry began to emerge, first among the Navajo Indians and then among the Zuni silversmiths, who by 1915 were establishing their own jewelry styles. The rest of the Pueblos were soon to follow. With this development the first period (1868–1900) of first phase Southwestern silver jewelry ended.

Initially the infant tourist market was a stimulus to fine craftsmanship. Tradition and the isolation of many of the silversmiths in the remotest regions of the Navajo Reservation and Pueblo villages kept much of the workmanship of the highest order. Cheaper silversmithing material furnished by the traders (such as Fred Harvey) had not yet affected these areas. There was an aura of excitement among the silversmiths who faced the challenge demanded by the mastery of continually advanced tools and techniques. By the 1920s the tourist trade in the Southwest began to reach large proportions and Indians started to design and make jewelry mainly for non-Indian use. Because the market for their jewelry had significantly increased and reached some measure of stability, more Indian silversmiths could expand their pastime into a profession. During the 1920s many imaginative and varied pieces were created.

In the transitional period, from about 1900 to 1930, the tourist market finally dominated the production of jewelry and brought an end to first phase jewelry-making. Indians were no longer making silver jewelry solely for their own use, and manufactured material, modern techniques, and ornate new designs were prevalent. By 1930 the second phase of Southwest jewelry-making was firmly established. Even the Indians were wearing the newer styles. Nineteen-thirty is a relatively arbitrary date, but is chosen because new techniques

5. This photograph, labeled "Man in costume: Nai-u-chi," shows a Zuni Pueblo Indian wearing both a double-crescent and single-crescent naja strung on one strand of silver squash blossoms and beads. The najas are of the old style and gleam against his old, hand-woven woolen shirt. A small strand of beads, possibly made of brass, is around his neck. Courtesy Museum of the American Indian, Heye Foundation, New York.

6. Two squash blossom necklaces, with the blossoms placed closely together and next to the najas, adorn this Navajo woman from Arizona. The jewelry dates from the 1920s. The front naja is most probably sandcast, with a silver star as a drop. The blouse ornament consists of a string of silver quarters. The woman is wearing a pair of unbezeled turquoise earrings. Courtesy Museum of the American Indian, Heye Foundation, New York.

7. This photograph is labeled "Portrait of Juana Maria, circa 1912. Isleta Pueblo, New Mexico." Her magnificent Pueblo Indian silver cross necklace teems with myriad silver crosses and a double-barred silver cross pendant. She wears a second double-barred cross pendant with a round base, hanging from a necklace strung with turquoise beads. Isleta was one of the main pueblos where these silver cross necklaces were made and used. Courtesy Museum of the American Indian, Heye Foundation, New York.

were in widespread use and the momentum and vitality of the older styles had ended.

A determined effort has been made in this book to study some of the changes in styles and techniques of first phase Navajo jewelry-making. The later Pueblo jewelry is not covered as fully in the text, which emphasizes the earliest developments. However, many Pueblo Indian items are illustrated and are discussed in the captions. Although the Apache Indians made a certain amount of silver jewelry in the Southwest, mostly of German silver, their jewelry is not treated here. The captions to the photographs are essential to the

reader's understanding of the subject, for they impart much historic and artistic information about the hundreds of pieces illustrated.

Considerable attention and study have been directed to the history of silver jewelry-making, and notable contributions have added to our knowledge of the early silversmiths (see Selective Bibliography). But this book focuses on the early jewelry itself, an approach that is long overdue. This neglect is caused in part by lack of perspective in the 1930s and 1940s about the importance of Indian jewelry: why it should be collected, and in what directions modern jewelry would develop. Few pieces were collected by museums before 1900 and even fewer were recorded with adequate collection data. Although all documentation is helpful, many of these items were acquired haphazardly or by donation, and at a relatively late date.

Even when collections are intact with a proper provenance, it is difficult to date Indian jewelry according to styles and techniques. Specific attributes may be identified, but because they occur repeatedly, it can be said only that a design motif or a kind of tool was in general use within a certain period and not when the use began or ended. Styles and techniques changed at a rate that depended on how close the silversmiths were to relatively populated centers serviced by railroads. A style would continue to be utilized in a remote and isolated region of the Navajo Reservation for some time after it had been abandoned in the cities. Gallup, with its gathering of Indian traders and its railroad lines to larger markets, caused rapid changes in local jewelry styles and techniques.

This book does not include modern or contemporary jewelry, but some comments about them are in order. As markets changed and tastes evolved, Southwest silver jewelry has become a national cultural success. Through its regionalism and its origins deep in Navajo and Pueblo Indian lands, it has been adopted by the American public as the only distinctive American jewelry. Millions of Americans receive pleasure from owning contemporary Indian jewelry, even though it is made with a wide variety of professional standards. Some modern jewelry is made by non-Indians or manufactured on assembly lines, and some is created by individual artists working with untraditional elements such as gold and various gems. It is obvious that such jewelry has effectively appealed to popular taste because of its uniqueness, diversity, vividness, reasonable price, and, one might add, basic aesthetic quality. The price structure varies, but most Indian jewelry caters to the average pocketbook. No longer need a marriage be sealed by a diamond ring; a woman can be married with an Indian turquoise ring instead, either old or new. The incorporation of an exotic, so-called primitive style into our life-style (again

one is reminded of Arab jewelry) has in part displaced our American-European practice of shopping at middle-class jewelry stores selling middle-grade diamonds. Although the popular vogue might change to a degree, there is no doubt of the permanent imprint Southwest Indian jewelry has made on American taste.

First phase jewelry occupies a significant niche in jewelry-making of the world. Several factors have contributed to its stature. While not necessarily prolific in their output, the early silversmiths made a good amount of quality jewelry well into the first years of the twentieth century. Collectively the jewelry forged an original style that caused a considerable impact. Jewelry-making became a popular and integral part of the Navajo and Pueblo economy and way of living, and by means of its explosive vitality it won for itself world recognition.

Most of all, however, the aesthetic quality of Navajo and Pueblo silver jewelry is responsible for its fame. Whether the jewelry owes its origins to Spanish, Mexican, or Plains Indians roots, or a combination of some or all of these sources, the fact is that at its finest it possesses a rich artistic integrity and imagination. The great variety of designs on beaten silver, often coupled with an extraordinary profusion of turquoise stones of all shades, colors, and textures, emerges in the hands of Navajo and Pueblo artists as strikingly strong and unerringly right in pattern and design. Motifs abstracted from nature — suns, flowers, leaves and petals, stars and moons — are caught in a stunning diversity of dynamic forms and spatial relationships. For all its range of design complexity, the jewelry usually manages to avoid a baroque busyness and fussiness that often mars other well-executed styles of jewelry. Its essence is expressionistic. Long-standing Indian traditions shape the jewelry and engender a certain thrust of concentrated power. That is why Indian jewelry holds its place and fascination; it goes beyond mere ornament and makes a forceful and imaginative statement of a creative people.

Techniques and History

ALTHOUGH the Indians of the Southwest probably began making personal adornment out of bone and shell upon their arrival in the area over ten thousand years ago, they did not work metal to any great extent until relatively recently. As we have seen, silversmithing and the wearing of silver jewelry became an important part of their life only during the last quarter of the nineteenth century.

The techniques used in the first phase of silversmithing can be divided roughly into those of construction and those of decoration (see the chronology on page 205). The chief construction techniques developed in the following sequence: using existing metal (usually wire, coins, or sheet metal cut from brass pans); casting ingots to be forged; casting into shape; and soldering and bezel setting. The major decorative techniques developed in this order: filing, rocker-engraving, chisel-marking, repoussé, stamping, and embossing. Although there seems to be evidence that confirms this sequence (e.g., collection dates on pieces in the Smithsonian Institution, the Field Museum, and the School of American Research), it should be remembered that all of these techniques were in use within fifteen years after the return from Bosque Redondo. Sequencing thus can help in identifying or dating a piece, but it is not foolproof.

Because distances were great, natural resources few, and populations sparse and often nomadic, trade with the eastern United States did not develop and the equipment and techniques of the early smiths remained quite limited until about 1900. Their tools included bellows to raise and concentrate the heat of a charcoal fire, a crucible in which to melt the silver (a fragment of a Pueblo pot or a small, thick-walled vessel made for the purpose), and an anvil (either a smooth hard rock or a heavy piece of iron). A hammer, iron tongs to lift the hot crucible and to hold stamps or punches during forging and tempering, one or more files, and a cold chisel or two completed the inventory.

◈ Construction

Some of the very early metalwork was done using copper or brass, but silver was always preferred. The primary source of material for jewelry

8. This photograph, circa 1900, is labeled "Navajo silversmith and grandson working the bellows." The silversmith is displaying his recently made wares and his collection of tools. All the jewelry seems to be made out of plain silver without turquoise, and there are a great many silver spoons. The hammers are of the modern type and what seems to be an anvil made from an old sledgehammer is set on the wooden log. The man is wearing a string of silver beads with old squash blossoms strung at the bottom. Courtesy Southwest Museum, Los Angeles.

was silver coins, since no mines were being worked in the area, as Coronado found out. An interesting mystique has developed concerning the use of coin silver in early jewelry. It is often heard that the beauty of the early coin silver is due to its unique shine and color, to say nothing of its guaranteed age (restrictions were placed on the use of coinage in this manner by the United States government in 1890). The truth is that any differences among United States coins, Mexican pesos, and sterling silver (which was used after 1900) are impossible to discern by visual examination. Variations may indeed be noticed, but they are probably caused by the texture of and wear on the silver, or result from the alloys added or burned off by the smith during the casting process. The presence of coin silver, even if established by chemical analysis, is of little value for indicating age, since U.S. coinage continued to be used by some smiths after World War II, and the fakers use it even now.

Due to the size and thickness of jewelry preferred by the Southwest Indians prior to 1900, it was necessary for a smith to melt down several coins and cast them into an ingot, which he then hammered into a sheet and worked into a finished piece, rather than fashioning the ornament from a single coin as craftsmen throughout the world have done.

The earliest work was hammered to as smooth a finish as possible, then ground with stones or filed, and finally polished with sand or ashes, sandpaper not being available until the 1880s, and scarce even then. On most old silver that we see today the surfaces have been smoothed by use and repeated polishing. When an object that was collected at an early date and never used is examined, the rough, irregular marks left by the stones, used instead of files, can often still be seen. Throughout the first phase files were used whenever available; by 1900 stones were seldom used to smooth silver.

Since Frank Hamilton Cushing, who lived in Zuni Pueblo from 1879 to 1881, is the only early observer to mention the Indian technology for the production of sheet metal and wire his observations are of particular interest:

[I] practically and thoroughly learned the art of metal-working as practiced by the Zuni Indians, having often seen and helped them make perfectly uniform plates as well as extremely thin sheets of copper and silver by alternate hammering and annealing, then grinding with sandstone, first one face, then the other, to form uniform leaves of the metal. . . .[1]

Draw-plates made from the scapulae of deer were formerly used by Zuni and other Indian metal-workers of the Southwest in forming silver and copper wire from slender hammered rods of those metals. The holes in these draw-plates were very numerous and nicely graded from coarse to fine, and wax mixed with tallow was freely used to facilitate the passage of the rods through them. The rods were not, however, unless very slender, drawn through merely, as in our corresponding operation with the steel draw-plate, but were passed through by a combination of pushing and pulling, accompanied by a twisting motion, just as arrow-shafts are rounded and straightened in a perforated horn plate.[2]

Although Cushing was well aware of the importance of the annealing process in shaping silver, many observers since then have not understood the process. All work, such as thinning by hammering, bending, stamping, and drawing wire, is done on silver while it is cold, since it becomes very weak and crumbly when at a dull red heat. Working the metal cold creates internal stresses that make it very hard and will eventually cause it to crack if the tensions are not released. This is done by annealing, or heating the silver to a barely visible red color and then quenching it in water.

In addition to hammering cast silver ingots into sheets, Navajo silversmiths made pieces directly from stone molds into which designs were carved. Carving a design in the mold took considerably more time than simply preparing it for ingot casting. Cleaning up the piece after casting was also very time-consuming, so the technique was not used as often as forging ingots.

Sandstone was apparently used first for these molds, followed by tuff, or tuffa. In order to get a successful cast, several things had to be done that were not necessary when casting an ingot. Instead of a simple depression in the stone into which molten metal was poured, a two-piece mold had to be constructed, complete with sprue hole and air

[1] Frank Hamilton Cushing, "Primitive Copper Working: An Experimental Study," The American Anthropologist 7 (Jan. 1894): 93.
[2] Ibid., p. 99.

9. Enhancing the strong features of this Hopi Indian is a pair of old silver loop-and-ball earrings. His necklace is composed of old U.S. Liberty Head dimes or possibly fifty-cent pieces, which were easily converted into cash in order to buy goods. Photograph taken at Mishongovi village between 1903 and 1911. Courtesy Field Museum of Natural History, Chicago.

10. The silver squash blossom necklace on this man from Sichomovi village (Hopi) has a naja with a silver fluted drop, shaped and grooved like a shell, and silver buttonlike forms soldered onto the terminals. As seems to be common in those times, he is also wearing a long necklace of U.S. Liberty Head dimes. Photograph taken between 1903 and 1911. Courtesy Field Museum of Natural History, Chicago.

vents. The stone also had to be coated with a finely powdered charcoal, or smoked, so that the molten metal would flow into the entire design rather than freezing up in the more deeply carved spaces. Pieces cast in this manner were not flattened into a sheet but were filed and sanded until smooth, then bent into the required shape by hammering over an anvil or other rounded form. Buckles, bracelets, buttons, rings, *najas*, and *ketohs* (see Glossary) were all produced by this technique during the first phase. A similar method of casting was used by the Chinese during the Shang Dynasty (ca. 1766–1122 B.C.) to make weapons. The use of this technique in the manufacturing of jewelry, however, seems to be uniquely Navajo.

An important tool for even the most basic work was the cold chisel. Like the file, it was used in both silver construction and decoration throughout the first phase period. Because saws, even hacksaws, were not readily available until the turn of the century, all cutting on early work was done with a chisel. There were several advantages to its use: it cut fast and caused no loss of material as sawdust, and it was readily available or could be made from a scrap of steel. The cold chisel had a straight edge, usually about one-half inch in length. Cuts made with the tool were smooth and tapered in from top to bottom. The fact that tightly curved lines could not be cut with it probably accounts for the straight-sided "diamond slot" openings on early conchas. The versatile tool was also used to cut sheet silver to shape, and to remove sprues from castings.

Most contemporary silversmiths would probably agree that by far the most difficult technique to master in making jewelry is soldering. If silver soldering is hard today, using modern torches, easy-melting solders, and fluxes that have been formulated by chemical engineers, think what the early Navajo silversmith was confronted with. Each smith had to make his own solder by combining silver filings with brass filings from old pans or cartridge cases. This mixture was then placed at the joint to be soldered, together with some rudimentary flux, usually borax. The prepared pieces were placed in the coals of the forge and the whole works brought to a red glow, just a few hundred degrees below the melting point of the material. At this point, if the smith was lucky,

the solder would flow and the pieces stick together. More often than not the solder needed additional heat; the smith supplied this with a small wick lamp and a blowpipe with which he blew the flame onto the solder. If things went right, only the solder melted, and the joint was successfully completed. All too often, though, the separate pieces were knocked out of position as the coals shifted, or the solder did not adhere to the silver because the pieces had become oxidized during the heating. When the soldering process failed, the smith had to start over again, hoping the next try would be more successful, or to abandon the soldering and find another way to do the job. The first attempts at soldering were made no later than 1875, with little relief from the problems mentioned above until the early 1900s, when better solders, fluxes, and torches were introduced.

Evidence of alternative solutions to soldering includes bracelets and ketohs which appear to have been designed for a setting but were left blank; conchas attached to the belt by a bar that was an integral part of the piece rather than by a loop soldered on the back (see Figure 198); and najas that were suspended from a hole drilled in a part of the casting rather than an attached loop. Although it is usually assumed that the use of copper or brass for loops on buttons and later on conchas was a matter of economy, there was another good reason for not using silver. Both copper and brass have a higher melting point than silver, making the soldering job much easier, since the smith did not have to worry about the loop melting at the same time the solder started to flow. Where soldering was attempted, work can be seen that has been overheated almost to the point of melting the piece, and large patches of a poor-flowing granular yellowish solder are often left as evidence.

Just before 1880 Dr. Washington Matthews, an early observer, watched smiths who, despite these difficulties, were doing complex construction and soldering on powder chargers and miniature silver canteens (popular curio items made to order for soldiers), tasks that would be considered difficult even with today's equipment.[3]

[3] Dr. Matthews was an assistant surgeon in the U.S. Army stationed at Fort Wingate, New Mexico, where he hired two Navajo silversmiths to make various objects in silver to observe them firsthand. His findings as well as other information from observers and general study in the area were published in the B.A.E. Annual Report of 1881.

By the turn of the century, these early soldering problems were mastered, and the improved technical ability of the smiths was reflected in the increasing complexity of the jewelry being made. One of the most significant developments was the setting of stones in silver jewelry — an impossibility until the rudiments of soldering were learned. By the 1880s there were smiths proficient enough at soldering to make bezels, or "housings," for stones. The first sets were usually small garnets or turquoise beads. The bezel came up straight along the sides of the stone and was then bent over the top or face of the stone to hold it in place. Until the turn of the century stones were not widely used in Southwest Indian jewelry. Most turquoise cutting at that time was done by the Zuni and some of the other Pueblos located along the Rio Grande River, the stones being strung into necklaces or stuck to wood or shell with pitch — mosaic fashion — for pendants, earbobs, and other ornaments. In fact, Indian jewelry made well into the 1940s can usually be identified as Navajo if the silver is emphasized, and Zuni if the emphasis is on lapidary work. In time the Navajo smith did use turquoise in his work, at first trade pieces that had been ground by Pueblo Indians, and a short time later large cabochon forms that he ground himself or obtained from traders.

Altered and imitation turquoise appeared soon after the stone came into use. Many stones naturally became darker and greener with wear as they absorbed skin oils, and this process was sometimes speeded up by the application of mutton fat or lard to lighter-colored stones. The first actual imitation turquoise was introduced by Lorenzo Hubbel about 1900 when he imported glass beads and cabochons that looked enough like fine turquoise to fool many people even today. These were the major forms of enhancement or deception concerning turquoise until plastic began being used in the 1940s.

◈ Decoration

The two decorative techniques that were most often used prior to 1880, when they were superseded by stamping, were rocker-engraving and cutting designs into the metal with a file. Rocker-engraving is done with a small, flat, chisel-edged tool, approximately 2 mm. on edge, which is placed on the metal and pushed forward while at the same time it is "rocked" from corner to corner, producing a zig-zag line that can be run straight or traced around a curvilinear design. By 1875, rocker-engraved decoration had been more or less abandoned, probably because the design did not show up as well as stamping and, being quite shallow, tended to wear away rapidly. Filing continued to be used occasionally for decoration, but the longer time involved, compared to stamping a design, probably accounts for its lack of popularity.

There is evidence that some of the earliest decorative stamping was done with only a cold chisel, but by 1885 there is no doubt that other stamps were being used. Most of the old photographs lack sufficient detail to show stamped designs on the jewelry being worn, which has led some people to the conclusion that stamping was not used during the 1880s. Careful observation of the jewelry styles in photographs from that period, however, indicates that the pieces then being worn are indeed those that, when examined in the museums today, have very competent stamp work on them.

Stamps and cold chisels were both made in the same way. A piece of carbon steel, usually a section of a worn-out file, was heated until it turned a glowing orange color. It was then pulled from the fire with iron tongs and held on the anvil, where it was shaped by hammering. After the rough shape was obtained, the tool was heated again to a glowing red color and allowed to cool very slowly. The slow cooling took the temper out of the steel and allowed the smith to file in the final details of the design. After the filing was completed, the design end of the tool was again brought to a red heat and quenched immediately in water to harden it. The tool was then cleaned down to the bare metal and again heated very gently, until the exposed metal turned a golden yellow color, and was again quenched. This last step put the temper in the metal, giving it enough hardness to keep it from bending but leaving it soft enough to prevent it from splitting or chipping when struck. A variation of the design process, which is occasionally seen on stamp work of about

1880–1900, was to strike the end of a red-hot or annealed stamp-blank against the face of a file. This left the impression of the file teeth on the punch. The tool was then tempered in the usual way. When a punch made in this manner was used, it produced the so-called end-of-a-file design referred to by Harry P. Mera.[4]

A technique frequently used to give dimension to silver, prior to the use of dies, was repoussé. Buttons, bow guards, headstalls, bracelets, buckles, and other ornaments were decorated in this manner. Repoussé was done by placing the blank sheet of annealed silver face down on a piece of wood and then doming the metal from the back with a hammer and rounded punches. After the design was hammered in from the back, the piece was turned over and shaped and the repoussé design was sharpened or further defined by filing. Stamp decoration was often added at this time to complete the piece.

The look of Southwest Indian jewelry was altering constantly during the first phase. With most objects the difference was stylistic or aesthetic, but with buttons the main factor was changing technology that enabled the maker to turn out work more rapidly. Several different methods were used to make and decorate silver buttons. The earliest buttons were domed out by hammering them into the end of a log with a punch or ball peen hammer. By 1880 sets of male and female dies were made to form plain-dome buttons. Buttons marked with a radiating design, made with a cold chisel and sharpened by filing, came within five years, and then around 1900 a single punch was designed that could put the entire design on at one time. Both the cold-chisel and single-stamped buttons were placed in a male-female die and domed out after being decorated.

Another variation of button decoration, used about 1900, was heavy fluting. This was first done one ridge at a time by punching a section of the button into a notch filed into an anvil or a small block of steel. All the tools used to decorate buttons were made in the same manner as the punches, with the exception of the female dies, which often were not tempered (see Figure 12).

[4] Harry P. Mera, *Indian Silverwork of the Southwest Illustrated — Volume One* (Globe, Ariz.: Dale Stuart King, 1960), pp. 10, 72, 91.

11. This pair of old forged-iron snips used to cut tin or sheets of silver has marks on the blades showing that it was made out of old files. Most of the iron used to fashion tools came from files, sections of railroad track, and pieces of scrap iron. The wooden bow drill with its metal tip (made out of an old file) was used to drill turquoise, coral, and shell beads in order to string them onto necklaces. Private Collection.

Much of the jewelry created during the first phase are superb works of art. The smiths used great care and precision in executing their work. Seldom is a stamp misplaced, a shape out of balance, or an unwanted file or hammer mark left to distract the viewer. First phase work is often found to be worn and damaged from use but it is seldom crude, a fact often missed by the contemporary counterfeiters of this work.

The early smiths put to their own uses the techniques and designs learned from other cultures. The ornaments they made were heavy, in order to withstand wear, and the designs were bold and clean. Within fifteen years after the beginning of the first phase, there were smiths creating designs

12. Tools used by Navajo silversmiths to fashion first phase silver jewelry. The upper tool in the group of three to the left is a cold chisel used throughout the first phase period. It was used for cutting, stamping, and incising. The bottom right-hand piece of that group was used for repoussé work. The left-hand piece of that group is a slightly later type of button stamp which was used for stamping a piece of silver while it was flat and which was later domed with ball peen hammer on wood. This procedure was used circa 1900, before the male-female-type dies to the upper right (1910, male examples). To the center right is an old Navajo clay crucible used for holding melted silver. At bottom right are three early stamps and a later arrow stamp (circa 1900). At bottom left is a rectangular piece of scrap metal with patterns on all four sides (two sides shown) for decorating silver studs and small silver buttons. Metal was rare and the early silversmiths were economical. Often they collected scrap metal and utilized every inch of surface available. Many of the tools were fashioned from worn files. Also at bottom left are two early crescent-design stamps. The center block of scrap iron was used on both sides during at least three different periods for three different purposes; on the side showing, the wedge-shaped indentation was used for fluting buttons like the fluted one shown; the round hole was employed for punching out cone-shaped buttons and was very much used; and the female part of a male-female die was added later and serves to stress the scarcity of iron. Above at left is a round hole used for doming out early silver buttons like the two shown. The two top pieces are small embossing dies. Except for the later fluted female-type die, circa 1910, these tools date around 1890 to 1900. Private Collection.

by incorporating extensive stamped and filed elements. Despite this complexity, the decoration maintained a unity that gives the viewer a single design concept rather than a cluttered display of technique for its own sake.

◈ Origins

The Mexican *plateros* (silverworkers) are usually credited with teaching the Navajos silversmithing, in spite of the fact that the filigree and heavy reliance on delicate soldering that typifies *platero* work of the second half of the nineteenth century is absent in first phase Indian jewelry. But the Mexican influence can be explained in another way. The Indian silversmiths, hammering shapes out of silver, cutting them with a cold chisel, shaping them with a file, and decorating them with file, stamps, and occasional rocker-engraving, followed exactly the same processes that were then in use by Mexican blacksmiths to produce ironwork. Even the process of soldering, although not usually associated with blacksmithing, has a close corollary in the technique known as forge-brazing, by which small iron objects such as keys are put together with a "solder" of copper or brass.

In the austere frontier environment of the Southwest, the work of the Mexican blacksmith was not always strictly utilitarian — many personal items and the hardware on doors and furniture were often decorated. Filed decoration and silver inlays with rocker-engraving occur on eighteenth- and nineteenth-century spurs. Perhaps the most telling comparison is between the hardware on old chests and first phase conchas. Virtually every detail on the conchas can be found on much of the old ironwork — the scalloped edges, the stamped crescent designs, and even the curious holes around the edges (see Figures 205, 206).

A great deal of attention has also been drawn to the similarity of silver stamps used by the Navajos to stamped designs on Mexican leatherwork. The entire range of stamp designs used on first phase silverwork is also found on nineteenth-century Mexican leatherwork. With the exception of a few designs introduced by traders about 1900, notably the swastika and arrow designs, even today the stamps in use are limited to the original Mexican inventory. This comparison again leads us to the Mexican blacksmith, for it was he who made the leatherworker's stamps. He also made stamps for use on tinware and on his own forged iron articles. Making a stamp is a complex procedure that goes beyond simply copying designs from leather or having access to fine files. The Mexican blacksmith, not the leatherworker, had to teach the Navajo how to make stamps, and with this technical knowledge went a design vocabulary as well. This theory is supported by a statement made by Grey Moustache, recorded by John Adair in 1938.[5] Grey Moustache said that his teacher, known to the Navajos as Atsidi Sani, was the first Navajo to learn silversmithing and that Atsidi Sani's teacher was Nakai Tsosi, a Mexican blacksmith. Thus, based on visual evidence and the Navajo oral tradition, it seems apparent that the Mexican *plateros* and leatherworkers probably had very little to do with the beginning of Southwest Indian jewelry.

Although Nakai Tsosi taught Atsidi Sani both ironworking and the techniques applicable to silversmithing, neither Nakai Tsosi nor any other blacksmith made jewelry. That idea was Navajo — and within ten years after their release from Bosque Redondo in 1868 the making and wearing of silver jewelry by many of the Southwest Indian tribes was firmly established.

At least three objects — the concha belt, the crescent pendant or naja, and the metal-covered bridle — seem to be derivative of similar items used extensively by the Southern Plains Indians. The evolution of the concha belt is particularly interesting. Disklike silver ornaments, called hair plates, were being traded to the eastern Indians by white men as early as 1750. At first these ornaments were worn singly, attached to the hair close to the head. By 1820 the use of hair plates had spread to the Central and Southern Plains area, and rather than wearing a single ornament, the men would string several together on a piece of cloth, horsehair, or leather. The decoration was still attached closely to the scalp but continued to grow in length until the 1880s, when the total length of a hair plate might reach six feet (Figure 13). While a man wearing such a hair plate was sitting, the ornament was

[5] John Adair, *The Navajo and Pueblo Silversmiths* (Norman: University of Oklahoma Press, 1944).

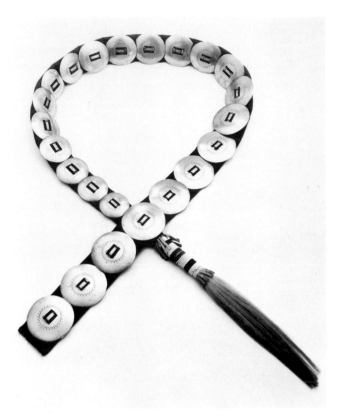

13. The early Kiowa Indian German silver hair plates resemble early Navajo silver concha belts. This excellent example even has center slot–type openings. The rocker-engraved conchas relate to the early conchas shown in the Smithsonian Institution's collection (see Figures 42, 43) and to the rocker-engraved conchas on the headstalls in the Museum of the American Indian (Figure 79) and in the Laboratory of Anthropology (Figure 116). The hair plates belonged to Wooden Lance, a Kiowa chief, and are attached to folded red trade cloth. Courtesy Denver Art Museum; photo by John Youngblut.

pulled under the right arm and draped across his lap, looking very much like a concha belt. In fact, Plains Indian women did, on occasion, wear hair plates wrapped around them as belts, with the excess length trailed down to one side (Figure 14). The Navajos took the Plains Indian idea of a decorative belt of metal disks, changed the material from German silver to silver, and decorated the conchas with techniques and designs learned from the Mexicans. The result was so successful that for years the concha belt has been synonymous with Navajo silversmithing in most people's minds,

while the Plains Indian origin of the concept has faded into seldom-mentioned and often confused academic footnotes.

The idea of taking a basic practice and changing the material, working techniques, and decorative elements occurred with two other objects from the Plains: the crescent-type naja decoration (see Figure 179) and the metal-decorated bridle (see Figure 80). Both the open and closed crescent design used by the Southwest Indians occurred frequently in Plains Indian metalwork, at the end of ear pendants, as a center pendant on headstalls, and as the bottom-most decoration on pectorals, where it was used singly or in number. Navajo bridles made in the last quarter of the nineteenth century were constructed in almost exactly the same way as the metal-covered bridles in use by the Indians of the Plains throughout the century. Mexican horsemen of the nineteenth century used similar decorations. Whether the Navajos got the headstall design from the Mexicans or the Plains Indians is not known.

Norman Feder has concluded that the Plains Indians were wearing and making their own metal adornments at the beginning of the nineteenth century.[6] Silver and brass were the metals most often used until the 1860s, when German silver, or white brass, was introduced. Until 1880, metalworking flourished among the Plains Indians, but then nearly died out because of the ready availability of such ornaments and their subsequent drop in prestige value. The bulk of early Plains metalwork was accomplished by hammering, cutting with a chisel, occasional file work, and decorative engraving utilizing the rocker, or scratch, technique. The use of stamps began sometime after the introduction of German silver. Hard soldering, casting, and the setting of stones were never utilized in the Plains area.

While the technology needed to produce Southwest jewelry could only be learned through close contact over an extended period of time with a person skilled in the craft, style concepts, such as those which apparently came from the Plains Indians, could be passed on in a much faster manner. The raiding and trading that took place whenever Navajo and Plains Indians met are probably where these ideas were exchanged.

[6] Norman Feder, "Plains Indian Metal Working," *American Indian Tradition*, vol. 7 (1962), nos. 2, 3.

14. Labeled "Navajo woman and daughter, Chaco Canyon, New Mexico," this photograph was taken by William C. Orchard in 1900. A superb, large, round, first phase concha belt is shown with the extra concha or conchas hanging down the girl's side much as the Plains Indians displayed their silver hair plates. The center slot opening is round. Courtesy Museum of the American Indian, Heye Foundation, New York.

15. This picture, taken in 1907 at the Hopi village of Hano, Arizona, during the annual summer Butterfly Dance, shows the center dancer wearing a first phase concha belt of the round variety. Other silver jewelry can be seen among the dancers. The Hopis eagerly traded for jewelry with their neighbors, the Navajos, and those who could afford to own pieces commonly wore their treasures to important occasions such as the dances. Courtesy Museum of the American Indian, Heye Foundation, New York, the Churchill Collection.

Although there does not appear to be any firm evidence at this time, it seems quite likely that the use of stamps on metalwork by the Plains Indians was learned from the Navajos. This conclusion is based on the observations that the designs on the stamps used by Plains Indians were the same as those used by Navajo smiths, and that there appears to be no Plains Indian stamped metalwork until after the Navajos were using the technique, starting around 1880.

In Adair's dialogue with Grey Moustache, we find that Grey Moustache named nine other smiths who were taught by Atsidi Sani. At least one of these — Atsidi Sani's son, Red Smith — was noted as being both a good salesman and a prolific craftsman. Technology and good salesmanship were not the only factors involved; a whole culture had just changed its course. Prestige and wealth could no longer be derived from raiding. A new form of economy was evolving and jewelry was to play an important part in it.

Many young men who might have been warriors a generation earlier were becoming herders, and in their free time, silversmiths. The sheep and goats provided food, a cash or barter income, and, to a lesser extent, clothing in the form of blankets. The Navajos proved to be excellent herdsmen and within a short time were producing enough wool to take care of their own needs and provide a surplus as well. The surplus went into silver jewelry. Silver jewelry soon became so important that neither men, women, nor children felt properly dressed for a social occasion unless they were wearing many objects of silver. Ben Wittick, an early Southwest photographer, recognized this concern among the Navajos and was never without a selection of silver jewelry, which they were welcome to put on while posing before his camera (Figure 16). Although this consideration enabled him to take photographs that might otherwise have been refused, it also created a problem for researchers today. Studying his portraits, suddenly one realizes that every Indian from Arizona and New Mexico is wearing the same necklace, men and women alike. Was there no jewelry in the possession of these people? They probably all owned jewelry, but with the exception of a few favorite rings, buttons, or bracelets, it was not worn on an everyday basis. It was too valuable an item to be subjected to the hard wear and chance of loss over hundreds of miles of sheep trail. The silver jewelry that we think of in terms of wearing apparel probably spent a good deal of its time buried beneath the earth floor of the winter hogan, or on the pawn racks at the trading posts.

To the Southwest Indians, silver and turquoise jewelry was the finest form of personal adornment, but it also represented an asset with a known value that could be held by a trader to secure credit for dry goods, exchanged for religious and medical services, or traded for livestock. This was only the first step in the growth of economic importance for silver jewelry. There were soon to be others who admired the shine of silver with its blue and green turquoise settings almost as much as the Indians of the Southwest.

In 1899 Herman Schweizer, who was in charge of the Fred Harvey Curio Department, conceived the idea of providing lightweight silver and turquoise jewelry for tourists. To accomplish the necessary output, precut turquoise and thin sheet silver was "farmed out" to some of the silversmiths working around Thoreau, Sheep Springs, Smith Lake, and Mariano Lake. The first "light" jewelry, which consisted mostly of rings and bracelets, was immediately popular with the tourists. A new phase of Southwest Indian jewelry had begun.

Soon the introduction of precut turquoise, machine-drawn wire, commercial solder and flux, machine-rolled sheet silver, saws, files, sandpaper, and the blow torch (which replaced the charcoal forge) revolutionized the jewelry craft. One might think that dating a piece of work using these criteria of new tools and materials would be both easy and accurate, but the transitional phase lasted until 1930. Some smiths, and even entire areas, continued to make the simple, heavy, first phase jewelry thirty years after the lighter tourist-type jewelry came to dominate the commercial market. Later designs, such as arrows and swastikas, are seen on work which obviously utilized some of the earliest techniques. The great distances covered by the Southwest Indian jewelry tradition in 1900 probably had only a partial effect on this time-lag phenomenon. Among the Navajos, rapid communication over great areas was a characteristic noted by many visitors, and certainly the Pueblos had no problems in this regard. The differences were

16. Ben Wittick usually staged his portraits with artificial sets and backgrounds, which is often distracting. But this Navajo woman, Anselina by name (photographed at Fort Wingate, New Mexico, around 1890), has strong appeal. Wittick normally overdressed his models and used his own supply of jewelry so that the same pieces appear in many of his photographs. Nevertheless, the jewelry is of the period. There is a round first phase concha belt, a plain old-style silver naja, two najas with double crescents (one oddly placed below the left shoulder), and two plain silver necklaces. At the shoulders are manta pins holding together the two pieces of the hand-woven woolen dress. Courtesy Southwest Museum, Los Angeles.

probably caused by a universal tendency to leave unchanged a method that has been found effective until outside influences intervened. This same process was taking place with the silversmiths. If a smith learned how to make a bracelet a certain way, he continued to do it in that manner because relearning took time and meant new problems to be worked out.

And so the production of first phase work continued, even though the makers were well aware that new designs, techniques, and materials were being used by others. Probably the greatest force of change was economics. When the Indian people themselves started wearing the new, lighter silver with machine-cut stones, first phase work was no longer salable and its production ceased.

The photographs of Navajo and Pueblo Indians shown on the preceding pages and in the following selection from the Field Museum are beautiful testimonials to a proud, free, and even wild people. They were taken long ago and their strength derived from the people seems never to wear away. The jewelry the Indians wear in the photographs still gleams for us today, no less than it did for the Indians who loved it then. Almost no Indian went unadorned. Theirs was a wise strength that included jewelry in its every fiber.

The Collections

THIS chapter gives a new, long perspective on the collections of historic Southwest Indian silver jewelry existing in various major museums and private hands throughout the United States. There is a good deal of general documentation on the development of silver jewelry in the words of the intrepid adventurers and historians who roamed the Southwest during the last four decades of the nineteenth century. However, many of their reports are vague and unclear, and some are contradictory. It is difficult to pin down what is being described, and the sharp image of a good, early photograph was essentially not available until the 1870s, when photographers started to venture into the Southwest with professional equipment and when their interest in recording Indian life was aroused. Most of the photographs were taken relatively late, as late as the 1880s to the 1900s, and by that time jewelry-making was already popular and well established. But some of the early observers and historians did manage to collect the elusive artifacts themselves, and these often wound up in museums or private collections. Some collectors donated their finds to museums or foundations at a later date, thus making it difficult to ascertain when the items were made or collected.

For the purposes of this book, the jewelry selected to be photographed has its roots in the older material that has been preserved and recorded. But we have sought a balanced representation of jewelry throughout a period of some sixty years, from 1868 to around 1930, when the creation of jewelry was perhaps most original and vigorous. Jewelry made before 1900 is extremely rare, and it took a determined effort to discover and exhume what has survived in museums. The Navajos contributed to the disappearance of the old jewelry by traditionally burying their best examples with the dead (and most of this has been lost). Almost no Southwest travelers went out to collect jewelry in the way that James Stevenson (who in 1879 visited Acoma, Laguna, and Zia Pueblos) collected what contemporary pottery existed at that time. Jewelry was quite incidental to the larger quests for anthropological and ethnological data. If an anthropologist, United States Army officer, or member of a geological survey team happened, out of curiosity, to secure an excellent item of jewelry, he

17. Silver jewelry often is interspersed with turquoise, coral, and shell necklaces. This Hopi man from Mishongovi is wearing little tube-shaped beads of silver intermingled with a coral necklace. His silver naja is of the flat, old style but the necklace is strung with silver crosses instead of squash blossoms. Photograph taken between 1903 and 1911. Courtesy Field Museum of Natural History, Chicago.

18. If the amount of jewelry one possessed was an indication of the owner's wealth, this Hopi man has made a good start. He wears a pair of old-style silver loop-and-ball earrings, a silver naja with flat disk terminals strung on a strand of silver beads (a few have become unsoldered through wear), and a long necklace of domed silver buttons (made from coins), not to mention a white shell (*heishe*) and turquoise necklace. Photograph taken between 1903 and 1911. Courtesy Field Museum of Natural History, Chicago.

or she would record a treasure which we, the public today, should look for and appreciate. That is exactly what has happened; a handful of documented pieces have led us backward in space and time and forward to the visible and knowable history of Southwest Indian jewelry.

The photographs are organized by collection because most of the pieces have been gathered by museums or foundations over many years, and they offer a balanced and historically oriented selection of material. Illustrating the collections as they have been assembled, with their different emphases on certain objects, allows them to become personalities unto themselves and offers a stronger

visual effect than if the items were grouped by type. A list of the illustrations by object is on page 209.

One factor that should be emphasized is the significance of the collection and accession dates used in this book. The collection date, when available, signifies when the piece was actually collected "on the Reservation," while the accession date shows only when the museum added the piece to its collection. Thus, most items are a good deal older than their accession dates would suggest, and often even older than the dates of their collection. Many of the jewelry pieces show signs of stress, wear, or a patina that take years to ac-

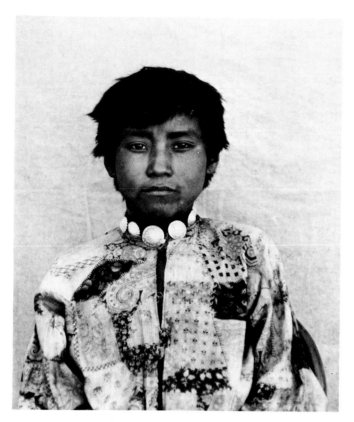

19. Southwest Indian children also wore jewelry and silver buttons. Some matched buttons accent this boy's patchwork shirt. Men wore silver jewelry and, in the early days, perhaps wore even more than did the women. The Hopi boy is from Shipolovi village. Photograph taken between 1903 and 1911. Courtesy Field Museum of Natural History, Chicago.

20. The matched, stamped silver button necklace worn by another Hopi boy from Sichomovi village, with the exception of the four domed buttons forming a pendant, is similar to the button necklace from the Smithsonian Institution (Figure 24, at left). But in the case of Figure 24, the buttons are strung on two sides and worn as beads with a naja. Photograph taken between 1903 and 1911. Courtesy Field Museum of Natural History, Chicago.

cumulate. In such instances the item considerably predates either its collection or acquisition. There are no foolproof criteria to go by when dating Southwest Indian jewelry. It is by studying old collections that one can give dating priority to certain jewelry traits over others. What dates are attributed in the captions are approximate, based on a combination of elements analyzed and background history.

Although not large, the collection at the *Smithsonian Institution* in Washington, D.C., consists of the largest group of pre-1900 jewelry available today. The core of the collection comes from no more than a half-dozen persons: James and Matilda Cox (Mrs. T. E.) Stevenson, a prominent anthropological team; Thomas V. Keam, trader, settler, and founder of Keam's Canyon Trading Post, Arizona (Hopi); James Mooney, an anthropologist known for his research on the Plains Indians; Dr. Edward E. Palmer, a director of Harvard University's Peabody Museum; and George F. Kunz, whose collection (procured from Charlie, "Indian scout") was purchased by Tiffany and Company in New York. Tiffany exhibited Mr. Kunz's collection at the World's Columbian Exposition in 1893, and Mr. Keam also exhibited his considerable collection there. The exposition had created a public forum for exotic material to be collected and exhibited,

21. The elaborate silver squash blossom on this Navajo man, Good Luck ("age 48"), stands out against his dark shirt. The double-crescent naja has two sets of domed disks soldered onto the terminals and a loop bar joining the crescents together, becoming at the top a single squash blossom. The stone drop was a pierced earring and has serrated bezels. A single silver button closes the top of his shirt. Photograph taken between 1903 and 1911. Courtesy Field Museum of Natural History, Chicago.

22. This Navajo mother and child seem to be wearing their best clothes for this photograph. The mother, Mrs. Vincenti Begay, wears a three-crescent naja with primitive hands and a loop with two curving appendages. The squash blossoms are extremely large. On her fingers are three rings with stones and on her left wrist is a silver bracelet. The little boy is wearing silver buttons on his shirt. Photograph taken between 1903 and 1911. Courtesy Field Museum of Natural History, Chicago.

and Indian jewelry — luckily for us — fell into that category. Mr. Victor Justice Evans rounds out the group with jewelry he collected on the Navajo Reservation in the early 1920s.

An analysis of the Smithsonian's collection reveals that the one strong, binding cord running through it is the abundance of Navajo-made jewelry which closely resembles Plains Indian material. Sometimes it is difficult to distinguish between the two, and yet the items are always clearly recognizable as Plains Indian in spirit. The evidence that heavy Plains Indian influence was exerted on the Navajo silversmiths from the late 1860s to the 1890s is overwhelming and undeniable.

Side by side, Navajo and Plains Indian jewelry, collected by Thomas Keam and George Kunz and labeled Navajo, coexisted, the distinction obliterated by the use of the same designs, tools, and materials. Brass and copper bangle bracelets; the wider, real silver, rocker-engraved bracelets (see Figure 31); and engraved silver rings as well as buttons all bespeak a design heritage common to these two distinct and different peoples. Even the Navajo silver najas echo the Plains Indian styles. Many Navajo silver bracelets, rings, and buttons are direct copies of Plains Indian prototypes. Some of the Smithsonian's pieces actually may be Plains material acquired by the Navajos. One Navajo needle or awl case has brass cone-shaped dan-

23. The elaborate hair style of this Moki girl from Sichomovi village (Hopi) augments the effect of the lovely squash blossom necklace she is wearing. The silver naja, made of two silver triangular wire crescents with interesting hands as terminals, has a fluted silver drop in the center. The stems of the silver squash blossoms are filed. Below the necklace her blouse is held together by a safety pin. Photograph taken between 1903 and 1911. Courtesy Field Museum of Natural History, Chicago.

gles and a perforated trade disk, all of which hail from Plains Indian sources or from those farther east (Figure 51). The Navajos particularly benefited from an exposure to Plains concepts, since their fledgling silversmiths were quick to respond to the strong outside influence of the more experienced Plains smiths. A meeting place of jewelry styles and types resulted. The Navajos used Plains jewelry essentially as a catalyst to project themselves firmly into their own clear, bold jewelry patterns. This is not to argue against a long-standing Spanish influence on the development of Navajo jewelry but it is certainly evident that a surprising amount of acculturation took place whereby the Navajos received the advantages of learning, mas-

tering, and going beyond Plains Indian styles and techniques. It is quite possible that in one case the Plains people borrowed from the Navajos the technique of applying stamps on metalwork.

The main contributors to the jewelry collection in the *Field Museum of Natural History* in Chicago are the dauntless Edward E. Ayer, who traveled in New Mexico and Arizona in 1895; the Reverend H. R. Voth, who stayed at the Hopi villages between 1893 and 1899; and Charles L. Owens, who collected in 1903 during the Field Museum Columbian Expedition at the White Mountain Apache Reservation and also in 1911 for the Stanley McCormick Expedition at Hopi. The material collected from the Apaches and the Hopis also shows marked Plains Indian influence. Here, too, as shown in the Smithsonian's Navajo jewelry collection, the Hopis were at home with Plains Indian jewelry styles (see Figure 61). The Edward Ayer collection, which came from the Navajos of New Mexico and Arizona, also confirms the strength of the Plains Indian cultural contact with this tribe. Some of the Navajo-made and Plains Indian-oriented jewelry was traded to the Hopis. Even though the Hopis were late to learn jewelry-making from the Navajos, by the late 1890s they had begun to fashion their own jewelry, although the items cannot be readily distinguished from Navajo work.

The jewelry collection at the *Museum of the American Indian, Heye Foundation,* in New York City is basically anchored by the material of Donald D. Graham, collected during his term as first United States agent in Zuni from 1880 to 1885. At Zuni, Graham collected early earrings, buttons, rings, conchas, hair pieces, manta pins, necklaces, and copper, brass, and silver bracelets in current use. A surprising amount of this jewelry was composed of early rocker-engraved pieces, of both Navajo (or Zuni Pueblo) and Plains Indian origin. Some Plains German silver items were also sprinkled among the contents. Graham labeled many of these pieces as "Navajo," thus implying that the Zunis received much of their jewelry through trade with the Navajos, and that even the Plains jewelry items labeled as Navajo were basically Navajo-owned. Much of the mixture of Southwest and Plains Indian jewelry types so prevalent in the Smithsonian's collection is evident here. Early Navajo silver bracelets, buttons, and rings and their

Plains Indian counterparts were all fashionable at Zuni Pueblo. Collections from Major John G. Bourke, who visited Zuni in 1881 to 1884, and from Frank Hamilton Cushing, who stayed at Zuni from 1879 to 1884, confirm the early Navajo Indians' familiarity with Plains jewelry styles. At the time it was being examined, the jewelry collection of the Museum of the American Indian (almost totally unphotographed) was going through a process of complete inventory. Thus, it was impossible to obtain photographs of most of the collection. The photographs used in this book had already been taken by the museum's photographer.

There are two separate collections housed at the *Museum of New Mexico's Laboratory of Anthropology* in Santa Fe, New Mexico. One is owned by the Museum of New Mexico and one by the School of American Research, a privately operated research center. A good portion of the museum's large jewelry collection is included in this book. There is little early collection data on either of the major jewelry collections at the Laboratory of Anthropology. However, the museum's material does include a wide range of excellent examples and gives variety and depth to the illustrations. In 1932, museum personnel went on buying trips to the Navajo Reservation and brought back a group of fine pieces made in the 1920s, some of which are revival specimens from the early 1900s. Witter Bynner's well-selected jewelry collection is also at the Museum. A few of the pieces from the School of American Research are also shown.

Besides holding a fine collection of its own, the *Heard Museum* in Phoenix, Arizona, has a large part of the superior Fred Harvey jewelry material collected in the first half of the twentieth century. No background information comes with the collection but perhaps some could be obtained by researching the Fred Harvey sales journals as they relate to early jewelry collected and sold.

The *Wheelwright Museum* in Santa Fe, New Mexico, has a solid collection of Southwest Indian jewelry. Mrs. Mary C. Wheelwright on occasion bought jewelry from the Navajos in the 1920s and 1930s. A difficulty encountered here, and with most museums, is that there is little or no collection data or provenance available on accessioned pieces, even though they may be old or have been given as gifts or donations some time ago.

The *Millicent Rogers Museum,* near Taos, New Mexico, falls into the above category. Its choice jewelry collection has little provenance, although Millicent Rogers diligently and with superb taste collected jewelry and other Southwest material in the 1940s and 1950s. Both Mrs. Rogers and Mrs. Wheelwright (as well as Mabel Dodge Luhan) were early appreciators of Southwest Indian and Spanish Colonial art and had the vision and conviction to collect distinctive material unavailable today.

The private collections of *Lynn D. Trusdell* in Philadelphia and of the *Graham Foundation for Advanced Studies in the Fine Arts* in Chicago provide an extra dimension of carefully acquired items as do those of anonymous *private collectors,* which close the illustrations. An individual collector's taste is often less concerned with scholarly values important to museum-type research and more based on aesthetic considerations. The collector's roving eye is freer to follow the course of his or her intuition and personal feeling.

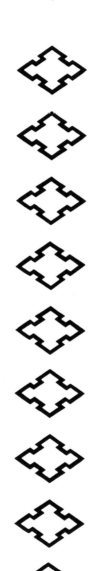

Illustrations

All the jewelry illustrated is considered of Navajo Indian manufacture unless labeled otherwise. If not otherwise stated, the pieces are all hand forged and hammered (wrought). Sandcast items are always listed as such. The term "bowguard" is reserved for the actual item used in the early days as an authentic guard against the snap of the bow and not used later as a personal or dance ornament. The latter item is called a ketoh. Museum accession numbers are listed on page 213.

Unless otherwise credited, all the photographs are by William J. Salman. The backgrounds for these photographs are early Navajo and Hopi weaving (blankets, rugs, and dresses), some of which is worn to the warp. The degree of enlargement shows normally invisible specks which cling to the wool.

24. The sandcast naja to the left is strung on a necklace of old stamped buttons (see Figure 20). The bar that joins the two crescents and forms the loop on top is stamped, and there is even some stamping where the inner crescent joins the larger one. The naja's terminals consist of stamped buttons. Acquired from Benjamin H. Frayser in 1937. The right naja has two crescents soldered at the terminals to stamped and embossed buttons. The loop bar is also soldered on. The crudely made beads have large holes. George Kunz Collection, property of Charlie, Indian scout; purchased by Tiffany and Company, New York, for the 1893 World's Columbian Exposition.

25. The top piece has a half-formed outer crescent tooled and soldered onto the central crescent. The stones are crudely set and the naja itself has a primitive bearing. Circa 1900. The other two najas are sandcast. Right, a flower petal center and incised loop, circa 1910 (see Figure 6 for another version). Left, a handsome diamond-shaped turquoise stone in a thick bezel on a loop soldered to the naja, circa 1920. Instead of hands for terminals, later najas such as these had button-shaped knobs or turquoise stones. All collected by Victor Justice Evans in the early 1920s; acquired in 1931.

26. These two graceful najas show early characteristics and were most probably made before
1880. Each has crude hands, a gracefully tapered
crescent — particularly the smaller one — and
raised middle sections in the upper part. Each connecting loop is soldered on; the larger piece has a
silver connecting ring. Both najas are oversized,
one enormous (see Figure 16). Both are tufa cast.
Collected by Thomas V. Keam before 1893 for the
World's Columbian Exposition, Chicago.

27. The crude naja to the left is completely flat with primitive hands. The loop is soldered onto the naja. Often these early najas were worn strung with beads but without squash blossoms, as shown by early photographs of Southwest Indians. Collected by Mrs. T. E. Stevenson, circa 1880. The middle piece is formed by two crescents, one embracing the other, joined together by a vertical bar. It has an attractive and more complicated design than the left-hand piece but retains the small, rudimentary hands. The loop and naja are one piece and very flat. The mellow silver beads show much wear, with one bead even completely unsoldered. Collected by James Mooney in Arizona in 1893. The naja to the right is slightly smaller than average and is raised down the middle. The loop is very small and soldered on. The naja has no hands, representing another type current in the 1870s and 1880s. The crescent is wide rather than tall, generally an early trait. Collected by Emil Granier before 1890; acquired in 1899–1900.

28. The three separate strands of small beads show the painstaking work involved in their manufacture during the 1920s. The tiny strand in the middle of the two larger necklaces has stamped beads. Collected in 1941. The largest beads have large holes; the two short, stubby squashes with thin, simple loops connecting them to the string are typical of early squash blossoms. Collected by Cosmos Mendeliff in the 1880s.

29. These four silver bracelets, made circa 1900, show relatively heavy and strong treatment. Except for the nicely stamped child's bracelet in the middle, the others have deep stamp work. The child's bracelet and the piece at top left also show file work. The bracelet at upper right has stamp work of primitive arrow forms in the center. The bottom bracelet was collected by Victor Justice Evans in the early 1920s.

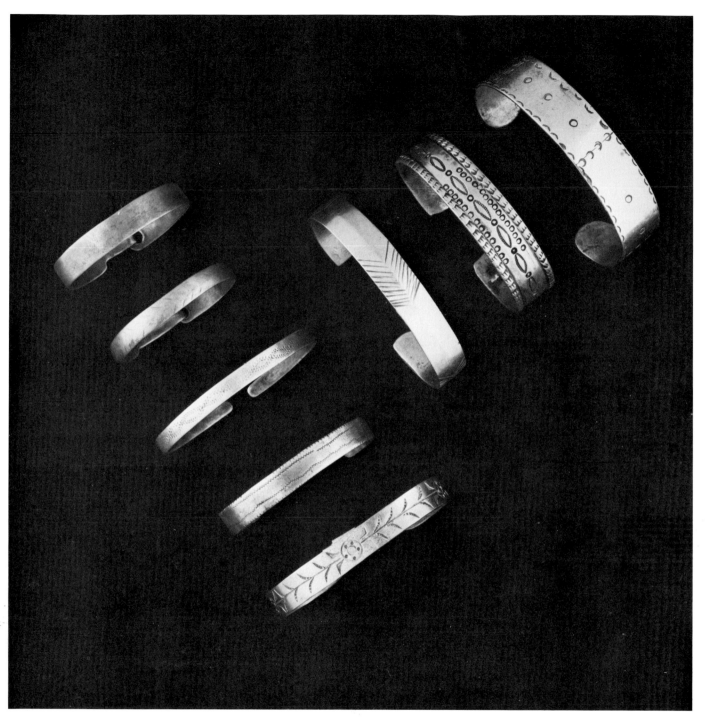

30. In the row of five silver bracelets, the first four from the top are rocker-engraved and the first two have an ingenious clasp device for closing the bracelet also found on Northwest Coast silverwork. All were made in the 1870s and show a very strong relationship to Plains Indian silver jewelry. The fifth bracelet is not quite so old as the others and has been attributed to the Copenhagen Royal Ethnological Museum. The busily stamped center bracelet in the group of three has no available history but probably dates in the early 1890s. The bottom bracelet in the group of three was cast and then decorated with a cold chisel. Six of the bracelets were purchased by Tiffany and Company, New York, for the 1893 World's Columbian Exposition from the George Kunz Collection, property of Charlie, Indian scout. The second bracelet of the five was collected by Mrs. T. E. Stevenson and labeled "Tesaki" and "Cherokee"; the latter is a Plains Indian attribution.

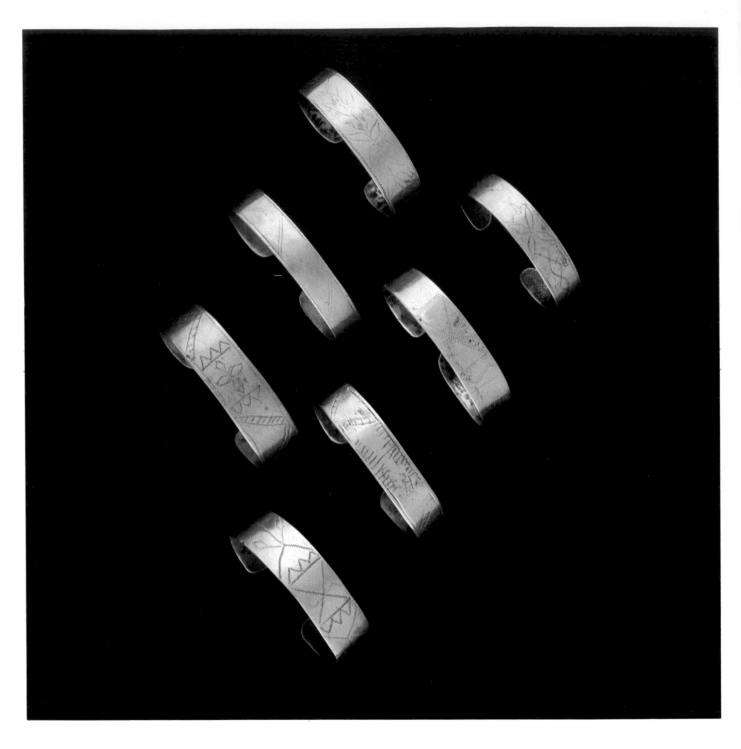

31. These seven silver bracelets were assembled before 1893 and are remarkable in that they form one of the clearest links to the silver work of the Plains Indians and show its influence on the early manufacture of Southwest jewelry, particularly on that of the Navajos and the Zunis. These bracelets as well as others are labeled "Navajo" and were obtained in the Southwest. Yet they are either Plains examples traded to the Navajos or Zunis or they are copies after Plains Indian material. The lower bracelet is most distinctly "Plains" in character. All are made of sheet silver and decorated with rocker-engraving. They are all well worn. Circa 1870s. George Kunz Collection, property of Charlie, Indian scout; purchased by Tiffany and Company, New York, for the 1893 World's Columbian Exposition.

32. Copper and brass bracelets are the earliest types made in the Southwest. The copper piece on the bottom, with its punched and filed butterfly designs, is a revival of earlier specimens and was acquired from Mrs. C. B. Gatewood in 1930. The second copper bracelet, with its simple, chiseled design, is considerably earlier, acquired in 1901 from Mrs. G. Carr. The simple, early bangles, made from silver rods, are filed and cold chiseled and are an early form of Southwest Indian bracelet. Two of them were collected by Mrs. T. E. Stevenson at Zuni Pueblo in the early 1880s and two by Thomas V. Keam for the 1893 World's Columbian Exposition.

33. Oddities like these crudely made bracelets do exist. The top sandcast bracelet has six crudely bezeled light blue turquoise stones, circa 1915. The other one is perhaps a tourist piece, circa 1910. The buttons are not soldered but are riveted to the bracelet, which is made out of a silver alloy. The balance of the decoration was applied with a cold chisel. Collected by Victor Justice Evans in the 1920s; acquired in 1931.

34. The five old silver rings with turquoise stones (the center one was meant to have a stone) are early examples of the crude workmanship in setting turquoise in silver. Even by 1900 many silversmiths had not mastered this art. The stones are crudely cut and the bezels crudely made. The stamp work on two of the rings is of technically superior quality. Most rings with stones attributed to the period 1880–1900 were actually made in the early 1900s or later. The ring in the center was collected by James Mooney in 1894 when it was still being made — it lacks a turquoise stone, the stamped design and the smoothing and polishing of the surface. The ring on the top left is made out of a silver alloy and was acquired from Mrs. Louis Salter Codwise in 1915. The handcut stone is clearly shown. The rings at top right, bottom right, and bottom left were gifts of Mrs. Charles Grindell to the Smithsonian in 1920.

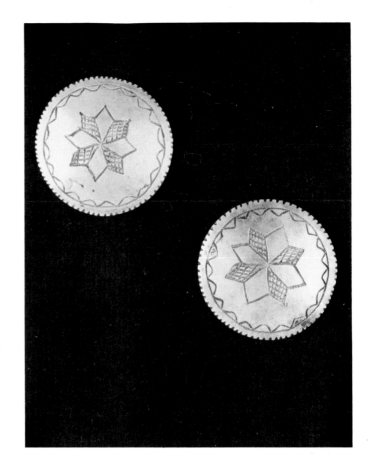

35. These two large German silver buttons with rocker-engraved, star-patterned floral designs and notched edges show direct Plains Indian influence and might possibly be of Plains Indian origin. They resemble Plains Indian hair plates in size and are "Plains" in the use of German silver. Circa 1870s. Collected by Thomas V. Keam before 1893, when they were exhibited in the World's Columbian Exposition.

36. The pair of buttons at top left and bottom right was collected by Victor Justice Evans in the early 1920s. The scalloped lower left button was collected by Victor Mendeliff in 1884, and the top right button, made from a United States fifty-cent piece, was collected by Mrs. T. E. Stevenson in the early 1880s. All the pieces have been filed, three have rocker-engraving, and three have center punch marks.

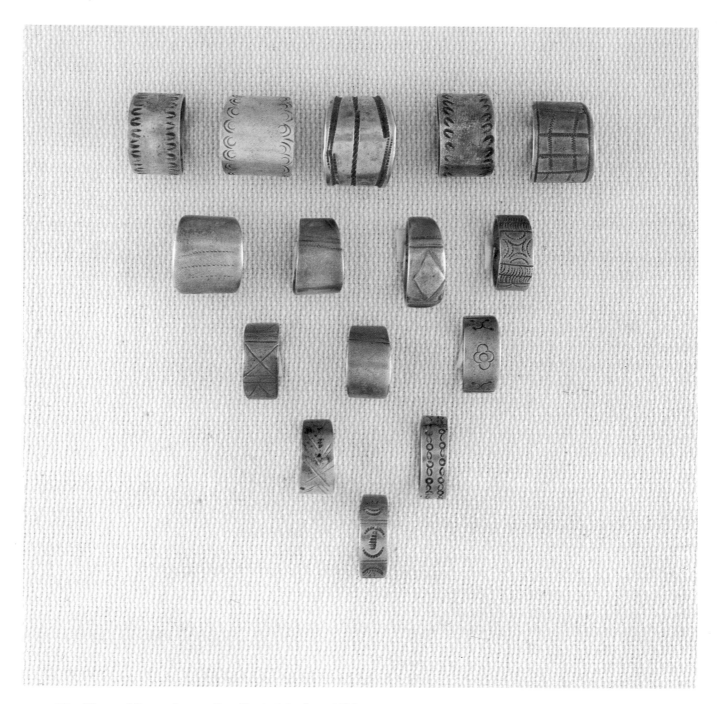

37. These fifteen rings, all collected before 1893, represent one of the finest collections of early Southwest silver rings available. For the most part they are crudely yet charmingly designed, decorated by rocker-engraved and stamped and filed patterns. The wear on the majority of the rings is apparent. The silver is thin but pure, not German silver or any other mixed alloy. The designs are fresh and free, not cluttered or overworked. There is an obvious affinity to Plains Indian silver jewelry although these rings were made in the Southwest. The lack of turquoise stones along with the rocker-engraved and filed designs, and the poor solder work in connecting the ends of the rings reaffirm the early period of 1870–1893. The large top center ring shows stamp work of the "end-of-a-file" variety. Eleven rings were purchased by Tiffany and Company, New York, from the George Kunz Collection, property of Charlie, Indian scout, for the 1893 World's Columbian Exposition. Three of the rings were collected by Thomas V. Keam for the same exposition and one by Mrs. T. E. Stevenson at Zuni in the early 1880s.

38. Many of the rings here are "sculptured" and only one has a turquoise stone (far right). All of these pieces are crudely soldered together and indicate that soldering technique was not mastered until the first decade of the twentieth century. With the exception of two rings (center and top left), they are decorated with soldered appliqué. They were all made before 1893 except the largest ring with the silver plate, which was collected by Victor Justice Evans in the early 1920s and acquired in 1931. The top ring was collected by Mrs. T. E. Stevenson at Zuni Pueblo in the early 1880s and the rest were purchased by Tiffany and Company, New York, from the George Kunz Collection, property of Charlie, Indian scout, for the 1893 World's Columbian Exposition.

39. The center button and the oval one on the top appear to be miniature conchas with their punched holes, scalloped edges, and simulated twisted wire effect. The two United States coins are dated 1863 and 1877. Some of the buttons are crudely and simply rocker-engraved, and a few possess unusual shapes. Twenty of these buttons were purchased by Tiffany and Company, New York, from the George Kunz Collection, property of Charlie, Indian scout, for the 1893 World's Columbian Exposition; one was collected by Mrs. T. E. Stevenson in 1887; and two by Victor Mendeliff in 1884. The history of two of the buttons is not known.

40. A group of nine conchas taken from Figure 41. The oval first phase conchas differ in the importance of the punched holes to the border designs, the prominence of the scalloped borders, the fineness of the wire effect, and the shapes of the cutout openings. A superb example is the middle concha in the upper left row. Both the round and the oval concha belts were in use from the early 1870s up to the turn of the century. The early concha on the far right shows evidence of long use which has worn the cross bar through, necessitating its replacement by using a mechanical attachment since soldering was still beyond the skill of most of the silversmiths of that time. Six of the conchas were collected by Thomas V. Keam for the 1893 World's Columbian Exposition; one by Dr. E. Palmer in the 1880s; one by Victor Mendeliff in 1884; and one is of unknown origin.

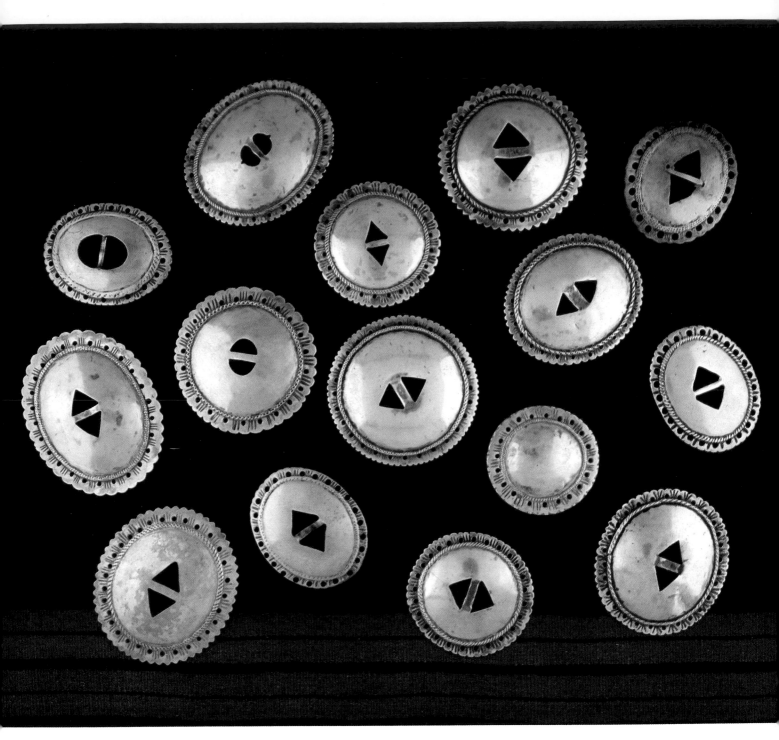

41. A gleaming array of first phase silver conchas, both oval and round in shape, catch the eye. It is difficult to distinguish between the ages of oval and diamond-shaped first phase center slots since they were manufactured concurrently. None of these conchas has stamping around the center slot openings. The center slots have been cut with a cold chisel. The one first phase concha with a raised solid center replacing the center slot area is unusual. All are circa 1880s. Twelve conchas were collected by Thomas V. Keam for the 1893 World's Columbian Exposition; one was purchased by Tiffany and Company, New York, from the George Kunz Collection, property of Charlie, Indian scout; one by Dr. E. Palmer in the 1880s; and one by Victor Mendeliff in 1884. The history of one of the conchas is unknown.

42. The six round silver conchas taken from Figure 41 were collected by Thomas V. Keam for the World's Columbian Exposition in 1893. They are all superb examples, particularly the center piece with its fine work and minimally scalloped border, which shows the silver area to its greatest advantage. The small, unique, high-domed concha with no center slot is a choice item. This unusually early closed-center concha dates no later than those with center slots. It has file work on the edge which is exactly what one finds in Mexican ironwork.

43. The beautifully proportioned first phase concha belt, circa 1880s, on the right is markedly contrasted to the fine rocker-engraved German silver concha. Both were collected at the same time in Arizona, and the early German silver piece, although completely characteristic of Plains Indian silver jewelry, was most probably made in the Southwest. It might have been copied from a Plains Indian hair plate. In the late 1800s there was a considerable Plains Indian influence on Southwest jewelry-making. The three conchas were purchased by Tiffany and Company, New York, from the George Kunz Collection, property of Charlie, Indian scout, for the World's Columbian Exposition in 1893. The German silver concha was collected by Thomas V. Keam for the same exposition.

44. Early belt buckles are usually very plain. The oval silver buckle belongs to a belt shown opposite (Figure 45, top). Collected in the early 1920s, acquired in 1931 from Victor Justice Evans. The rectangular silver buckle dates even earlier, circa 1880. There is evidence of stone-ground finishing which is an early trait. Purchased by Tiffany and Company, New York, from the George Kunz Collection, property of Charlie, Indian scout, for the 1893 World's Columbian Exposition.

45. The concha belt at top is typical in that the punched holes constitute a basic part of the border decoration, but these holes are more pronounced than usual. Circa 1880s. Collected by Victor Justice Evans in the early 1920s, acquired in 1931.

The other concha belt has a traditionally tight design with very fine twisted wire effect which in most cases was achieved by chiseling and filing the base metal; here, however, the metal has just been punched. The belt also has minimally scalloped edges, small punched holes, and a glorious patina. Like the top belt, it is strung on its original leather. Circa 1880. Collected by Mrs. G. Carr and acquired in 1901.

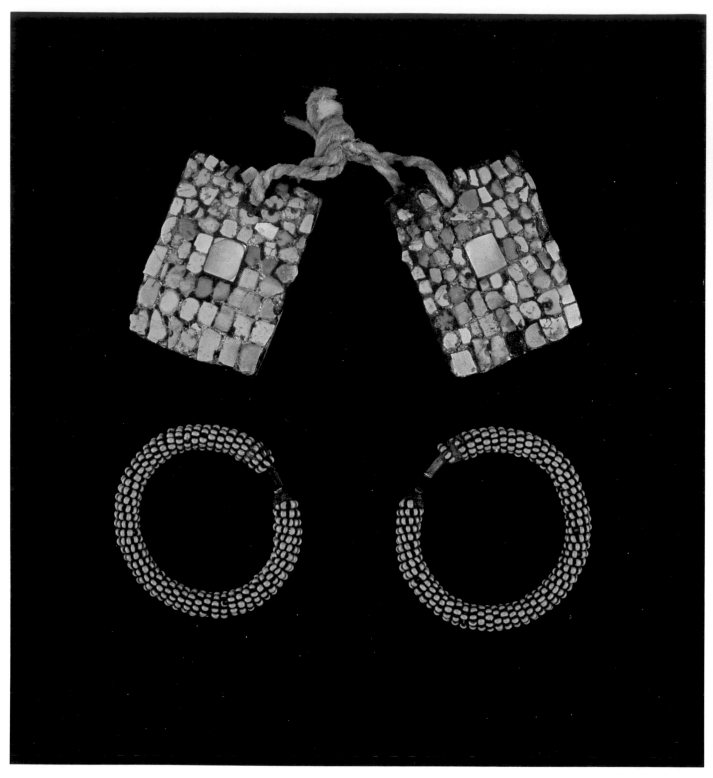

46. The top pair of classic earrings with turquoise stones inlaid in wood was collected by James Stevenson at Zuni in 1879–1880s. A number of drilled turquoise pieces in this item were once used as beads. There are two pairs similar to this one at the Field Museum (see Figures 66, 67). The pair with fine glass seed beads applied around brass wire is more unusual, and definitely Plains Indian in spirit if not origin, although the circular shape is similar to many Navajo and Zuni earrings. It was collected by Dr. E. Palmer in the 1870s in Arizona or New Mexico.

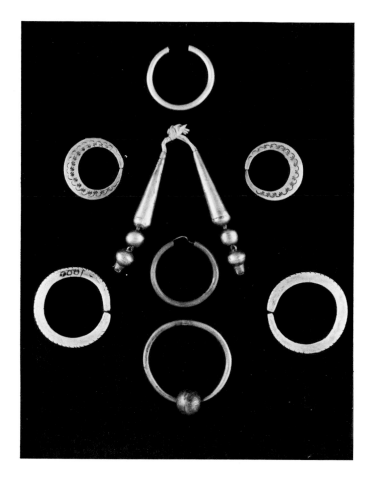

47. The various types of silver earrings consist of four pairs and one single piece. The cone-shaped pair with the silver bead and squash blossom dangling was purchased by Tiffany and Company, New York, from the George Kunz Collection, property of Charlie, Indian scout, for the 1893 World's Columbian Exposition, as was the finely stamped, tapered pair on either side of the cones. The silver loop with a bead and the pair of flat, cold-chisel silver stamped earrings on each side of it were acquired from Victor Justice Evans in 1931, collected in the early 1920s. The silver loop earring with the wire connecting the terminals, and its partner (without the wire), were collected in Zuni by Mrs. T. E. Stevenson in 1879–1880. These are smaller versions of the old silver bangle bracelets. The fine wire soldered on may well indicate non-Indian manufacture, perhaps a trade item.

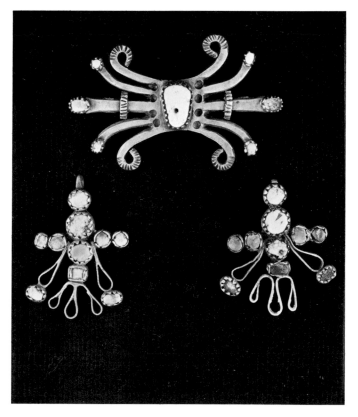

48. The top piece is a manta pin, which has a pierced blue turquoise stone once used as an ear-bob. The six small stones in serrated bezels, the chisel-stamped, curled finials, and the punched forms encircling each side of the bezel make this a strong and unique piece. All the cutting and decoration were done with a cold chisel. Purchased from Dr. E. Palmer in 1910, collected in Tampico, Mexico and labeled "Mexican." The bottom pair of earrings with serrated bezels and graceful silver forms with turquoise stones attached to their ends are most probably of Navajo origin, although they have a delicate feeling that could be early Zuni work. They are among the few first phase pieces that have stylistic connections with the filigree work of the Mexican *platero*. Collected by Victor Justice Evans on the Navajo reservation in the early 1920s.

49. These pleasing silver rocker-engraved hair ornaments are crudely soldered together. They could almost pass for Plains Indian pieces except that their round cylindrical shapes are not Plains Indian forms. Hair ornaments are extremely rare. Circa 1870s. Collected by Thomas V. Keam for the 1893 World's Columbian Exposition.

50. The sparsely stamped and rocker-engraved Navajo alloy silver bowguard at the top was collected by James Mooney in 1893 in Arizona. Although Navajo in character, the use of an impure silver and brass alloy was mostly employed by the Plains Indians. Circa 1870s. The wide ketoh below, circa 1890, was purchased by Tiffany and Company, New York, from the George Kunz Collection, property of Charlie, Indian scout, for the World's Columbian Exposition in 1893, and is unusually complex and sophisticated for that period.

The stamped floral patterns with the rocker-engraved internal designs stand out sharply among the filed columns. A silver button fastens the ketoh. The repoussé floral-designed bracelet at the left with the dark green turquoise stone also has deep and strong stamp work. Circa early 1900s. It was collected by Victor Justice Evans in the early 1920s and acquisitioned in 1931. The stamped ketoh with the oval design and fine turquoise stones, circa 1920s, was collected by J. Cooper in 1956.

51. This very unusual piece, a Navajo needle or awl case, 4½ inches long, makes use of brass cone-shaped bangles and a brass disk (probably a trade piece) shown at bottom. At the top are some small deer hoofs attached to hide thongs and a white button designed with tiny circles. The case is bounded by sinew at the edges. The deer hoofs, the bangles, and the needle case itself are completely within the framework of the Navajo culture, but the piece also has a marked affinity to Plains Indian work. Circa 1860s. Collected by Dr. E. Palmer in the 1870s.

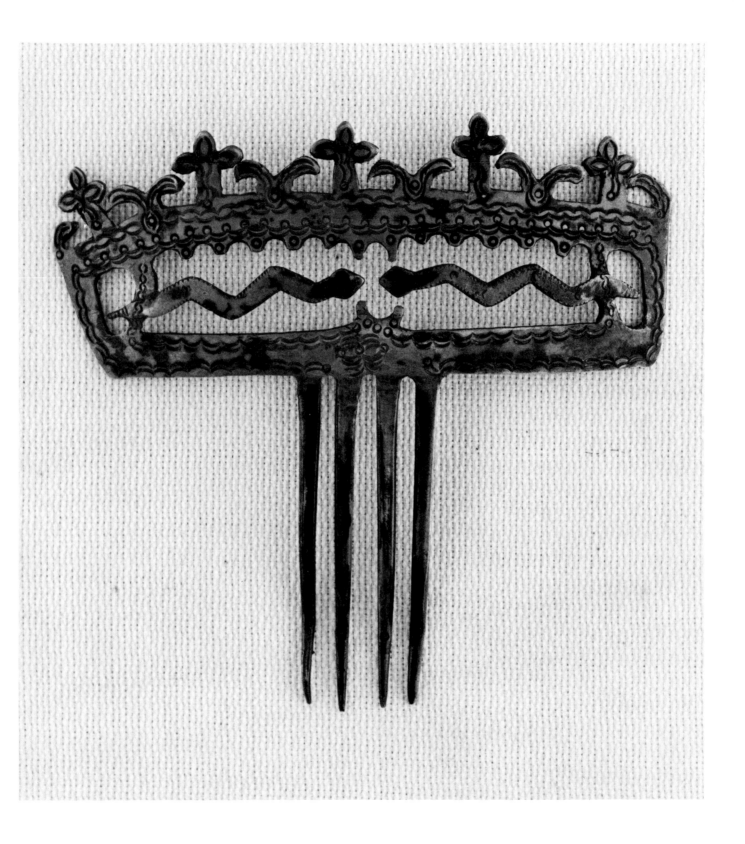

52. This silver comb with elaborate stamp work and silver cutouts resembles a Spanish mantilla comb. Although a comb of this sort was a White Man's style, it has figures of the sacred *avanyu* (sky and water snakes). The history of this piece was not available.

53. Dr. W. Matthews, while at the Fort Wingate, New Mexico, area in the 1880s, collected this copper powder measure with its chain. Also collected at the same time was a copper canteen with a chain (not shown). Very few of these were made, since their use was limited to the years that rifles had to be charged with powder. Slight rocker-engraving and punching can be seen.

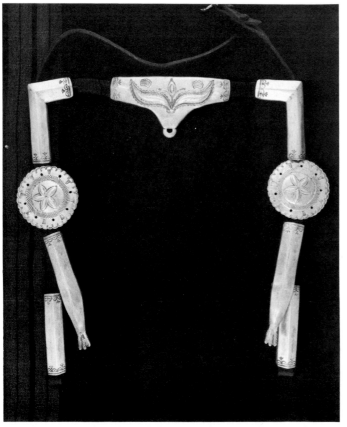

54. An early silver Navajo headstall with minimal stamping and broad, simple-patterned conchas corresponding to the end of the first phase period (see Figure 1). The finely executed center piece design flows toward the missing naja and notched loop, and the repoussé design is clear and bold with small marginal patterns. The terminal connectors, which would have joined the headstall to the bit, are also missing and the headstall is well worn. Najas, due to their movement on the horse's forehead, frequently fell off the browband; they were also dismantled and used in squash blossom necklaces. Collected by James Stevenson at Zuni Pueblo in the 1880s, gift to New York University in 1897.

55. Five silver bracelets, including one pair, show the complexity of stamped work on silver nearing the turn of the century. The deeply tooled designs are basically Navajo; the narrow, flat width of the silver and the thin, wavy designs, particularly in the bracelet pair, are precise and delicate. Labeled "Navajo," collected by Edward E. Ayer in 1895.

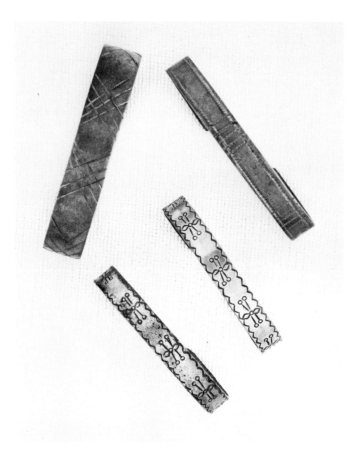

56. The bottom pair of delicately stamped brass bracelets, collected by S. C. Simons in 1901 at the White Mountain Apache Reservation during the Field Columbian Expedition, are most probably Navajo in origin but relate most strongly to Plains Indian designs. Circa 1885. The top right bracelet with crudely stamped lines is made of brass and was collected in the Apache Reservation by Charles L. Owens during the Field Museum Columbian Expedition in 1903. The chisel-stamped bracelet, upper left, was collected by Edward E. Ayer in 1895 in New Mexico or Arizona and has stronger and bolder designs more typical of Navajo work.

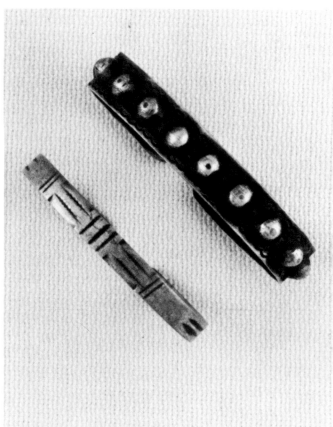

57. These two silver bracelets were collected by Edward E. Ayer before 1895 in New Mexico and Arizona. The small, flat bracelet is primitively and charmingly stamped. The bracelet with the domed forms making up the center band has stamped designs on the edges and punch marks in between each domed area.

58. The top left and the center right bracelets were again collected by Charles L. Owens in 1903 on the Apache Reservation, as well as the brass bracelet at the bottom which was collected in 1901. The top right and center left brass bracelets were collected by Edward E. Ayer in New Mexico or Arizona in 1895. Whether found in Apache or Navajo hands, the bracelets are quite similar and Plains Indian influence on both of these cultures is apparent. Several of these bracelets cost as little as 10¢ or 30¢ on the Reservation at the time of their collection. Both cold-chisel work and file work are evident here, and the heavy wear on both sides of the bracelets indicate that they were worn in numbers on the arm.

59. The top bracelet with four large sunburst button forms (one at each terminal not visible) and stamped designs flanking the center stone and at the sides was collected by Charles L. Owens in 1911 in Sichomovi (Hopi), Arizona for the Stanley McCormick Expedition. Although collected at Hopi, the bracelet is quite possibly Navajo. The other bracelet with attractive stamp work in the center and at the edges can be attributed to the early twentieth century. The price paid for this piece was $1.50. Since the Navajos quickly became the chief source in the early days for silver jewelry, much trading was done with them to acquire such coveted treasures.

60. This Navajo leather bowguard is ornamented with seven silver buttons. The leather is primitively and attractively tooled with a horse hoof-print design, a Plains Indian motif. The plain buttons hark back to the earliest forms with flared rims and are perhaps related to horse ornaments. Collected by Edward E. Ayer in 1895 in Arizona or New Mexico.

61. The smaller button, made for a bridle, is constructed out of a nickel with slightly notched edges. The larger German silver button, definitely Plains Indian in character with fine rocker-engraved designs, and the small button were both collected by H. R. Voth in Oraibi (Hopi), Arizona in 1893–1899. The silver cross, with a filed design around the edges, is said to be an amulet and was collected in 1903 at the White Mountain Apache Reservation for the Field Columbian Museum. It has strong Plains Indian traits.

62. The simple rocker-engraved silver manta pin with file decoration on the sides was collected by Edward E. Ayer in 1895 in the Southwest. The fine design resembles the work on early bracelets influenced by the Plains Indians. Manta pins were essential for holding women's dresses together at the shoulders and were used as dress ornaments (see Figure 16). Circa 1870s.

63. All of the simple loop earrings are silver except for the iron pair on the right. Iron was occasionally used by both the Navajos and the Apaches and indicates an early age. These items were most probably traded by the Navajos and were copied from Plains Indian earrings (see Figure 3). The largest of these earrings could have served as bangle bracelets. All were hand forged; the wire was hammered, not drawn. Collected at Hopi (Sichomovi and Mishongovi), Arizona, during the Stanley McCormick Expeditions of 1911 and 1913 by Charles L. Owens.

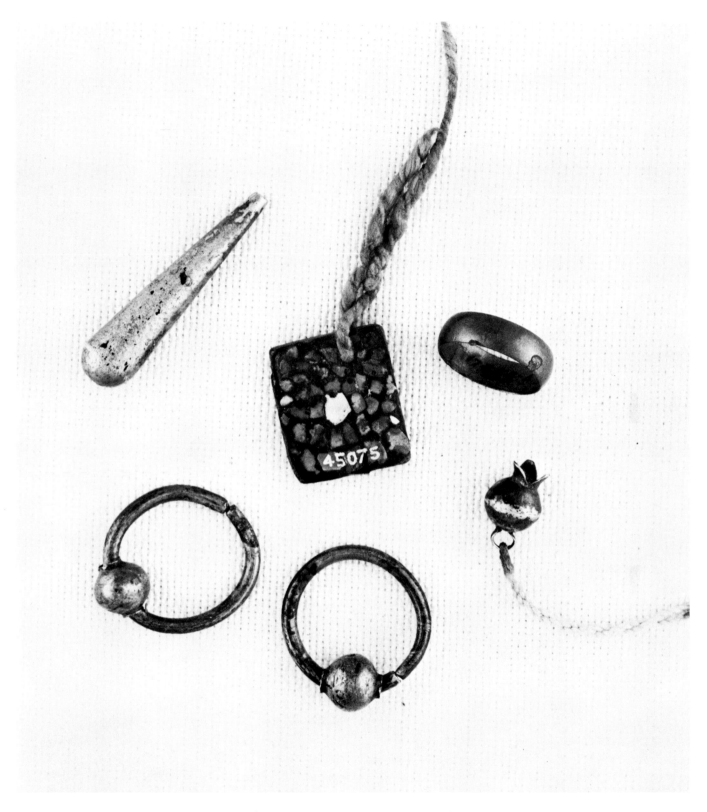

64. The Hopi turquoise earring was collected by Charles L. Owens in 1911 at Sichomovi (Hopi), Arizona, as was the traditional pair of silver loop earrings with the silver beads. The brass ring, probably a trade item made on the East Coast, was collected by Edward E. Ayer in the Southwest in 1895. The single stubby squash blossom earring and the cone-shaped earring were collected in the same period.

65. Edward E. Ayer collected this unusual pair of earrings in New Mexico or Arizona in 1895. Brass twisted wire loops support a pendant of shell, two types of trade glass beads, and a short extension of a brass chain. Trade beads were popular among the Plains Indians and metal chains were often used as Plains hair ornaments. A Plains Indian attribution is again in order here.

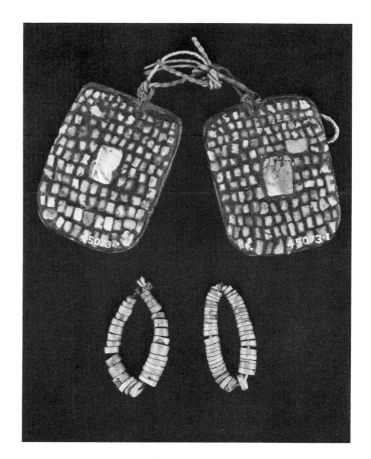

66. The handsome pair of large Hopi earrings consists of pieces of turquoise and a center piece of abalone fixed on a wooden backing by pinon gum mixed with the same ashes which color piki bread. Earrings of this type seem to have been the favorites of both the Hopi and Zuni Pueblos. The piece was bought for $1.50 by Charles L. Owens in 1911 while with the Stanley McCormick Expedition at Mishongovi (Hopi), Arizona. The museum's catalogue description attributes these earrings to the Hopis and says that they "were worn by maidens for festal occasions." The smaller pair of turquoise earrings was collected by H. R. Voth at Oraibi (Hopi), Arizona between 1893 and 1899 and acquired in 1899. These small, almost dainty, turquoise earrings are rarely found intact at such an early date.

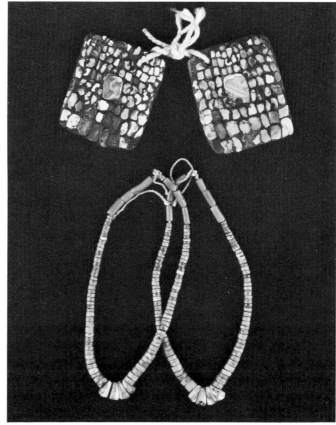

67. Another, smaller, pair of Hopi mosaic earrings collected in Oraibi (Hopi), Arizona, by H. R. Voth between 1893 and 1899. Pieces of turquoise and malachite were pasted onto a small block of wood. The two strings or loops of turquoise beads with graded sizes below have four shell beads at the center and three coral beads at each end. These are the popular "jacklases," turquoise beads once worn as earrings but later worn dangling from chunk turquoise necklaces as pendants, and they continue to be worn that way today (see Figure 14). On more modern loops of jacklases the old coral beads are now replaced by glass or plastic beads.

68. The set of six stamped buttons was collected by Charles L. Owens at Hano (Hopi), Arizona, in 1911. They are made of thick silver and are heavily oxidized. Their shape, four scalloped domes around a high domed center, is unusual. Circa 1890s.

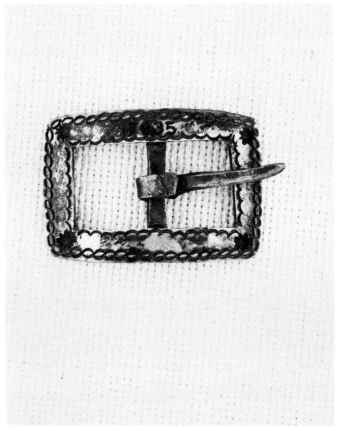

69. The stamped Navajo silver buckle was collected in Arizona in 1895 by Edward E. Ayer. It has simple stamp work, little wear, and would be worn on a first phase concha belt. At first buckles from old harnesses or old U.S. Army–issued buckles were used instead of the hand-wrought silver ones which were made slightly later. Circa 1895.

70. This stamped silver tobacco canteen catalogued by the museum as an "engraved silver bottle" was collected by Edward E. Ayer in 1895 in the Southwest. The early canteen has a simulated twisted wire effect going around it and on the cap which the later ones often do not possess. The canteen stamping clearly shows the "end-of-a-file" type design, which is another early trait.

71. This piece, which has no early collection data, is an unusually designed first phase silver concha. The pattern around the center slot opening, the twisted wire effect, the scalloped border, and the tiny punched stars on the scalloped edges themselves contribute to its distinctive features. Circa 1900.

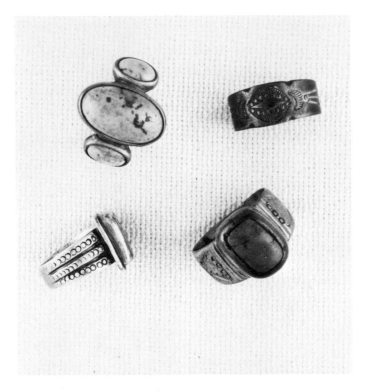

72. The ring at top left, with thick bezels around three oval stones, was collected by Herman Schweizer, chief buyer for the Fred Harvey Company, in 1930. The plain silver ring at top right, with stamped designs, was collected in 1911 by Charles L. Owens at Sichomovi (Hopi), Arizona and purchased there for ten cents. The stamping here is more advanced than some of the plain silver rocker-engraved rings shown in the collection of the Smithsonian Institution. The Navajo ring at bottom left, with a solid, charmingly stamped silver band and a square turquoise stone (not visible), is attributed to the early twentieth century. At bottom right, the ring with the large turquoise stone and bezel with stamped sides was also collected by Herman Schweizer in 1930.

73. The sandcast squash blossom necklace has an attributed date of 1920. The strong form of a squash blossom on top of the stamped bar just above the naja harks back to earlier styles current in the 1900s. The sandcast naja is graceful with its flower form falling from two silver curves, the tops of which connect with the crescent of the naja. The terminals have punched knobs. The flared ends still obvious on the silver beads show that this piece has had little wear. The clasp is a later White Man's addition.

74. This silver tobacco canteen, called a "silver bottle" by Edward E. Ayer when he collected it in the Southwest prior to 1895, was the first of its kind to be documented. Since then two other canteens probably made by the same silversmith have been found. All have the same design of a deer on one side and a rabbit on the other, but this canteen is rocker-engraved whereas the others are engraved. Here only the deer is visible. This canteen is of standard size while the other two are miniatures. (See Figures 80 and 182.) The canteen shown is circa 1890. Courtesy Field Museum of Natural History.

75. Labeled "Navajo leather wrist guard with silver plate," this bowguard was collected by Edward E. Ayer in 1895 in Arizona or New Mexico. The rocker engraved floral design, horizontal bar, and border designs all indicate an early date, circa 1880. The upper and lower scalloped border designs are punched, filed, and stamped, and resemble Navajo silver conchas of a later date. Rarely do bowguards have conchalike border designs. The headstalls in the Laboratory of Anthropology (Figure 116) and from a private collection (Figure 229) also have a combination of rocker-engraved interior designs and scalloped conchalike borders and come from a transitional stage in the development from the early rocker-engraved work, showing Plains Indian influence, to the stamped, filed, and punched work showing the influencé of the Spanish blacksmith. Courtesy Field Museum of Natural History.

Museum of the American Indian, Heye Foundation

Figures 76–84 all courtesy Museum of the American Indian.

76. The left-hand ring has file-notched decoration around the edge and heavy rocker engraving across the face. The right-hand ring shows evidence of tufa casting on the back. The piece was bent into shape and then filed and chisel-stamped. It is left open at the back, most probably unfinished because of the difficulty the silversmiths had with the process of soldering. Donald D. Graham, the first Indian agent at Zuni Pueblo, collected these pieces between 1880 and 1885 and said that a Navajo silversmith by the name of Chon (Atsidi Clon) instructed the Zunis to make silver jewelry and that these were among the first pieces made. Rocker-engraving is an early technique which the Navajos absorbed from the Plains Indians. Graham's collection of jewelry assembled at Zuni includes many other rocker-engraved pieces such as rings, earrings, buttons, and bracelets, plus engraved German silver items. Both the Navajos and the Zunis leaned heavily on current Plains Indian styles during the last four decades of the nineteenth century.

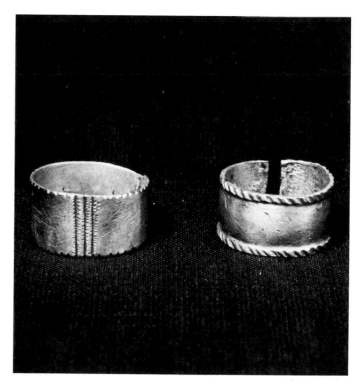

77. This striking early style bowguard (larger than later styled ketohs) has chisel-cut designs with a one-stamp design filling out the rest of the decoration. On the sides, silver tabs have been fashioned and bent over the leather to hold the silver in place. The piece is mounted on its original leather. The cutouts and designs hark back to Plains Indian silver brooches and hair piece ornaments. The bowguard was accessioned in 1936 but dates from much earlier, circa 1880.

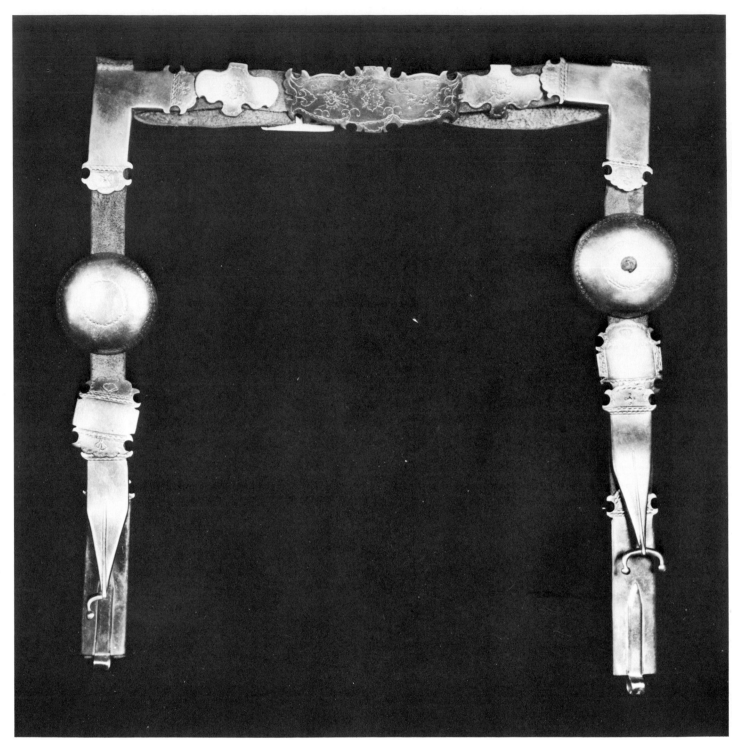

78. The Hunkpapa Sioux German silver headstall is quite elaborate with its center band and flanking German silver pieces cut out into involved shapes. Otherwise, the component parts are the same as in early Navajo silver bridles. Most Plains Indian bridles are simpler, without such ornate cutout shapes. The tabs of the German silver pieces under the conchas are similar to the tabs on Navajo bridles. The center piece and the conchas are rocker engraved. Often a German silver crescent-like naja (such as Figure 179) hung from the center pieces of Plains Indian bridles. A comparison with the Navajo silver bridle shown in Figure 79 reveals the strong connection between the Plains Indian bridles and the resulting Navajo ones.

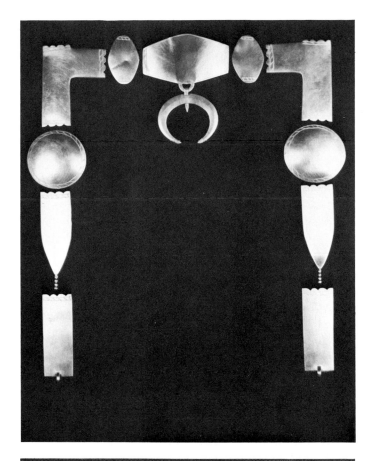

79. This is an early silver headstall dating before 1880 and most probably as early as 1870, made by Atsidi Chon, one of the earliest Navajo silversmiths. The headstall is basically rocker-engraved with minimal design content and large areas of silver. The naja is a simple, flat, wide silver crescent of the early style with plain pointed terminals. Plains Indian silver headstalls from the Colorado State Museum, the Museum of the American Indian (Figure 78), and the Smithsonian Institution resemble closely the Navajo headstall shown here. The basic layout of the pieces that comprise the headstall are the same, even to the extent of the tablike projections below the silver conchas. The conchas themselves also resemble the conchas of the Plains Indian bridles as well as their hairplates. Both the Navajo headstall and concha belt clearly originated from Plains Indian sources.

80. This miniature silver canteen shows a lot of wear. It was probably carried as a fob or a decorative piece, possibly by a soldier. The canteen has a heavily engraved figure of a rabbit on the front and a deer on the other side, with rudimentary stamping around the two loops and the spout. There is a crude, chiseled wire-effect design applied along the outside edge of the canteen. The chain is composed of heavy, hand-forged silver rods cut off with a cold chisel. The hanging loop at the top (not shown) shows extensive wear. The miniature canteen in the Graham Foundation collection (Figure 182) is most probably made by the same silversmith; see also Figure 74. Circa 1890. Presented to the Heye Foundation in 1936 by Mrs. Joseph Bancroft.

81. This is a full concha belt showing the first phase diamond-shaped center slots typical of the 1880s. The beautiful buckle, which was probably added about twenty years later, shows both cold-chisel and well-executed stamp work. Collected around 1910.

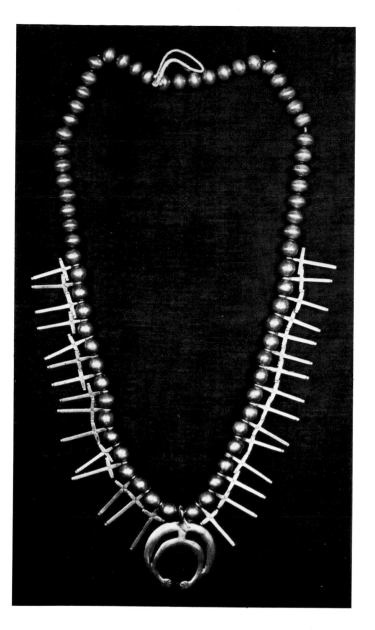

82. Here is a fine, early Pueblo-style necklace with a sandcast naja and crosses used as the Navajos use squash blossoms. The delicate crosses are lightly decorated with cold-chisel stamping, relating well with the simple and rather crude naja (see Figure 17). The necklace has been restrung; the more oval-shaped beads at the top were added later. This piece is said to have been made for the wife of Kit Carson. Circa 1885.

83. This simple and elegant early style necklace has a naja with hands, rounded beads, and a single cross strung between the beads. The typical early naja design at the terminals is complemented by a small third hand on the connecting loop soldered to the top. The necklace is strung on its original leather and dates circa 1890.

84. Collected in Ganado, Arizona, in 1910, this necklace was most probably shortened because of loss of beads. Many necklaces broke under wear and in the process lost beads and squashes. This accounts for necklaces restrung with different types of beads, such as this piece. The outstanding feature of the item is the four-handed naja which was first cast and then embellished with the use of a cold chisel. There is file work on the loop of the naja on the inner crescent, and on the stems of the squash blossoms.

85.   Three types of early squash blossom earrings used by Navajo and Pueblo Indians are shown here, all dating from 1900 or before. The pair at the end has heavy silver pomegranates hanging from thick forged silver loops. It was made by Gushgi, a Zuni silversmith, and collected in 1901 at Zuni Pueblo by H. E. Sargent. Next to it is a variation of the pomegranate where small ones hang from silver beads, suspended by hollow cones. The middle earrings are strung with two medium-size silver beads.

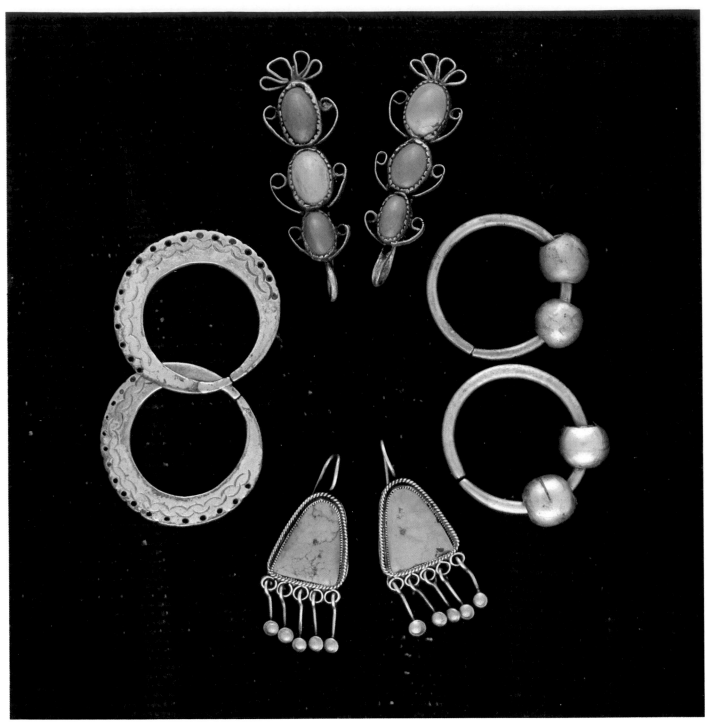

86. Top: this pair of Navajo earrings with large oval green stones looks particularly handsome with its serrated bezels and projecting wire-scroll forms. Circa 1915. Center left: a plain silver pair of flat scalloped earrings, simply stamped and punched. The well-worn early stamped design is quite effective. Both the Navajos and the Zunis wore earrings of this type. Circa 1890. Center right: one of the earliest earring forms is that of a silver ball strung on a silver loop. The two large silver balls here have wide holes and move easily around the loop (see Figures 9 and 18). The Navajos and the Pueblo Indians used this style extensively. Circa 1870–1880. Bottom: Zuni earrings with their intricate silver drops differ markedly from the bolder and stronger-appearing Navajo ones. Around the triangular blue stones is a fine border of twisted wire work. Circa 1930.

87.   These eight dark green stone rings with much wear date from the early 1900s except for the bottom square ring which belongs to the 1920s. Most of the bezels are appropriately thick and crude and many are serrated. The ring at right center with elongated oval stones and the one at left center with silver loops attached to the two outside stones are particularly attractive. The earrings, circa 1890, are typically scalloped and minimally stamped.

88. Shown here are seven rings with blue turquoise and two plain silver ones. The plain silver ring in the middle has simple engraved designs and is shaped like a seal ring, of which it is most probably a copy. The technique of engraving onto silver would indicate the piece to be early, but the thick seallike part of the ring places it circa 1900. The unset silver ring to the left has a square plate applied to its center, and soldered, cold-chiseled leaf-shaped pieces on each side. Circa early 1880s. The other rings date from the early 1900s to the 1920s and present a diversity of styles using soldered bars (early 1900s), a large plate with an oval stone in its center (1920s), and an oval twisted wire setting (1920s).

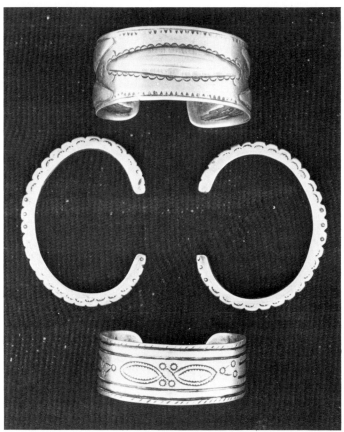

89. The gracefully filed and stamped bracelet on the bottom was accessioned in 1905, a good early date (around 1900 or earlier). The filed edges show considerable wear, and the space between the chiseled, thickly grooved lines is worn smooth. A stamped design of small circles with two elliptical figures occupies the center area. The pair of bracelets in the middle dates from circa 1895; accessioned in 1922. The notched or scalloped plain silver bangles show early stamped crescents and circles on the sides. These were made by casting and forging. In general, the stamp work and bracelet shape are similar to early silver earrings. The unset silver bracelet at top shows much wear in the middle repoussé form which is twice repeated at each end (not visible). The stamped designs at the edges are early, as are those outlining the repoussé forms. The repoussé forms have tiny stamped lines in their centers. At each terminal are two sets of three crudely stamped small arrows in between the repoussé forms. Circa 1905.

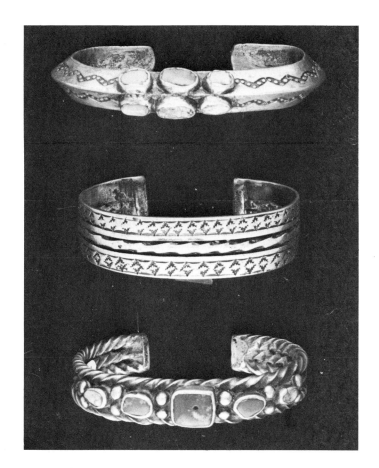

90. Above is a strongly visual bracelet with three stones on each side held by crude bezels. The zigzag stamp work down each side is pleasing. Circa 1920s. The middle unset silver bracelet has an elaborately stamped design which is offset by the simple, well-worn central band of twisted square wire. Circa 1910. Below is a finely twisted wire bracelet with five greenish stones, the center square one a pierced earbob. The crudely cut stones are each separated by two silver studs. Circa 1910.

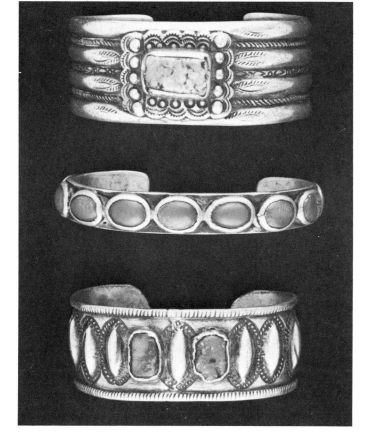

91. The top bracelet with the rectangular blue stone is set in a baroquely designed plate of stamped and studded patterns. Between the silver bands with well-worn stamp marks is fine filed rope work dividing the bracelet into four ridges. Between the two middle ridges is a subtly different stamped pattern. Circa 1920s. Thick silver bezels around matched, mellow green stones make the middle bracelet appealing. Circa 1915. The bottom bracelet has two oddly shaped green turquoise stones in crude bezels (one an old pierced earbob) and thirteen embossed forms around the bracelet, with elaborate stamping bordering each embossed form. The chisel-stamped edges nicely frame the piece. Circa 1915.

92.   All three of these sandcast fluted bracelets are heavy, well-made, and hammered Navajo pieces dating around 1920 (the middle bracelet is possibly a little earlier). In the 1930s there was a revival of this style. Each bracelet has a central silver plate holding turquoise stones soldered onto the silver band base. Strong chisel and stamp marks on the top bracelet are evident. It has a large, green, almost round turquoise stone surrounded by a sunburst effect. The three bands have minimal stamping while those in between have a simulated wire effect. The middle bracelet also has minimal cold-chisel stamping on the three bands while the middle plate holds a richer and more complicated design. The unmatched rectangular and square green stones are held by thick, serrated bezels, flanked by six silver knobs or studs on the long side and two flared and stamped extensions on the short side. At the terminals are rectangular green stones, each in a serrated bezel, inset in a smaller stamped plate (not visible). The bracelet on the bottom has a large sunburst effect enveloping an oval blue stone on a minimally stamped plate.

93. The top bracelet is immensely thick and heavy. The three bands, each individually stamped, have been soldered together and the unique busy designs are deeply stamped. There are four green stones (one is blue and has been replaced, two are not in view). The center pieces alternating between the stones are repoussé. Circa 1920s. Below is a large, wide, well-worn bracelet with a large green stone, crudely bezeled. Simulated deeply grooved rope designs and lovely, lacy stamped designs that are irregular in size — all add a nicely spaced and balanced effect. Circa 1915. Notice the similarity of this later piece to the bow-guard shown in the Smithsonian Institution's collection (Figure 50).

94. These three fine bracelets, inset with turquoise stones, show a 1920s style. They are heavy, even heavy-styled, and display a simple mastery in the use of stones. The bracelet on the top, with three greenish stones, two oval and one square, is nicely stamped, four studs setting the middle stone off. It is relatively thick and well worn. The middle bracelet is set with three oval spiderweb turquoise stones, the middle one set off, again, by two pairs of silver studs. The band has two rows of simulated twisted wire between two slender bars, each decorated with stamped crescent designs, all hammered into a simple band. The bottom bracelet, with five primitively set greenish stones (the center one a pierced earbob), is inset in a single silver band. The edges are simply filed to look like twisted silver wire.

95. Four completely silver najas are shown here. The top one is thin, with crude hands and simple but pleasing stamped designs. The central piece is soldered onto the naja and contains an embossed form. Circa 1920s. The naja to the left is gracefully stamped with a design on the large crescent and on the connecting loop. The inside crescent or inner naja is soldered onto the larger one. The terminal knobs are concave on the inside. Circa early 1900s. The thin naja on the right has unusual nearly heart-shaped terminals with holes. It is made of poor grade silver and is strongly reminiscent of Plains Indian jewelry material. Circa 1890. The sandcast naja at the bottom has a nice wide shape based on older styles and two perfectly matching crescents, enhanced by the simple stamped designs with file work on the terminals. Circa 1930.

96. The "squash blossom" necklace on top is strung with beautiful old oval beads instead of squash blossoms supporting a well-worn sandcast naja with hands at its terminals. It was accessioned in 1932, the naja belonging to the turn of the century while the beads are contemporary with it. To the lower right, the huge and unusual naja has a central design resembling a tree with a square turquoise stone at one end. Simple, attractively stamped designs adorn the very thin, flat, and round naja. Circa early 1900s. The lower left necklace has a naja with a stamped silver cross soldered on two crescents ending in two round turquoise stones which are almost joined. Circa 1910; the cross may have been added at a later date.

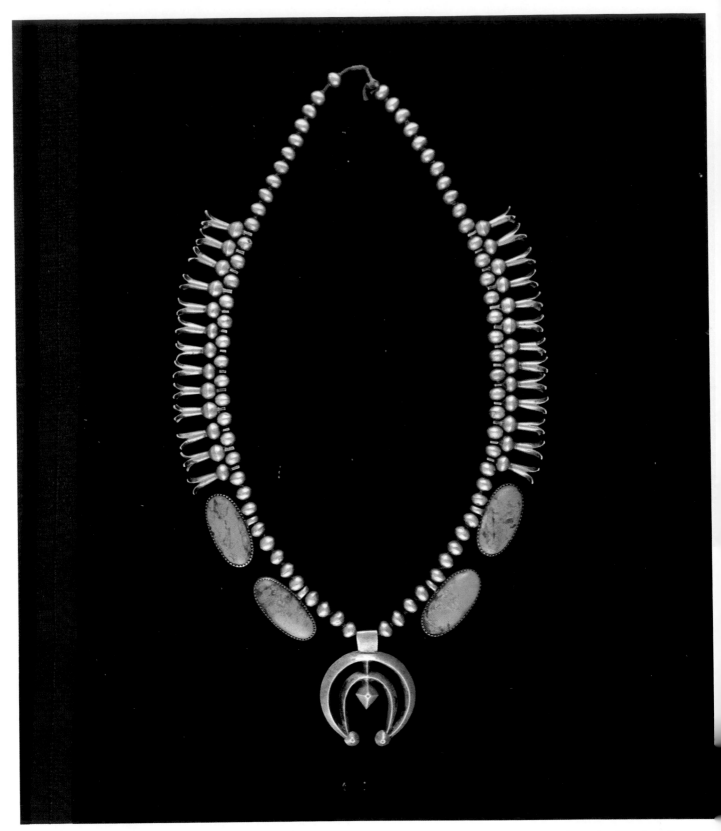

97. A combination of simplicity and ornateness is reflected in this unique squash blossom necklace. The plain sandcast naja is contrasted with the vivid oval turquoise "squashes" set in fine bezels and the delicate silver squash blossoms above. The craftsmanship here is of a high order. Circa 1930.

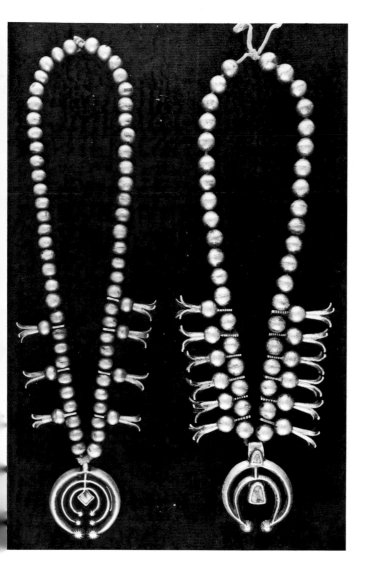

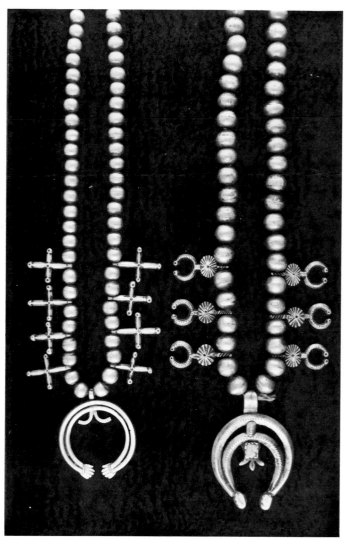

98. Two typical, well-constructed, sandcast squash blossom necklaces illustrate the excellent craftsmanship current in the 1920s. The necklace to the left has a naja consisting of three crescents with a diamond-shaped blue stone turquoise set. Each crescent has graduated button-shaped terminals. The other necklace has two nicely set triangular blue turquoise stones in chiseled bezels. The center stone drop is soldered onto the naja and both relate well together. The stems of the large squashes are notched.

99. These two fancy squash blossom necklaces each have unique sandcast "squashes." To the left, instead of "squashes," there are silver crosses with small stamp marks and a lightweight silver naja. Soldered onto the naja, as terminals, are hands with a center scroll form (see Figure 22). This piece is probably of Pueblo origin, maybe Isleta. There is a photograph taken by William H. Jackson around 1878 at Hopi of a Moki Indian Snake Priest wearing a squash blossom necklace with very similar sandcast squash blossoms. This necklace is a later revival of the style shown in the Jackson photograph. Circa early 1900s; accessioned in 1932. The heavy sandcast naja to the right has a square serrated bezel drop of green turquoise with leaf forms under it. The crescents are nicely stamped. The terminal green stones taper gracefully. The unusual sandcast "squashes" are in the shape of najas which are finely stamped. Circa 1920s.

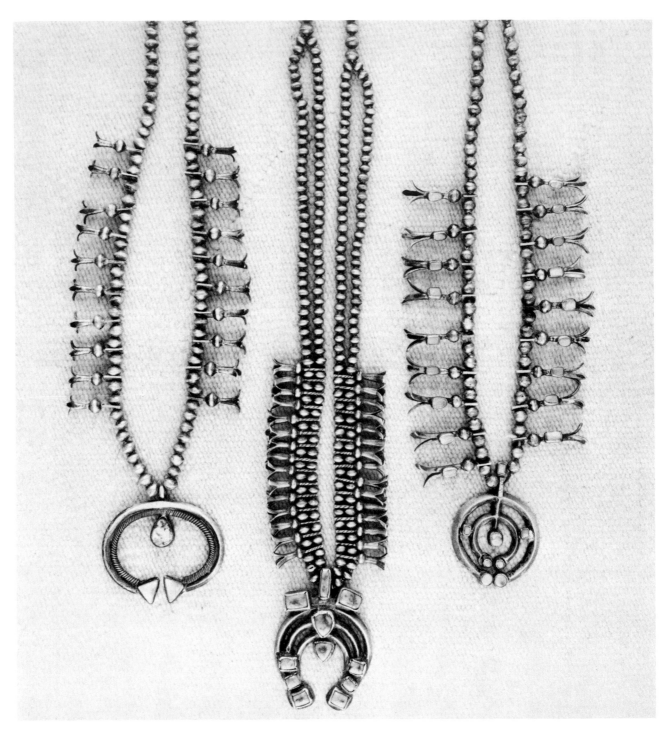

100. These three squash blossom necklaces are delicately proportioned with tiny squashes and small silver beads. The one to the left has a naja with two triangular turquoise stone terminals and one teardrop center stone. A fine wire crescent band edges the inside of the naja. Circa 1920. The middle necklace has fifteen refined squash blossoms on each side tightly compacted together and strung on two strands of silver beads; the stem of each squash blossom is notched. This dainty effect is contrasted with the more crudely conceived sandcast naja with eleven small turquoise stones in crude bezels. The cluster effect of the naja is needed to balance the baroque array of squash blossoms. Circa 1925. The necklace to the right has in each squash blossom a small, square green turquoise stone. The delicate effect of these settings is augmented by a small sandcast naja finely inset with seven small stones. Circa 1920.

101. This ketoh has a simple green stone and fine floral repoussé designs: Shown on its reverse side is the old leather fastened by copper loops secured by leather tabs. The leather strap that goes around the wrist is decorated with silver buttons and a unique silver cross bar. Circa 1910.

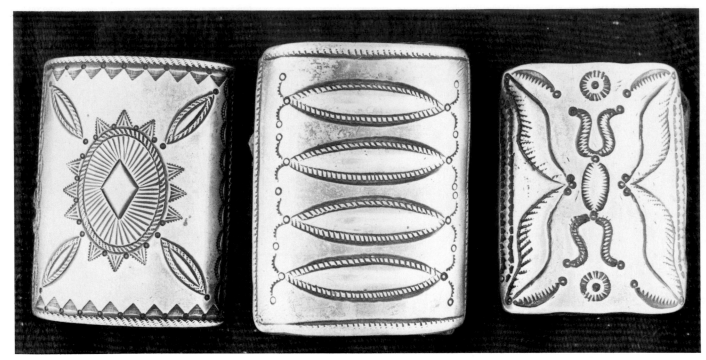

102.   Left: the well-worn small ketoh is made with thick silver and has heavy, crude stamp work. Circa 1900. Center: this ketoh has four attractive elliptical repoussé forms with lacy border designs. Circa 1890. Right: this ketoh has an elaborate re- poussé sunburst design around a plain silver dia- mond form. The four leaf forms and the involved border patterns give balance to the strong central design. Circa 1910.

103.   Seen here are three small ketohs. The stun- ning one to the left with the small blue stone is a sandcast example with cold-chisel work. Circa 1910. The wrought middle piece with an oval green stone shows strong stamp work of floral designs. The slightly scalloped edges match the stamped border designs. Circa 1920. The wrought ketoh to the right has well-worn stamped floral designs and is unusually small in size. Circa 1910.

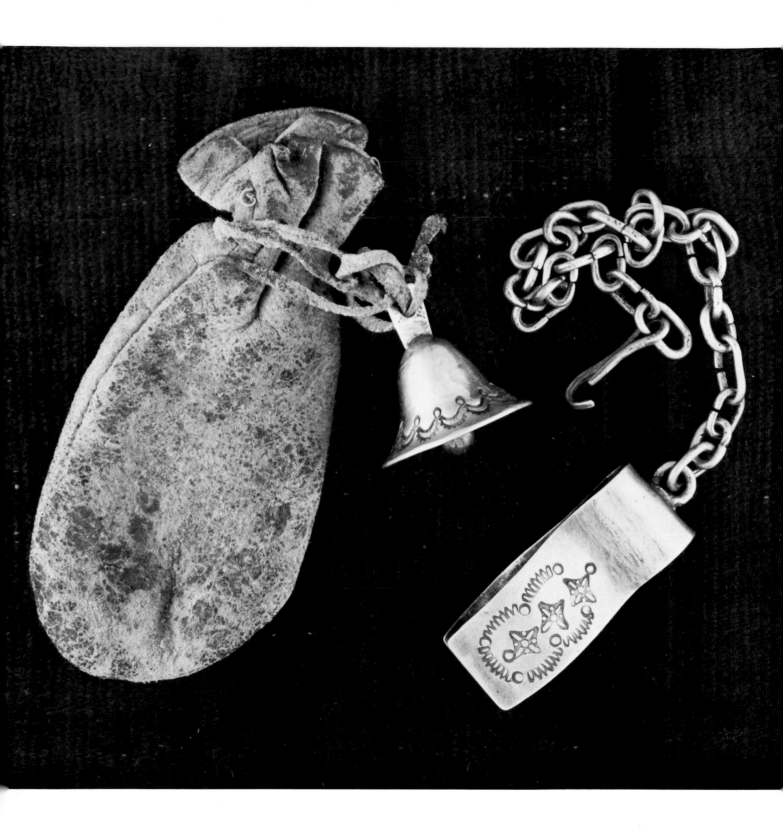

104. To the left is a Navajo "mother-in-law" bell with hide bag. The bell was supposedly used to warn a married man of the approach of his wife's mother. Circa 1915. Right: This is a fine example of silver Navajo tweezers, used for removing whiskers, together with a thick silver home-made chain with its hook. The stamping on the tweezers is quite attractive. Circa 1900.

105. This first phase concha belt, composed of round stamped conchas, has a handsome stamped buckle. Patterned like the conchas, it is pleasingly reduced in size. The conchas have cutout diamond slots which were made with a cold chisel and which contrast against the plain silver. The twisted wire effect is small and fine. Circa 1870–1880.

106. The first phase concha belt on top has bold scalloped and rope-work borders with a simple stamped design outlining the diamond-shaped slots of the oval conchas. Circa 1900. The other, older, first phase belt features finer scalloped border designs, twisted wire effect, and stamped designs around the diamond-shaped cutouts. Circa 1890s.

107. The thick, oval buckle on this first phase concha belt has an attractively simple stamped design. The conchas are oval with semioval center slot openings lightly rocker-engraved around the edges. The outside decoration is plain and crisp. Each concha is backed by an individual piece of old leather. The sparse decoration on first phase concha belts leaves exposed a wide expanse of rich plain silver. Circa 1880.

108. The finely stamped pattern around the diamond-shaped cutout openings of this first phase concha belt is of high quality. The border decoration has a fine wire effect and richly scalloped edges, yet is clear and uncluttered. Circa 1880s.

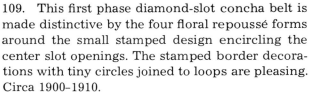

109. This first phase diamond-slot concha belt is made distinctive by the four floral repoussé forms around the small stamped design encircling the center slot openings. The stamped border decorations with tiny circles joined to loops are pleasing. Circa 1900–1910.

110. Both closed-center first phase concha belts shown here are very baroquely decorated. The one to the left has green turquoise stones in the conchas and elaborate oval petal-like patterns. The stamped border decorations are traditional. Circa 1900. The other has similar floral forms and a plain silver diamond area instead of the turquoise stones. The elongated oval stamped disks interspersed between the conchas are unusual. The scalloped border design is more involved than the center areas. Circa 1900.

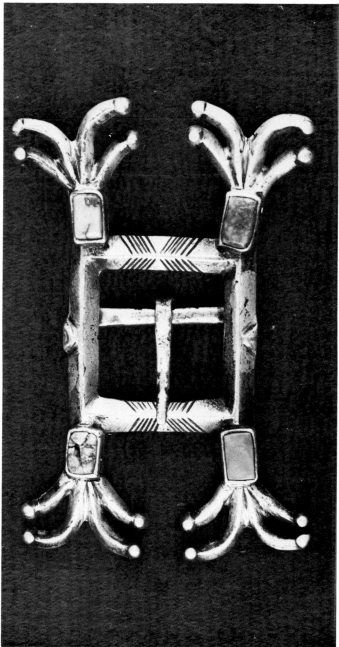

111. On the right is a small sandcast concha belt with airy tracery work, which allows the attractive leather to show. The conchas resemble abstract butterflies. The elaborate buckle has a pair of turquoise stones, one at each end. Circa 1910. The other small, finely executed belt has nice stamped and cold-chiseled work around a plain silver diamond area, giving a crowded yet integrated effect. The repoussé and stamped buckle is the same size as the conchas.

112. This quite large and beautiful sandcast belt buckle has four rectangular green stones and strong cold-chiseled designs. The elaborate prongs contribute to its graceful form. It shows good wear. Circa 1915.

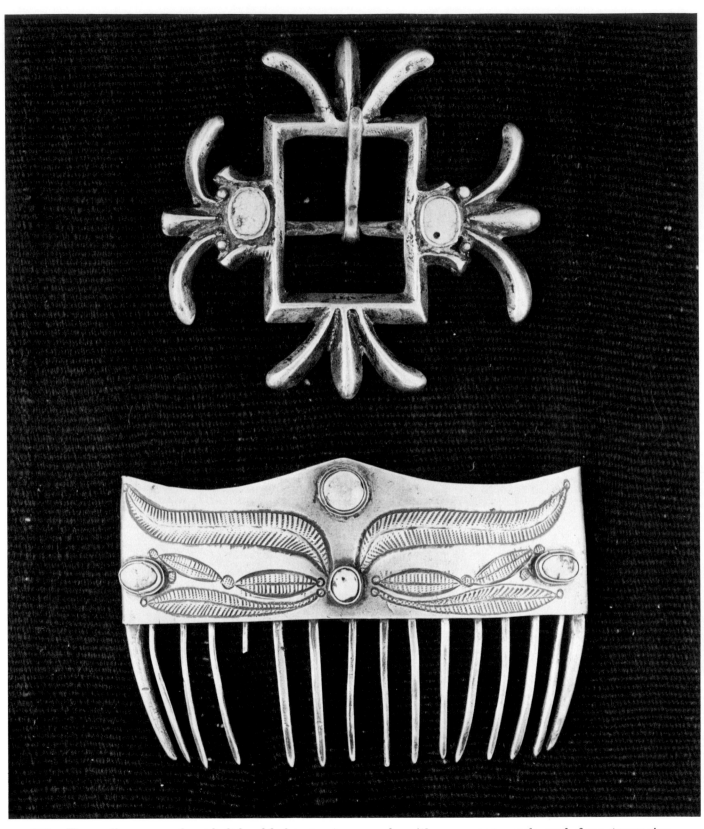

113. The well-worn sandcast belt buckle has a set of turquoise stones (one of which is pierced) enveloped by thick bezels. The stones give color to the buckle. Between 1920 and 1930. The silver comb with repoussé work and four turquoise stones is an adaptation of an early Spanish mantilla comb. Circa 1930s.

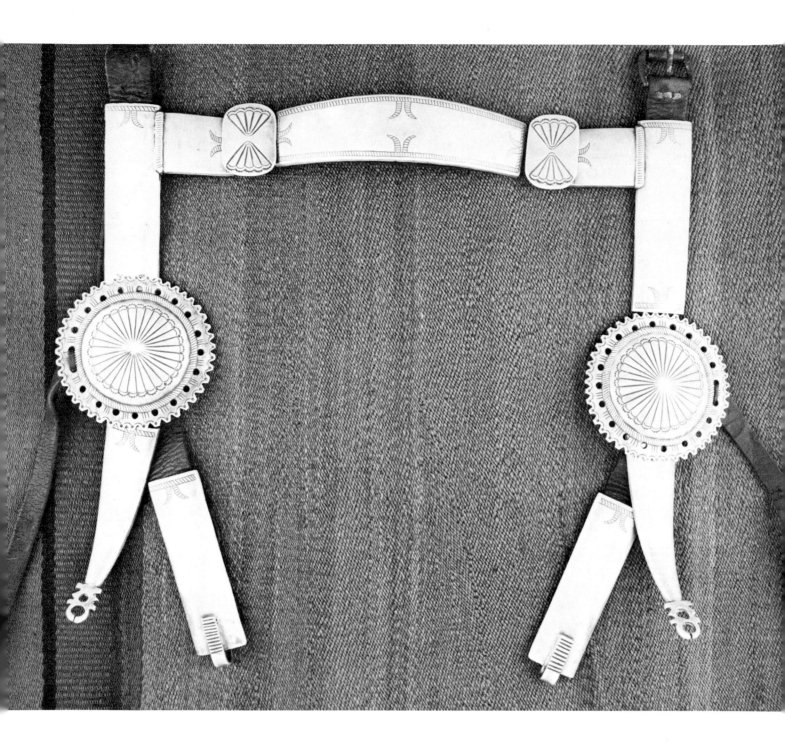

114. The simplicity of this bridle is refreshing. Except for the relatively sparsely patterned conchas, whose designs match the two oval silver pieces on either side of the curved antler center piece, the stamped designs are elegantly restrained. Circa 1885; accessioned 1939.

115. This bridle is similar to Figure 114. The plant form (corn) design on the center piece is exquisite as is the chisel-stamped single bar pattern. The small tabs below the conchas are attractively de-signed with a small raised center fashioned like traditional silver button forms. On the tabs below the conchas are chisel-stamped "cuffs" above primitive hands. Circa 1885; accessioned 1936.

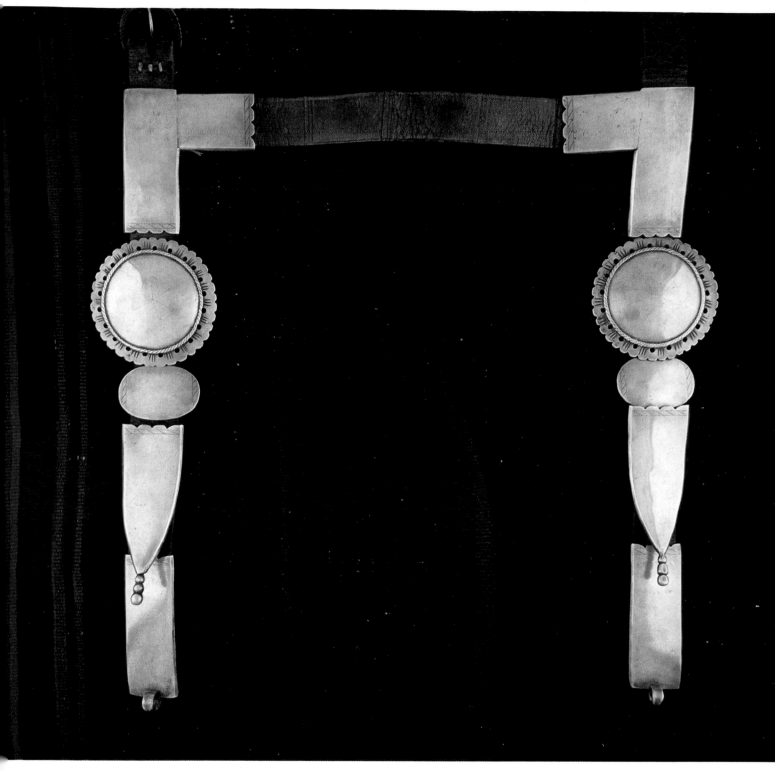

116. This simple headstall is rocker-engraved except for the stamped and filed early conchas which are similar to the closed-center concha in the Smithsonian's collection of oval conchas (Figure 42). The rocker-engraving of a three-triangle form in the middle of the conchas, almost completely worn away, attests to the delicacy and shallowness of the rocker-engraved design. This headstall is not quite as early as the one in the Museum of the American Indian (Figure 79), representing a slightly later stage in the development of the bridle from Plains Indian styles to Navajo ones. Circa 1870–1875.

117. The simple naja of two soldered silver crescents with buttonlike terminals contrasts strongly with the rest of the well-stamped bridle with file work. Stamped on the center piece are two pairs of simple arrow designs. The concha designs are bold and explosive, and the oddly shaped pieces under the conchas and the finely stamped end tabs add to the busy effect. The original stamped silver buckle is with the bridle. Circa 1915.

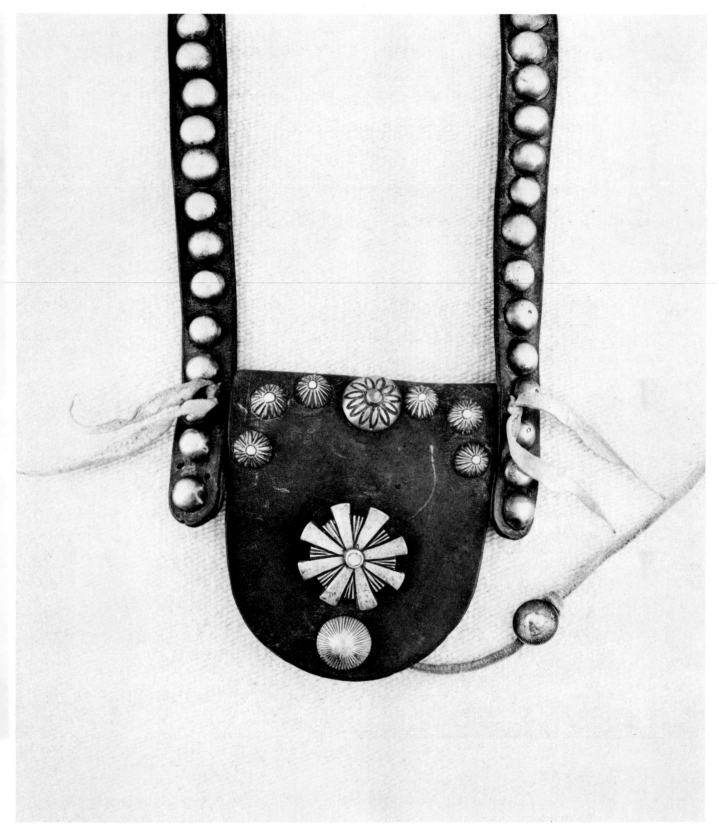

118. The small bandolier pouch is decorated with an assortment of silver buttons (only one with a turquoise stone) and a unique silver center piece of cutout forms with a stone in its middle. A single plain silver button similar to those on the strap is tied to the leather drawstring. Circa 1910.

Figures 119–126 are photographed by Glenn Short/Southwest Silver and Light Works.

119. This one-of-a-kind round bowguard was collected by Herman Schweizer of the Fred Harvey Company and purchased in 1906 for one dollar. It is a spectacular example of what artful complexity can be derived from a silversmith's chisel. The back of the leather band is also stamped with cross designs. Circa 1880.

120. The three stamped manta pins and the chisel-stamped pair of Navajo copper earrings resemble silver earring styles but are much rarer. The stubbiness of the copper pair and the thick, crude prongs that go into the ear lobes are unusual. The museum's inventory card reads, "1880–1890 — about the first ones made."

121. The squash blossoms have a refined appearance with filed stems. The naja has two notched strips of wire soldered together in a crescent shape. Five delicately shaped stones are soldered onto the naja, and soldered button-shaped forms serve as terminals. Circa 1910; purchased in 1929. The unusual ends of the upper double crescent naja terminate in triangular plates that are soldered and stamped. The loop is part of a filed, scroll-like plate soldered onto the crescents. Circa 1910. The lower double crescent naja has the early tapered form with a square turquoise stone joining the crescents together. Circa 1890s.

122.   A fine selection of old and different style belts is seen here. To the left, the cold-chiseled and filed conchas have a clear design with a center repoussé, a plain silver elliptical form which relates well to the wide swath of silver bordering the sunburst design. Circa 1890; purchased from the Frazier Trading Post in 1946. The twelve conchas on the next belt have small, elaborate border designs and a powerful, stamped center area which makes this belt particularly effective. The early stamped belt buckle has a visible leather backing on the underside, cut out to fit the buckle's shape. All the other conchas on this belt and the one next to it have a similar old fitted leather backing. Circa 1885. Third belt: the unusual shape, flattened, twisted wire soldered to the outer edge, the stamped and repoussé center and matching belt buckle, all add up to a splendid small-sized belt. Circa 1885. The belt to the right is also repoussé, chisel-stamped, and filed. The bold, raised sunburst predominates. The buckle with the stamped arrows is later. Circa 1900; purchased from Willis Martin, Two Gray Hills, Arizona, in 1925.

123. All these bracelets date from the early 1900s and are superbly designed and crafted with stamped, chisel-stamped, and filed techniques. The top and bottom left-hand items and the top right-hand bracelet have fine stamped sunburst designs with turquoise stones in the center. The two middle left-hand bracelets have a center band of strong, stamped designs centered by turquoise stones and flanked by stretches of plain silver with a nice patina. The bottom right-hand bracelet is crowded with a large rectangular stone with a serrated bezel, a center band of twisted wire, and four applied and stamped forms with stamp work on the outside bands.

124. The left-hand bracelet consists of two triangular bands made of silver rods with diamond shapes inset with turquoise and a silver pin. Stamped silver diamond forms appear at both ends. On the two silver bands are sparingly stamped arrow designs. Arrow designs originate around 1900, the date of this bracelet, and continue to be used through the 1930s when they were increasingly employed and tourist oriented. The two triangular bands of the second bracelet from the left have a simulated wire effect centered by a large triangular stone. Circa early 1900s; purchased at Rockpoint Trading Post in 1925. The baroque silver bracelet to the right has two triangular silver bands joined together by stamped silver bars with four rectangular turquoise stones and bezels set on silver plates. Six radiating arms are soldered and placed between the plates. Circa early 1900s; purchased from Garcia at Chinlee, Arizona, in 1926. The three stamped silver ridges of the right-hand bracelet support a round turquoise stone in a scalloped concha-type center piece with silver dots and stamped designs. Circa early 1900s. Some of these bracelets might be Zuni, particularly the last two.

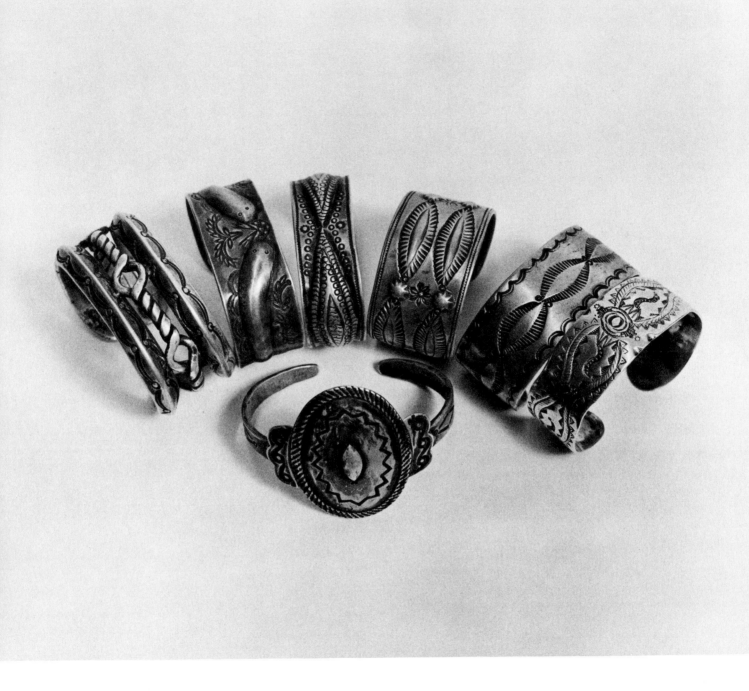

125. The bracelet at left utilizes two large twisted silver wires to form the central design. Two stamped triangular silver bars frame the wires. Circa 1920s. The second stamped silver bracelet with an elongated repoussé snake figure on each side is unique. The snake replaces the more traditional floral pattern. Circa 1900. The third bracelet has die-stamped, long diamond-shaped designs. Tiny circles and fine stamped designs beautifully ornament the piece. Circa 1900. Cold-chiseled and repoussé elliptical forms flank two raised center button forms on the fourth bracelet. Circa early 1900s. The fifth silver bracelet has stamped and punched elliptical forms and a scallop-design border. Circa early 1900s. The sixth bracelet is busily stamped with graceful and elaborate designs. Circa early 1900s. The bracelet below has a center concha-style disk with wire effect patterns, stamping, and narrow wrist bands. It is most probably a tourist piece. Circa 1920–1930.

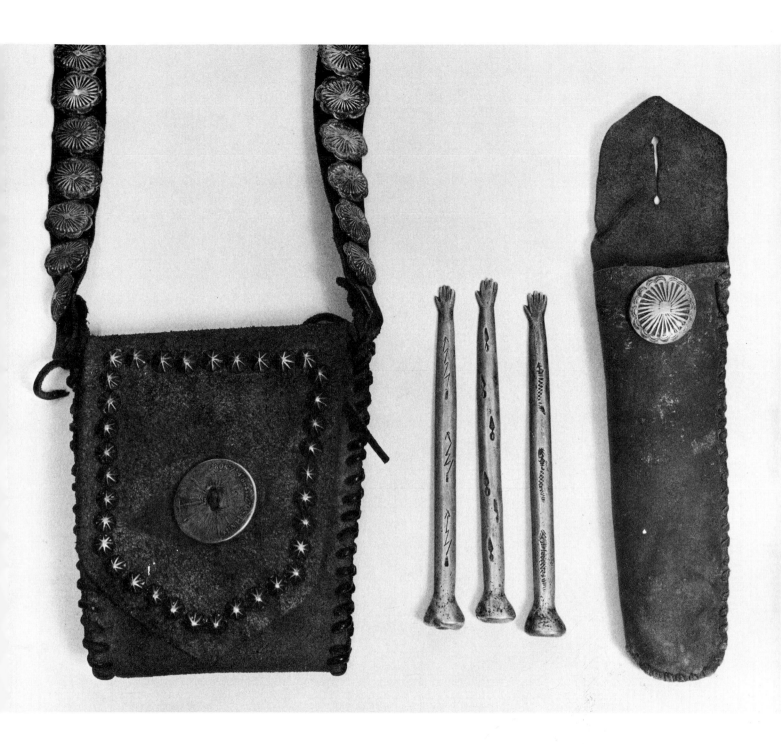

126. A unique piece is shown here — a Navajo medicine pouch. The three silver pieces in the center were made from straight bar ingots, cast in tufa, and then smoothed down with a file. Pieces such as these were also made from meteorite fragments and stone. They are stamped with designs resembling lightning, arrows, and snakes. On top the bars terminate in hands. To the right is the cylindrical pouch that houses the three silver bars. This pouch appears to be older than the bandelier pouch to the left, which holds all of the items and which might have been added later. The bars are labeled by the museum, "witch sticks and were used by Navajo Medicine men to exorcise spirits." Sometimes silversmiths went blind from their arduous work and then became medicine men. The "witch sticks" were most probably acquired before 1930 by the Heard Museum.

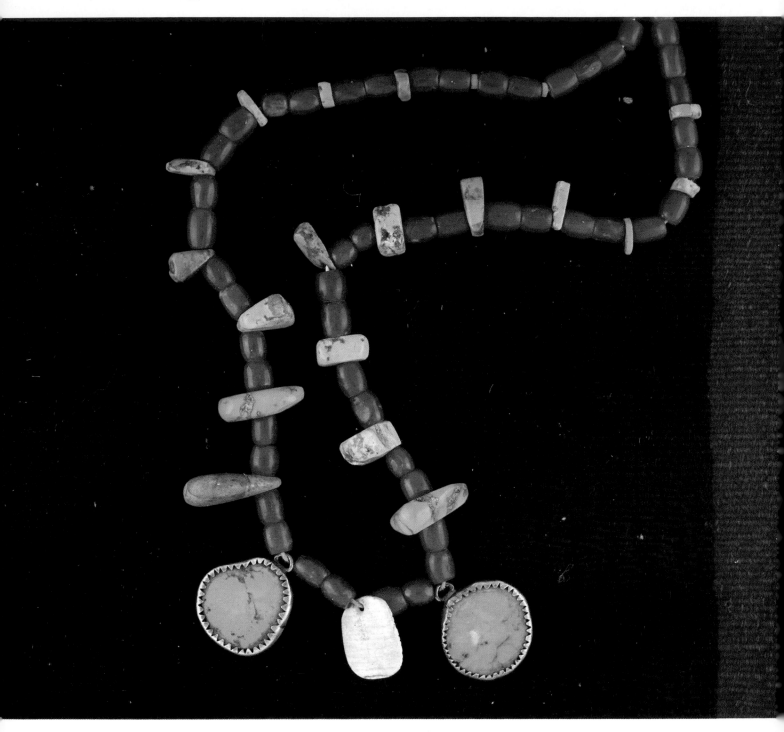

127. A fine, thick, dark red coral necklace with two superb blue turquoise stones set into fine serrated bezels and a white shell pendant. Earbobs such as these turquoise stones were often worn as pendants for necklaces or tied onto chunk turquoise necklaces. Circa early 1900s.

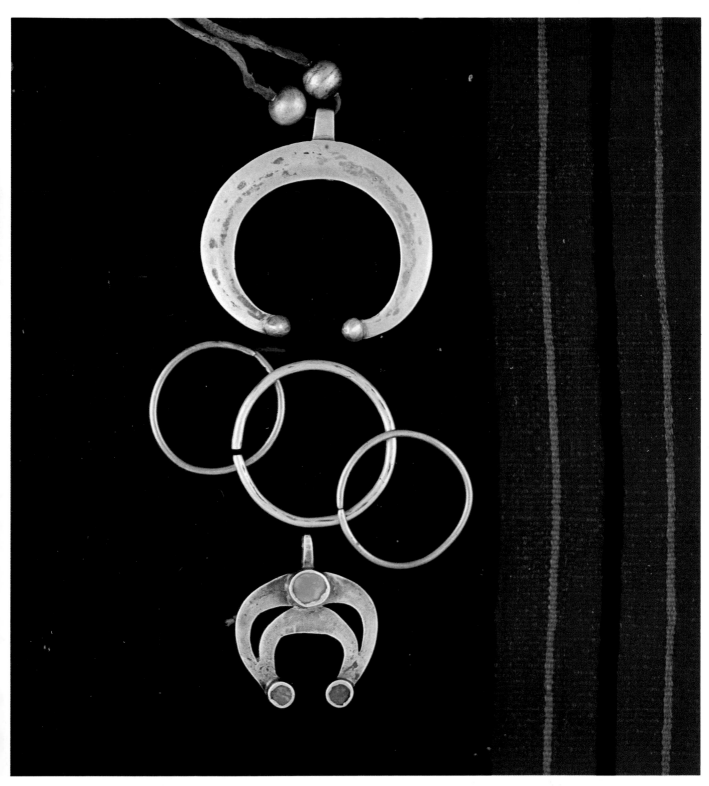

128. These two early najas, one large and tapered with a wide crescent shape and simple silver knobs for terminals (see Figure 4), and the superb smaller flat one with turquoise terminals, a center turquoise piece and a crescent attractively enfolding another, are both fine examples. The latter naja is one of the earliest examples known with turquoise stones. Circa 1880s. The three forged silver earrings are of a style typical of the 1870s and 1880s. Collected by M. L. Woodward, Gallup, New Mexico, in the 1930s on the Navajo reservation.

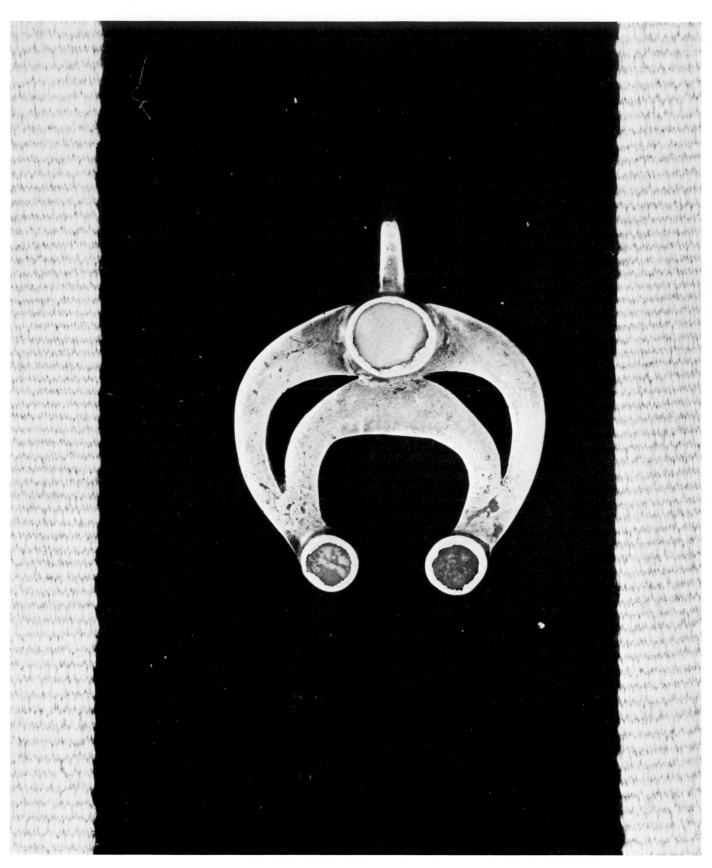

129.   A close-up of the bottom naja in Figure 128.

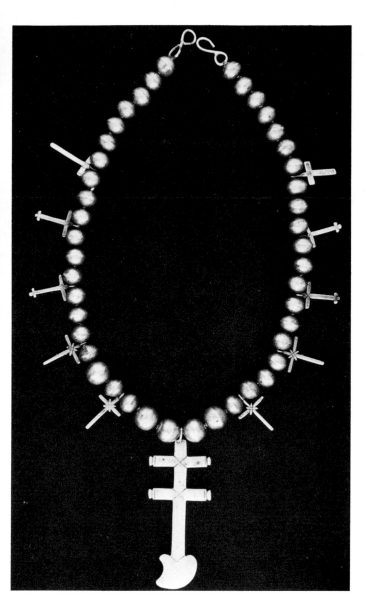

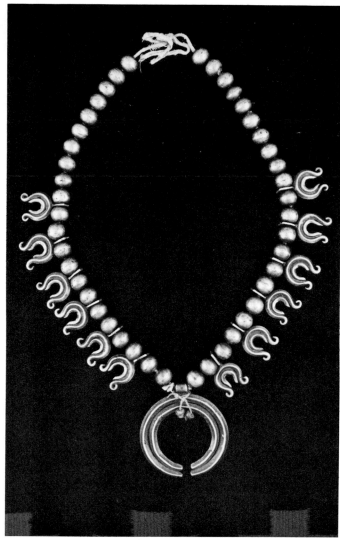

130. The Pueblo Indians made their necklaces by replacing the usual squash blossoms with crosses and the naja with a double-barred pendant. This classic example has three types of crosses. The double-barred cross pendant ends with an engraved sacred heart, a Catholic symbol. The Catholic religion was more readily absorbed by the Pueblo Indians than by the Navajos. The double-barred symbol and its heartlike bottom are also found in Plains Indian jewelry and are thought to represent a stylized dragonfly. The clasp on this necklace and the various types of beads and crosses indicate that it has been restrung. Circa 1915.

131. The simplicity of the triangular two-crescent naja hanging from silver beads coupled with the elegance of the sandcast "squash blossoms" in the shape of baroque najas make this necklace a stunning piece. Two turquoise beads have been tied onto the naja, forming a drop. Circa 1920s. The naja is probably earlier.

132. The fleur-de-lis sandcast blossoms with filed stems and the matching fleur-de-lis form on top of the naja nicely complement the elaborately constructed silver naja. The naja is closed by a turquoise setting but is visually dominated by the effect of the simulated twisted wire. The three turquoise stones in vertical order (the middle one is a pendant) add to the necklace's beauty. Circa 1920s.

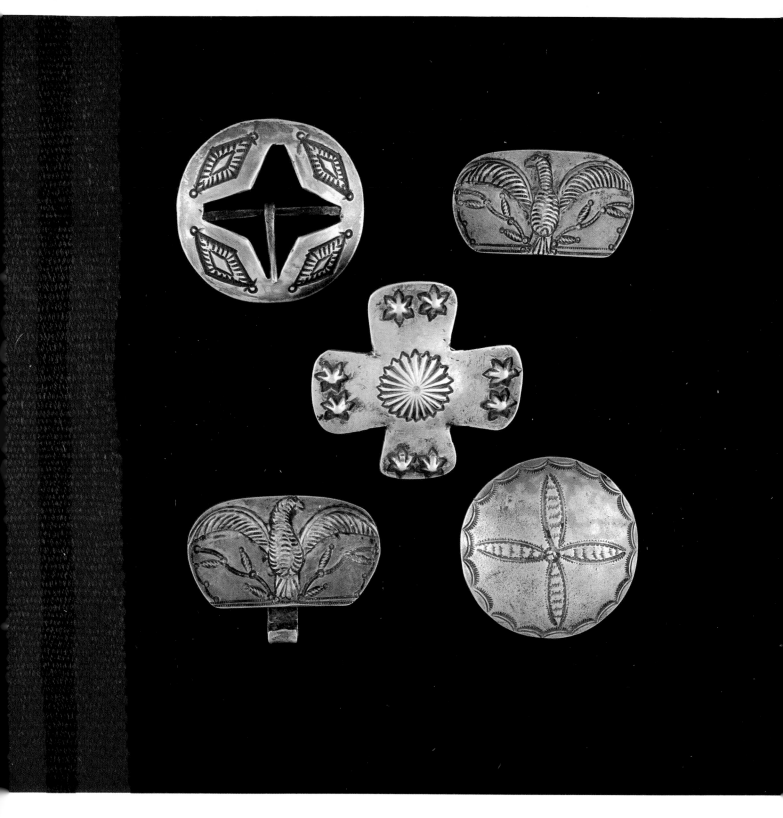

133. Five old silver items — a pair of repoussé eagle design pieces for a belt buckle, a concha in the shape of an embossed silver cross, a silver stamped button, and a belt buckle with repoussé work with a star-shaped center slot — show some of the more unusual designs found in Southwest silver jewelry. All of the pieces date circa 1900.

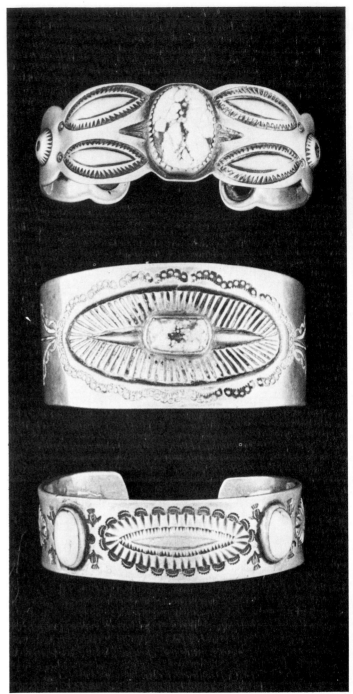

134. The top two bracelets are brass and the fourth is copper; all have various degrees of file and stamp work and date from the 1870s. The third bracelet with the very unusual stamped forms on a copper flat band with triangular terminals dates from 1870–1880. The fifth bracelet with the oval green turquoise stone set in a crude bezel and flanked by a crude swastika design is made of copper and dates circa 1890s.

135. These three bracelets, circa 1900, all show a predominance of cold-chisel work enhanced by stamped designs. The top bracelet illustrates a combination of repoussé and embossed techniques and a stone with a serrated bezel. The middle bracelet has a stone on a repoussé center form which is in turn surrounded by a chisel-stamped sunburst. A chain of stamped circles is arranged in small crescents. The bottom bracelet has an elaborate stamped and repoussé center in between two oval turquoise stones.

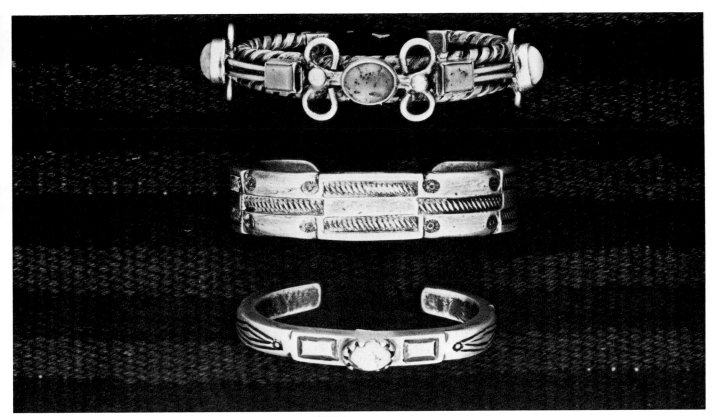

136. The bottom bracelet is a later version of an older traditional style plain silver bracelet. Although the chiseled designs and serrated bezeled stones are early in origin, the two cold-chiseled triangles are later inventions. Circa 1900s. The filed and chisel-punched designs are set nicely on the middle silver bracelet. The middle section of the bracelet is fashioned lower than the built-up side sections. Circa 1900s. Above, two twisted wires support three oval stones and two square ones separated from the middle stone by silver wire loops with silver studs. The effect is both rich and delicate. Circa 1915.

137. The two sandcast bracelets are thick and heavy. The bottom one has file work enhanced by stamping and a thick bezel around its green rectangular stone. Circa 1900. It is relatively simple compared to the top piece with its extensive file work and oval stone with serrated bezel soldered to a diamond-shaped plate. Circa 1920.

138. The child's bracelet at top with its large oval green stone and simple stamp work makes a direct and appealing statement. Circa 1920. Seven old turquoise stones, the center one pierced, dominate the middle bracelet. The stones do not fit their bezels and are replacements for the originals. Circa 1920. The dark, olive-green stone bracelet, its three large turquoise ovals richly contrasted against the thick silver bezels, has a filed silver border design and three supporting wire bands. Circa 1920.

139.   These three bracelets have unusually shaped stones. Each of the five turquoise stones on the upper bracelet are interspersed between fine silver bars set on two bands of twisted wire. The filed bars hold the ensemble and silver bands together at each point and at both ends. Circa 1920. The elegant sandcast middle bracelet has three dark green stones separated by an elaborate three-stud bar. The stones have profusely stamped silver borders and the terminals fan outward. Circa 1920. In the bottom bracelet rectangular and diamond-shaped turquoise stones alternate, separated by a row of four studs, and all are soldered onto a middle band framed by twisted wire. Circa 1930s.

140. Interesting cutout forms of blue glass dominate these bracelets. Bottom: four triangular glass "stones" with brass bezels are attached to a brass band with well-worn stamped designs. Circa early 1900s. Top: twelve hexagonal glass pieces soldered onto four strands of twisted wire adorn the top bracelet. Circa 1920. Glass was occasionally used as beads for necklaces or incorporated into bracelets and rings. Brass was used concurrently with and before silver.

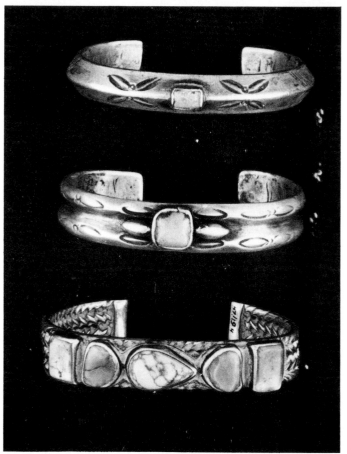

141. These three bracelets become progressively more complex: the top one with a stone and minimal stamping (circa 1915); the middle one with a two-section triangular band, more involved stamping, and raised silver nodules soldered onto each side of the larger stone (circa 1915); and the bottom one with five turquoise stones soldered onto a separate silver plate which is affixed to four strands of thick twisted wire (circa 1920).

142. The top two bracelets are typical of the period around 1920. Both are made up of triangular wire with sets of silver studs, serrated bezeled turquoise stones, and minimal stamping. The lower bracelet was collected in 1934 at the Navajo Kayenta area by Marie Chabot who accompanied Mary C. Wheelwright on trips to the Southwest Indian reservations. Five alternate blue and green turquoise stones are fitted into crude bezels on openwork silver. Circa early 1900s. Collection of Richard Dillingham.

143. Five blue matched turquoise stones with serrated bezels separated by pairs of silver studs give the top bracelet a delicate appearance. Circa 1900. The five crudely cut, crudely bezeled, and irregularly shaped stones in the middle bracelet are in marked contrast to the orderly ones above. This piece has chisel work on the band. Circa 1900. The heavy bracelet below has an oval turquoise stone in a serrated bezel, soldered onto a chiseled silver plate. The tooled middle decoration resembles twisted wire work. Circa 1900.

144. The upper sandcast bracelet is quite elaborate. Three triangular stones are soldered over a twisted wire going through the bracelet's center, complemented by silver loops which spring out from the center band and end in solid silver diamond forms. Circa 1920s. The other large bracelet is also sandcast and shows wear on the top and incomplete casting. Stamped borders, a large horseshoe-shaped turquoise stone, and looping forms on each side of the stone distinguish this piece. Circa 1920s.

145. The center piece with three oval shapes and the thin quality of the silver are the unusual features of this early headstall. The center piece has simple sunburst designs with minimal stamp work and rocker-engraving around the edges and a pair of silver ovals on either side which perfectly complement the center piece. Stamping is at a minimum throughout. An extra, delicate stamp-work design between the twisted wire work and the raised sunburst center design of the conchas is apparent. A pair of primitive hands form the ends of the tabs below the conchas. Circa 1880s. The browband is probably earlier than the conchas. Compare Figure 180.

146. The earliest tobacco canteens were made for the White Man's use out of hide, brass, or copper. The tops of both the larger brass and the upper copper canteen were, typically, made from casings from U.S. Army shells. Circa 1880s. Collected on the Navajo Reservation by M. L. Woodward, Gallup, New Mexico, around 1932.

147. The strong, filed and chiseled center designs of the conchas and the beaded wire effect give this belt much of its visual power. The superb buckle shows a predominance of chisel work with stamped designs playing a minor role. Circa 1890.

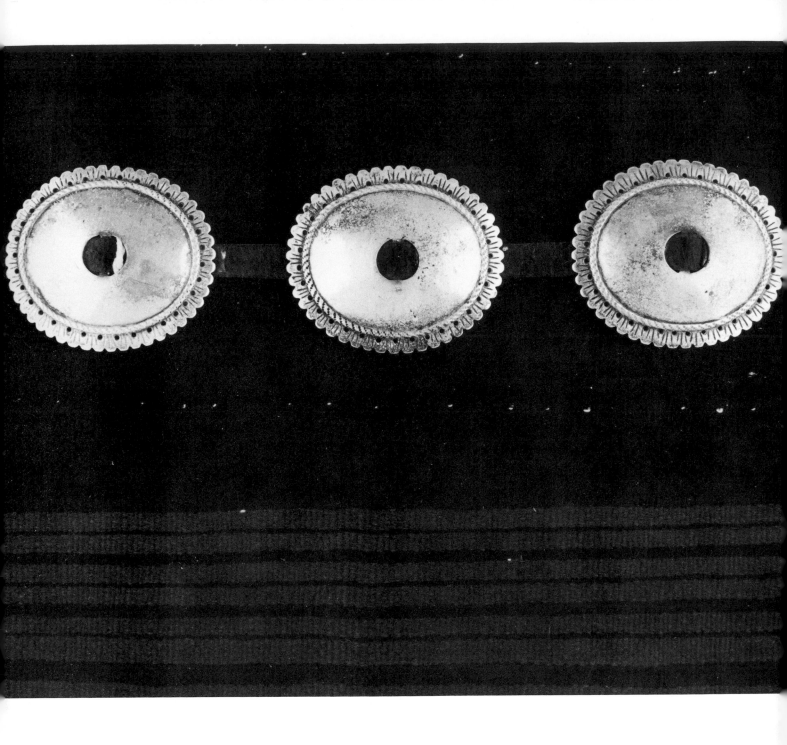

148. This well-worn first phase concha belt with pleasant proportions dates from the 1870s–1880s. The hemispheric rather than diamond-shaped center slots are unusual.

149. This saddle blanket with jewelry attached to it was acquired by the museum from a trading post in the Four Corners area. Some of the buttons, earrings, a necklace with pendants, an unusual belt buckle, and a bridle center piece have good age. A trading post often became a deposit box for Indian jewelry that was pawned and ended up at the post. The trader kept on adding jewelry pieces to the blanket as he obtained them. Collected by M. L. Woodward, Gallup, New Mexico, around 1940.

150. The ketoh to the left is constructed of soldered triangular silver wire with twisted wire soldered on either side of each piece. The solder-constructed piece is light and airy with much of the dark leather showing and contrasting with the silver, turquoise, and beaded border of the center oval. The fine wire designs on the silver bars and the tiny turquoise stones at each corner add a delicate flavor to this piece. This is a very unusual way of fashioning a ketoh. Circa 1920s. The plain silver child's ketoh has a cold-chisel stamped design of a sunburst and pleasing border patterns. Circa 1890. The crazy arrangement of the stones and their shapes on the third ketoh, all with holes or silver pins in them, as well as the odd repoussé forms, give credence to the humor or primitive qualities (or both) of the silversmith. Circa 1915.

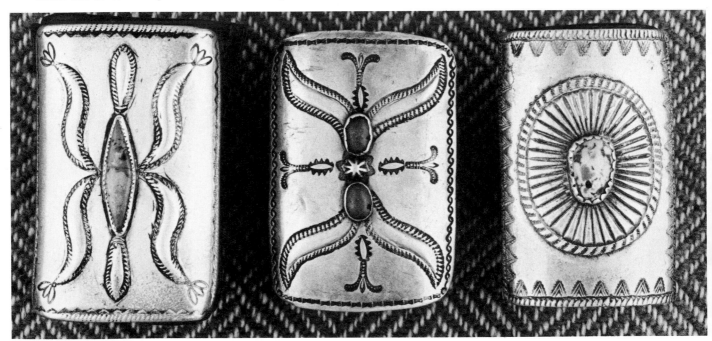

151. The first two ketohs from the left have design variations of four floral, repoussé petals with different size green turquoise stones. A button separates the two stones of the middle ketoh. The third ketoh has a turquoise stone with a serrated bezel (serrated more strongly than in the first piece) and a pierced hole, surrounded by a sunburst pattern. Circa 1920. The middle ketoh is slightly earlier.

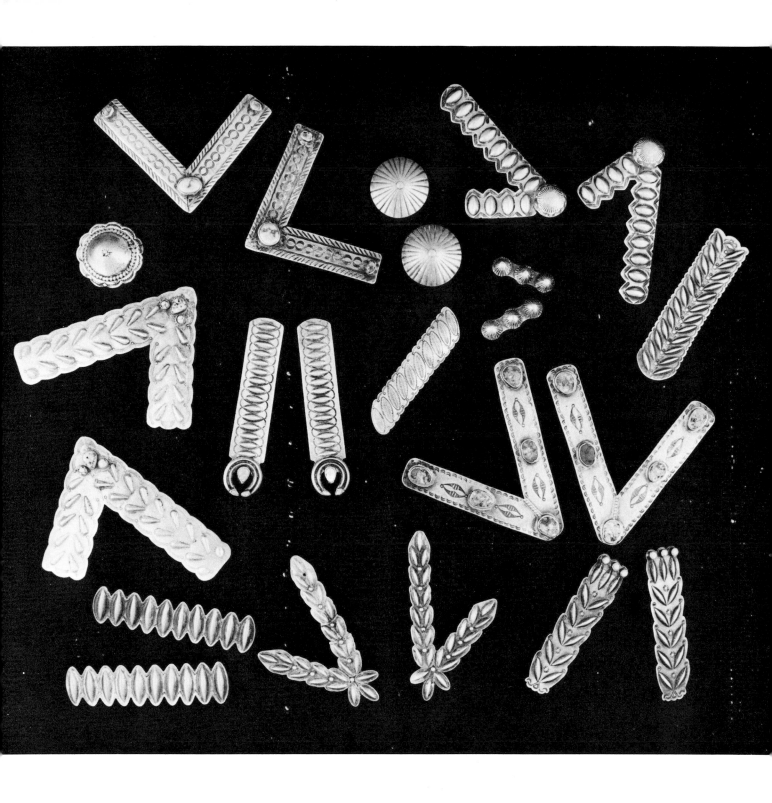

152. An array of collar tabs showing a wide variety of designs and some silver buttons are shown harmoniously together. Collar tabs were used as colorful ornaments on blouses. Circa 1920s.

153. Of the three choice bracelets shown here, the top one is the most sophisticated. It has a diamond-shaped, mottled green turquoise stone with serrated bezel flanked by punched finial projections and involved stamp work on the band itself. The terminals have turquoise stones set into them. Circa 1920. The plain silver bracelet has a diamond-shaped silver plate with pleasing chisel-stamped design soldered onto two triangular bars, which are soldered together. Circa early 1900s. The mellow hand-cut green stones of the bottom bracelet with their crude bezels are quite appealing. The differing intensities of the green are balanced between the large square stones and the smaller round ones. Circa early 1900s.

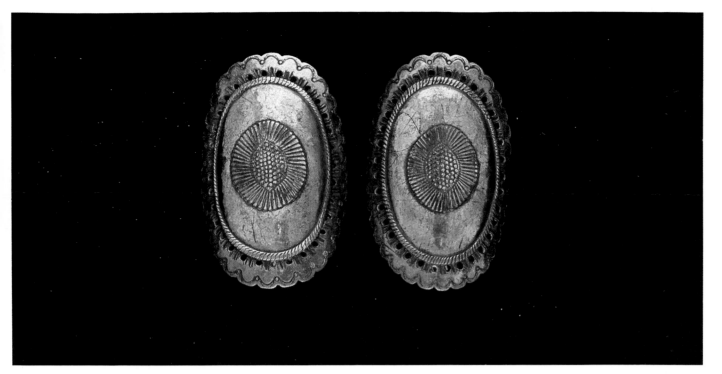

154. A unique and excellent pair of hair ornaments which resemble the conchas of old belts. The markedly convex oval form combined with fine border decorations, twisted wire effect and the intriguingly stamped and cold-chiseled center design particularly enhance these pieces. There is an enormous difference between the Plains Indian-oriented hair ornaments in the Smithsonian Institution (see Figure 49) and these, which are definitely Navajo. Circa 1890.

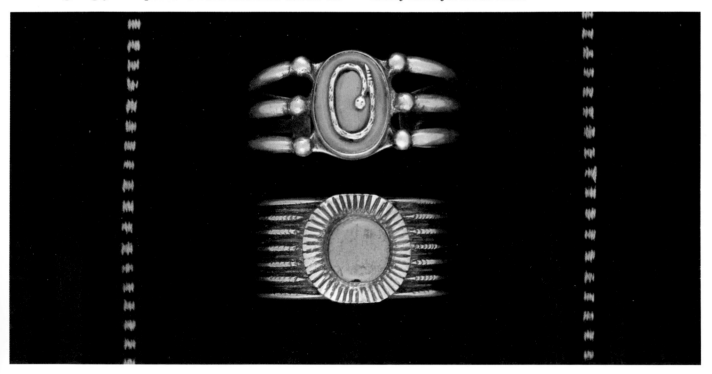

155. At top, the highly unusual stamped silver coiled snake matches the form of the oval green turquoise. The snake, stanced between six silver studs, dates around 1930. Below, a date prior to 1920 can be assigned to the well-worn chiseled bracelet with the round turquoise stone set on a plate with a sunburst design.

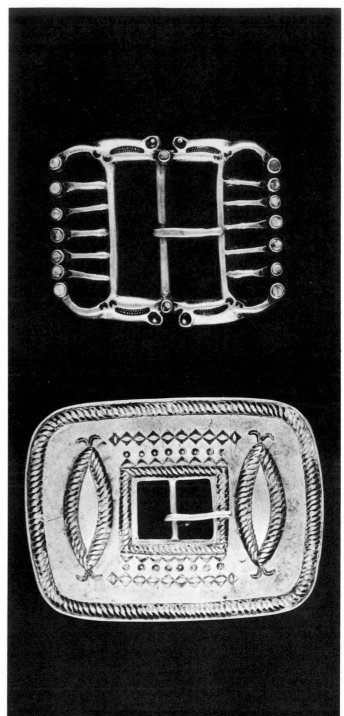

156. Of these two repoussé bracelets, the upper one is the oldest. Its crude bezel and simple repoussé forms speak for a date in the 1890s. The wider, more ornately stamped bracelet with odd-shaped stones is circa 1900s.

157. The solid, heavy silver belt buckle below has good wear. The two elliptical-shaped designs are repoussé (with stamped blossom forms on either end) and the stamp work between them and on the border is pleasing. Circa early 1900s. The delicate tracery work of the sandcast buckle on the top has some stamping on its only stampable surface. Sixteen tiny turquoise stones add to its airy quality. Circa 1900.

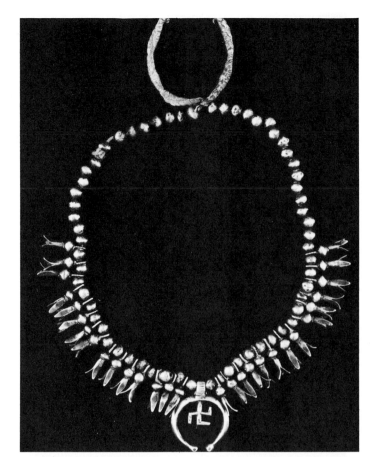

158. A sandcast naja with a swastika drop and a filed loop above centers this sumptuous necklace. The terminals consist of punched knobs. There are fifteen small, primitive squash blossoms on the left side of the naja and fourteen on the other, closely spaced together. Circa 1920.

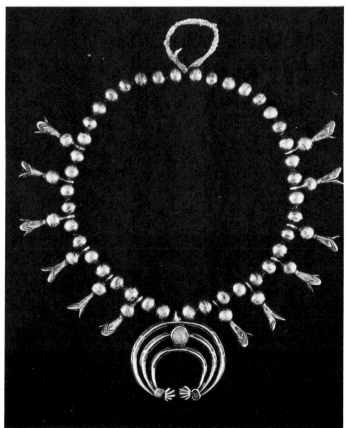

159. This quite large squash blossom necklace is perhaps a handsome revival of earlier styles. Although the naja has a primitive pair of hands, the stamped arrows on the crescents and petals of the squash blossoms indicate a later date, somewhere in the 1920s. One unusual trait is the small oval green stones (serving in lieu of the traditional "cuffs") flanking the hand terminals.

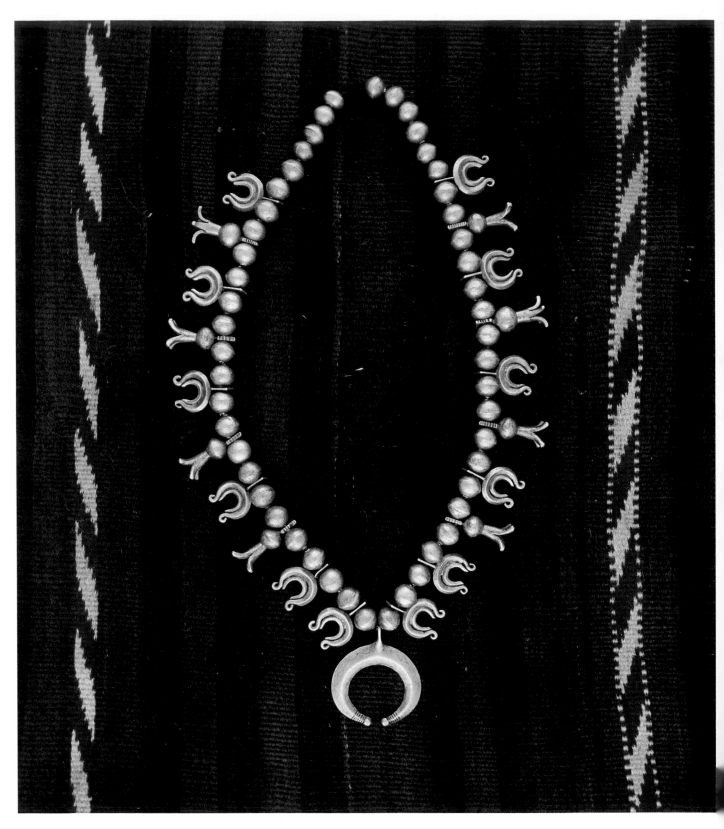

160. The sandcast naja and the sandcast "squash blossoms" in the form of small najas produce a harmonious effect. The fact that the small najas are interspersed between regular wrought-silver squash blossoms adds an extra richness. Circa 1920. The naja, decorated by fine rocker-engraving and file work on the ends, is probably an earlier piece. Circa 1880s.

161. This distinctive, symmetrical turquoise pendant necklace follows the general format of a squash blossom necklace, a large oval green stone replacing the naja and poor-grade green stones replacing the squashes. All the stones have old serrated bezels and the necklace shows considerable wear. The total effect is slightly European. Circa early 1915.

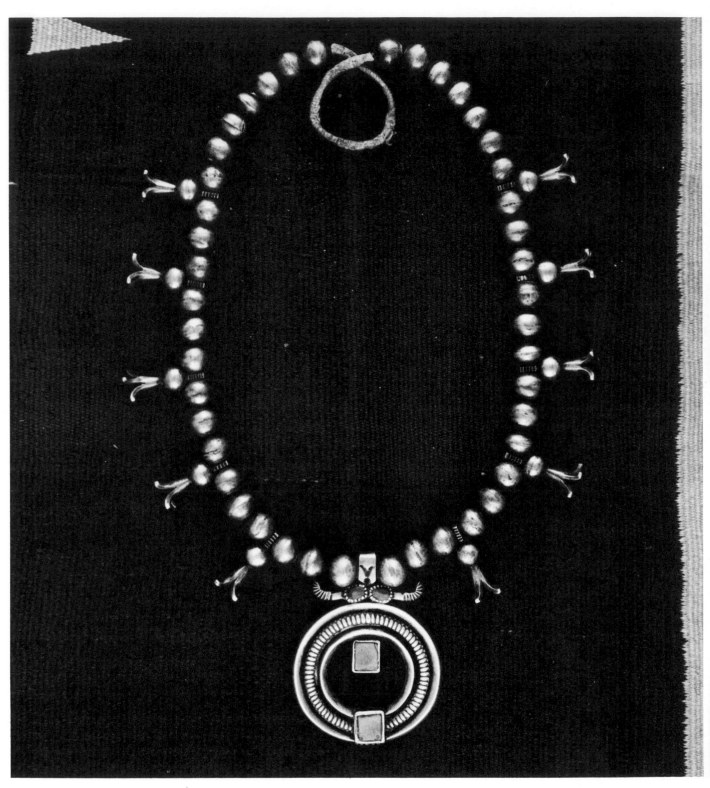

162. The naja of this beautiful squash blossom necklace is completed by a square green turquoise stone bridging the two terminals. A matching green stone above forms the drop and above it are two small oval green stones with serrated bezels flanked by two filed finial projections. The loop is nicely stamped. The simulated wire effect inside the naja creates the impression of three concentric circles with the wire circle between the others. The stems of the squash blossoms are notched on the sides and top. Circa 1920.

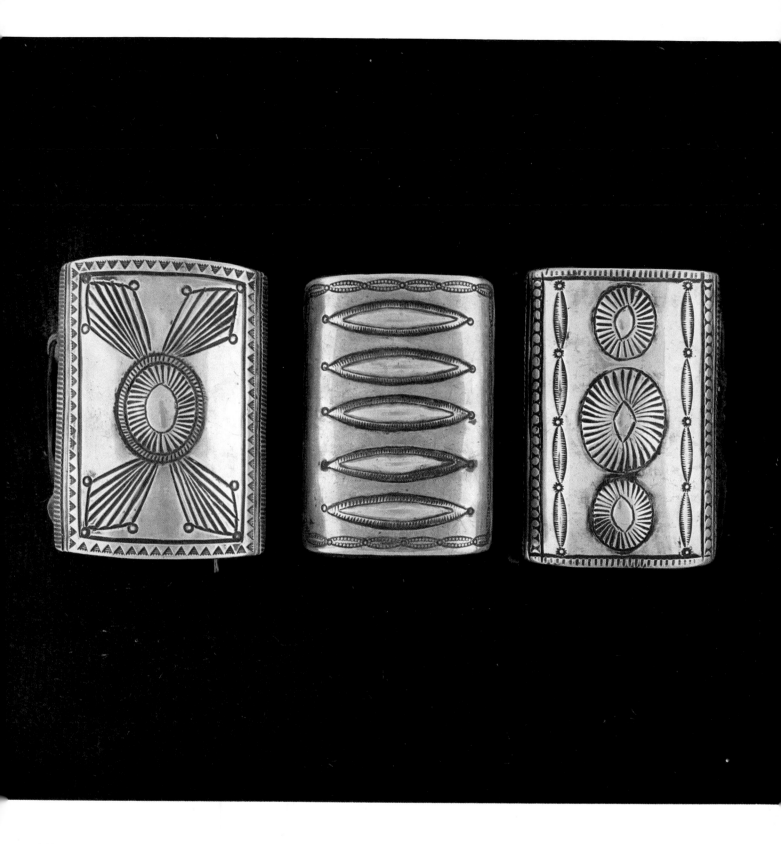

163. Three strong and clear-patterned ketohs are shown here with oval sunburst type designs exhibited in the pieces to the left and right. All the ketohs utilize repoussé to some extent. The middle ketoh has five interesting elliptical forms. The one to the right has an elegant column formed of miniature traditional elliptical forms. All are circa 1890.

164. The plain pair of early silver loop earrings, circa 1890, contrasts sharply with the two other handsome pairs. To the lower left, two round turquoise stones surrounded by thick bezels support two pendants in the shape of butterflies with twisted wires forming their antennae. Circa late 1930s. The delightfully primitive pair to the right with rough hand-cut turquoise stones and crude bezels dates from the early 1900s.

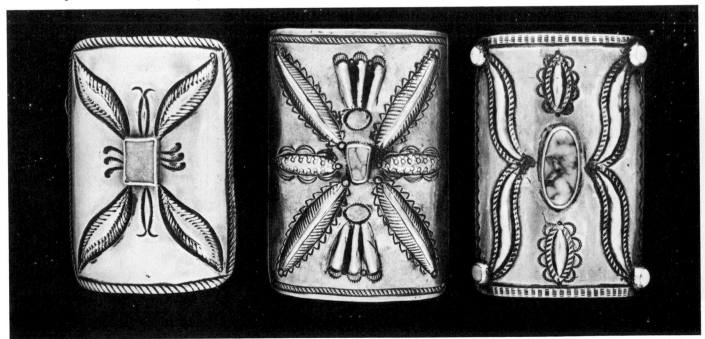

165. Three variations on the petal motif are shown progressing from the earliest and least involved ketoh on the left (circa 1910), to the intermediate stage on the right (circa 1915), and to the latest and most baroque in the middle. All the floral designs are repoussé. The middle ketoh has an extra lateral projection with tiny stamped circles, circa 1920.

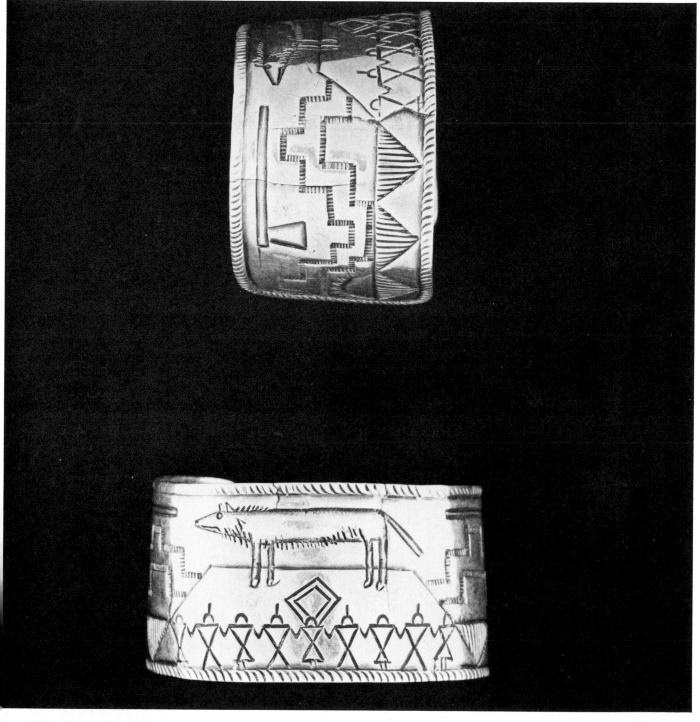

166. Early Hopi Pueblo silver work is rare and this bracelet, shown in two views, is quite unique in its own right. A chisel-stamped and rocker-engraved wolf with hair occupies the center with petroglyphlike men and women strung out below. Each male figure wears a feather, distinguishing him from the female figures. On the sides of this exceptional bracelet a tomahawk is chisel-stamped and, below that, rainclouds. At the bottom is an abstract design almost like rain and mountains. Circa 1900.

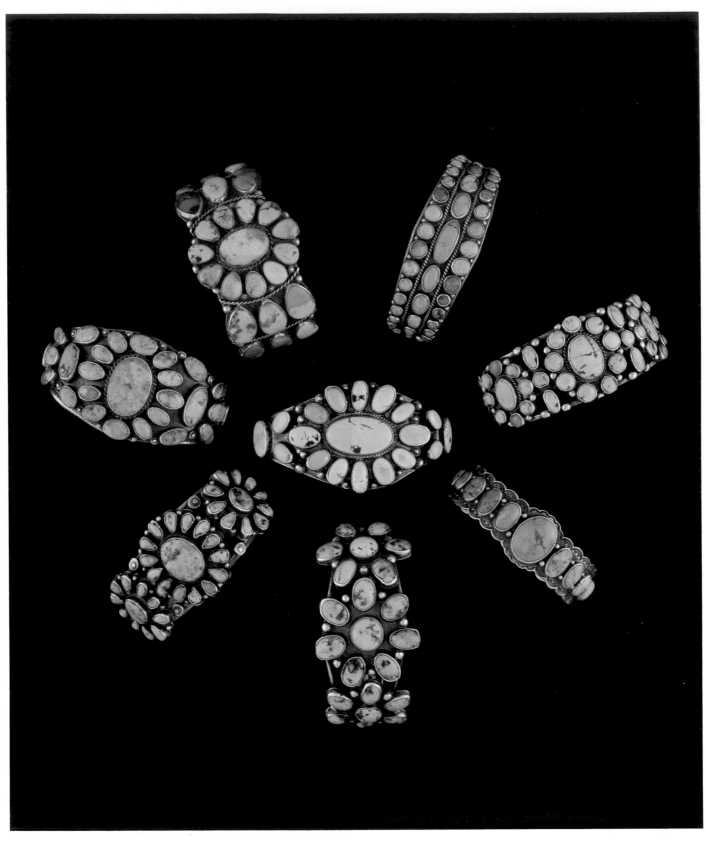

167. Six Zuni turquoise cluster bracelets and two turquoise row bracelets create a visual spectacle. The row bracelet at bottom right is possibly Navajo. Circa 1930s.

168. This is an extraordinary belt because of its imaginative designs and superb execution. The small, delicate, scalloped border, the unusual, finely drawn circle decoration under it, the tiny punched holes, and the delicate twisted wire effect all add to the masterpiece. To top it off, there is the restrained, unique design around the center slot opening and the small patterned, punched holes in the leather belt between the conchas out-lining the visibly scalloped edges. If one looks carefully at the center concha, one notices that at least two different stamps have been used. This is probably due to a broken or lost stamp for which another was then substituted, or sometimes a con-cha was added later to enlarge the belt. A normal-size concha belt consisted of between six and eight conchas. Circa 1880.

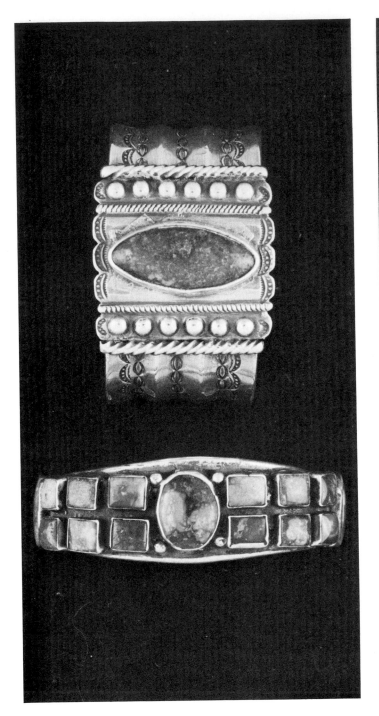

169. The large and wide bracelet has a single el-liptical dark green stone on the center scalloped silver plate. On the sides are rows of small and large twisted wire work and more stamp work. Circa 1910. The dark green turquoise row bracelet has an interesting arrangement of stones. The large round turquoise stone is flanked by parallel rows of square stones, with round stones appearing again at the terminals (not visible). Circa 1915.

170. All of these silver bracelets are either domed (the second and third from the top) or repoussé (the first and fourth; the fourth one also shows the repoussé effect at the back). They represent an early style of stamping with little use of stones except for the upper bracelet which has a primi-tively set green turquoise stone. All of the brace-lets are circa 1900.

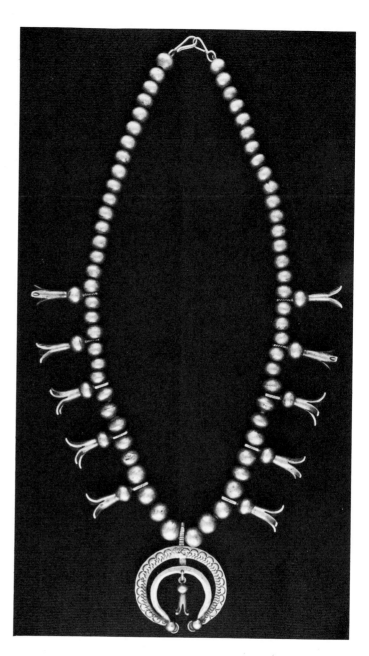

171. Of the two closed-center first phase concha belts, the one on the left is the most intricately executed. Both have raised diamond-shaped centers, but the left one has a fine border design around the dome, sunburst rays with their tips notched forming an extra circular design, an extensive area of plain silver, and an elaborate border design. Notice that, like Figure 168, this belt has a one-piece leather backing cut to flow with the conchas. The concha at the extreme top of the left belt was made with different tools and possibly by another silversmith. The belt on the right has conchas with a looser, stronger sunburst and border design, and it is contemporary with the conchas. These pieces show well-executed cold-chisel, file, repoussé, and stamp work. Both are circa 1885.

172. The attractive silver naja is notable because the terminals of the inside crescent curve gracefully into the terminals of the outside crescent and become one. The stamped pattern of the larger crescent contrasts with the plain silver smaller one, from which a squash blossom pendant hangs. The loop of the naja and the stems of the squash blossoms have filed designs. There also appear to be designs stamped on the tips of some of the squash blossoms. Many such necklaces broke from wear. Often some of the pieces were lost and composite necklaces were assembled using the remains of more than one object. This necklace was restrung as shown by the non-Indian clasp. Circa 1915.

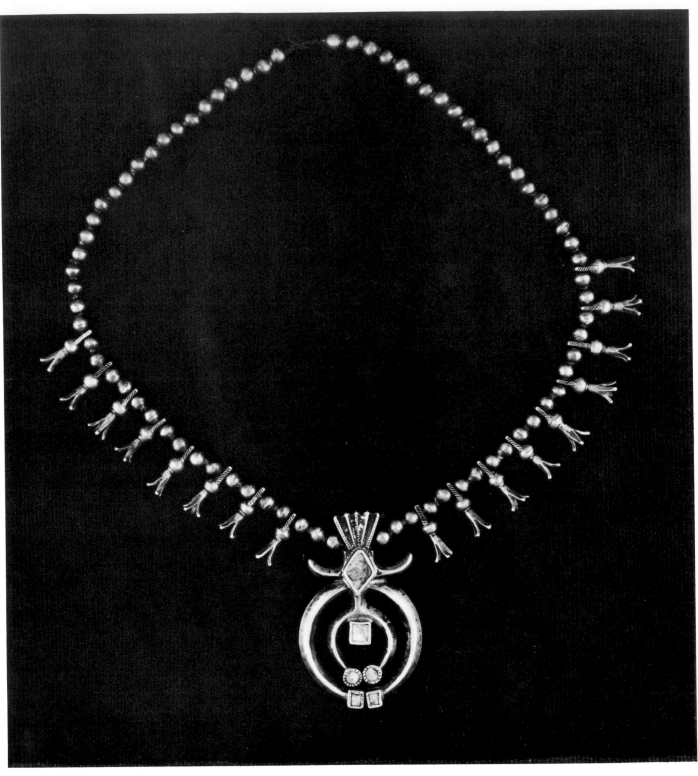

173. This heavy, sandcast naja maintains a delicate balance. The larger crescent has a diamond-shaped turquoise stone on the top with decorative silver projections and a small set of square turquoise stones at its terminals. Completely enveloped is a smaller crescent with a square turquoise drop on the top and round, serrated bezels and stones at its terminals. Small silver squash blossoms and beads maintain aesthetic harmony. The piece is made with very heavyweight silver and is strung on rawhide. Circa 1920.

174. This Pueblo Indian necklace has seven small silver crosses and a large cross pendant with a stepped and engraved base (without a sacred heart) at the bottom right. It is strung on the original leather. The odd German silver rocker-engraved cross at bottom left was attached to the necklace and could be of Plains Indian origin (see Figure 3). Other such pieces have been found on Pueblo necklaces, particularly from the Northern Pueblos. The necklace is circa 1890s but the German silver engraved cross dates around twenty years earlier. In the center is an unattached German silver cross of the double-barred variety; circa 1890.

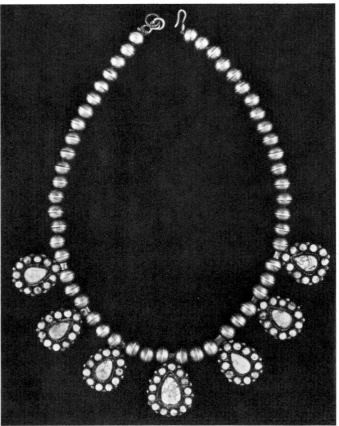

175. The delicate characteristics of Zuni Pueblo jewelry are evident here. The well-matched, deep blue turquoise stones in each pendant with small, finely cut stones around a large central one, intricately bezeled, are miniature versions of Zuni cluster rings and bracelets. Circa 1930s.

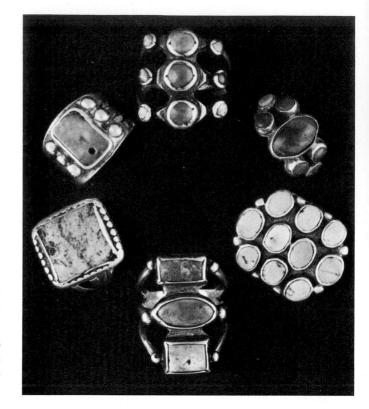

176. Six well-mounted rings with one pierced stone among them lie in partnership here. The top ring with its three center stones flanked by three tiny stones on each side is particularly effective. The top and bottom rings represent the earliest styles of this group and date around 1895, as does the ring set with an earbob. The other attractive rings were made fifteen years later.

177. Bandolier bags are still worn at some Pueblo Indian dances, particularly by the ceremonial leaders who take corn pollen out of them to bless the dancers. All the embossed buttons on this piece are identical except the four in the top row and the first button on either end of the strap and, of course, the early embossed center button. The buttons are old and the bag has good wear. Circa early 1900s.

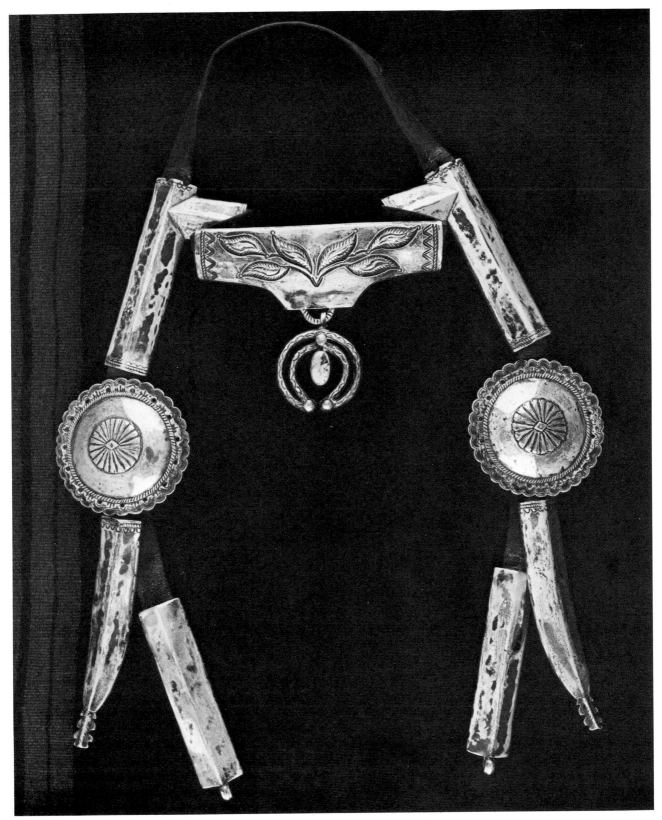

178. The floral design of the center piece of this silver headstall is intricate, with an almost realistically conceived plant. The naja with a turquoise pendant on a filed loop is heavily stamped and of a later date. The conchas with a center sunburst design expose a wide area of plain silver before they reveal finely executed border decorations. Circa 1900.

179. The German silver breast plate ornament (or pectoral or gorget), circa 1865–1875, made by Southern Plains Indians, is illustrated here because of the similarity of the naja with hands to those on Navajo najas. Within the naja is a circular form with a modified heart-shaped cutout opening. The crescent form was most probably copied many years earlier from similarly shaped European trade items coming from the eastern United States. The hands motif could have derived from the Spanish. Since the Plains Indians traded with the Southwest Indians from the 1870s up to the turn of the century, the influence the Plains Indian silversmiths had on the development of the Navajo naja is quite significant. The scalloped top piece is rocker-engraved.

180. This early headstall is made of thin silver with minimal, deep rocker-engraving. The central section of three scalloped pieces with a strong border pattern is similar to the early headstall in the Wheelwright Museum (Figure 145). The plain silver conchas with no designs are similar in appearance to German silver ornaments of the Plains Indians. Circa 1875.

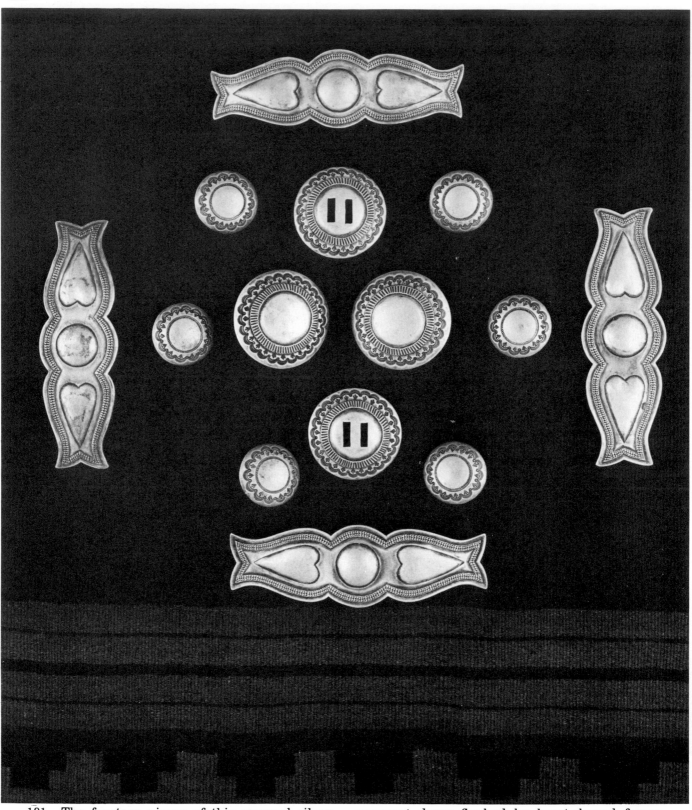

181. The fourteen pieces of this unusual silver bridle are presented almost as if they are manta pins and buttons, but at one time they did decorate a horse. The four large "scalloped" pieces have a repoussé dome flanked by heart-shaped forms. The various-sized conchas are stamped and filed. Very tight sophisticated work is presented here. Circa 1915.

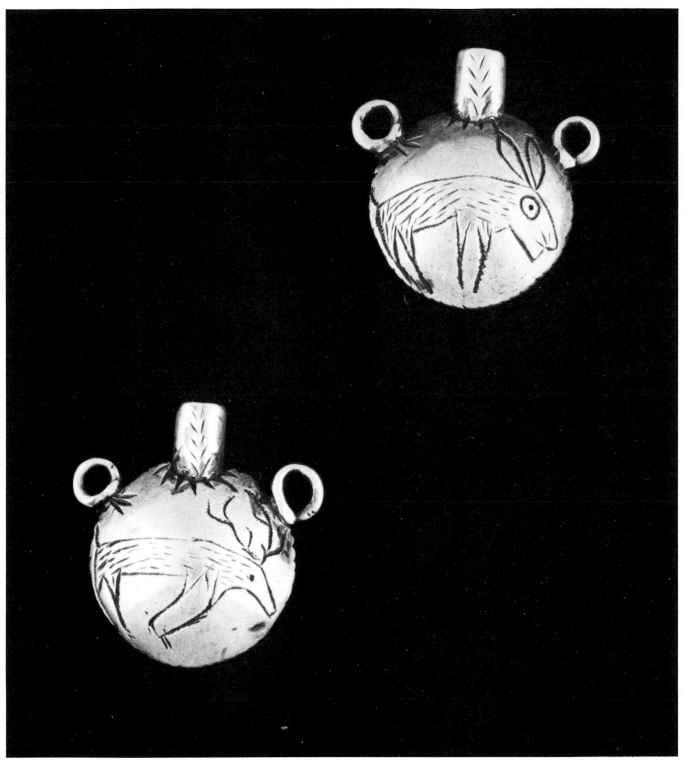

182.   There are three examples in this book of canteens with animal designs, one of normal size and
two of miniature size including this one. The designs of both domed sides are seen, one a rabbit
and the other a deer. Two suspension rings, which
would have held silver chains attached to the missing cap, flank the tubular neck. The designs are
primitively engraved and undoubtedly made by
the same silversmith who made the miniature canteen in the Museum of the American Indian (Figure 80). The other canteen is in the Field Museum
(Figure 74). Rudimentary chisel marks are apparent on the edges of the piece, serving as rope work.
Circa 1890.

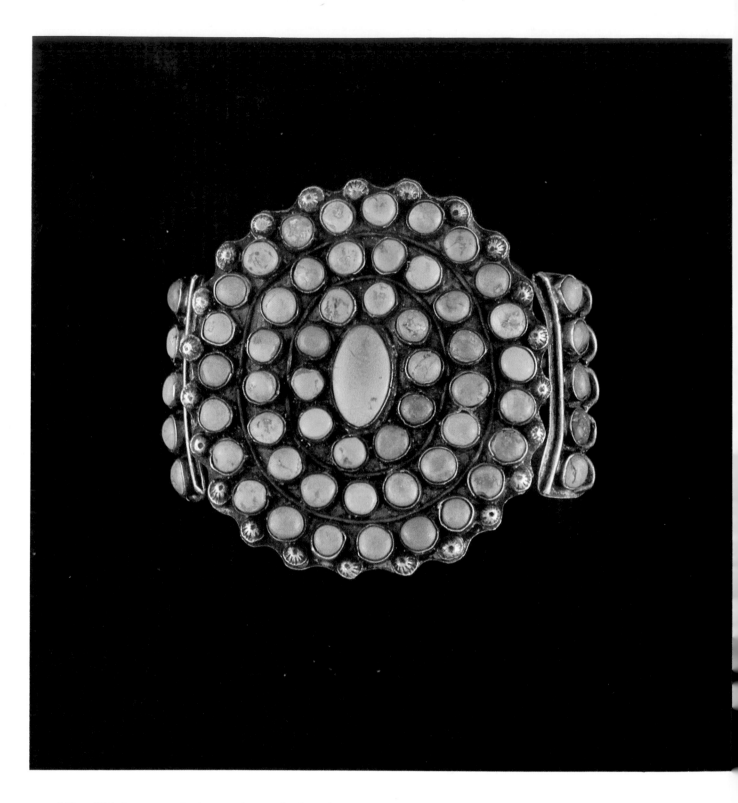

183.   This huge, explosive sunburst-design cluster bracelet is composed of three wire bands supporting a round, scalloped plate on which are set a central oval turquoise surrounded by three circles of round turquoise sets. An extra embellishment consists of the outer circle of small buttonlike forms and an outermost flat side-mount of five stones with line wire loops on each side. Circular stones slightly predate teardrop-shaped ones. Most probably Zuni, this bracelet dates from around 1930.

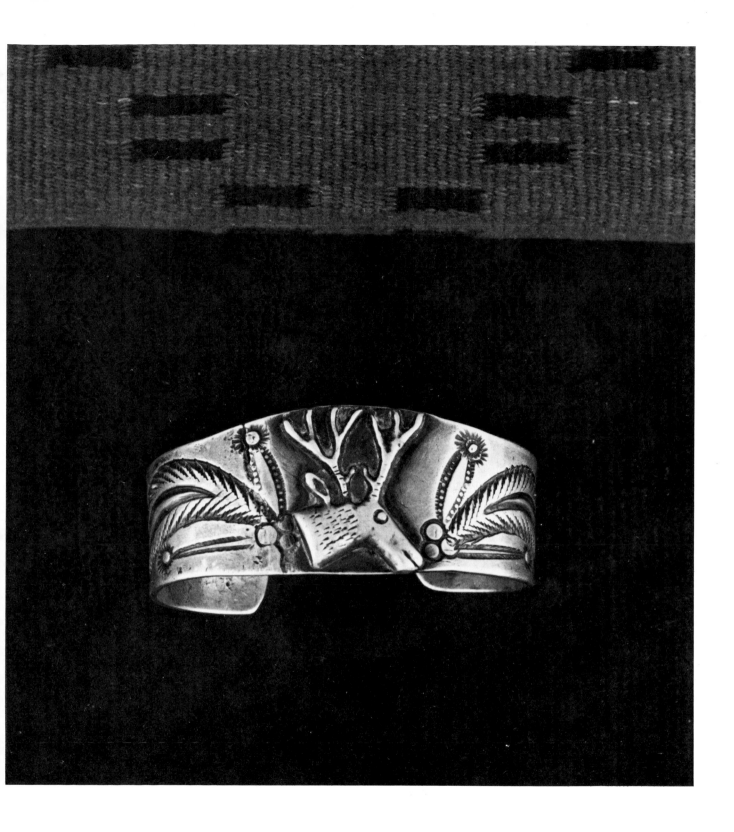

184. An intriguing deer's head is mounted in the center of this silver bracelet, flanked by stamped floral decorations. Animal motifs are usually incorporated in the form of stamp work and, on occasion, a cow's head may be seen on a ketoh, but this attempt at depicting a rather naturalistic deer is extremely rare. Circa 1900.

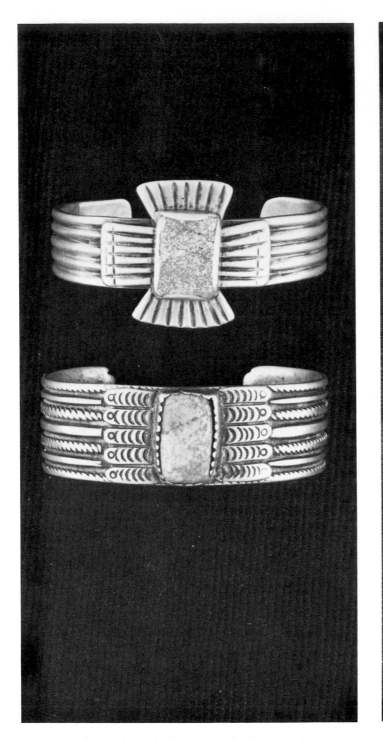

185. Both bracelets are early types with poor-grade turquoise stones and tooled, thick grooves on the bands. The plates holding the stones are soldered onto bands with the plate of the upper bracelet chiseled in the form of a partial sunburst and the lower one heavily stamped on either side of the serrated bezel. The bottom bracelet dates around 1915 while the top one dates slightly earlier.

186. The combination of the outer crescent of this silver naja having a twisted wire effect and an inner triangular silver cross bar gracefully relating the two crescents together makes this naja visually effective. The terminals are formed by file-worked buttons. Circa 1890.

187. These four stamped, chisel-stamped and repoussé ketohs (the lower right one is only stamped) are vivid examples of the four-petal floral (foliate) designs. The elaborate lower right ketoh is an abstract version of the floral pattern. Circa 1915. The ketoh on the upper right, austere with its four stark petals divided by a vertical bar (an early trait), is framed by a line border. Circa 1880. The well-worn lower left ketoh is finely executed. The petals and domed center diamond have an inner design, and the whole ketoh a stamped border. Circa early 1890s. The upper left ketoh has a pierced center stone. Circa 1890.

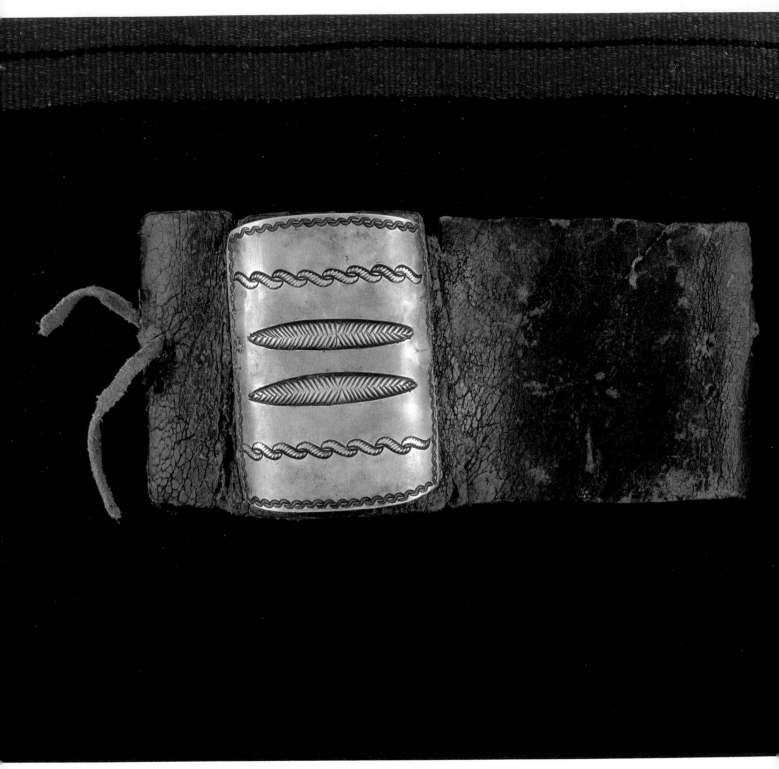

188. This stunning bowguard is an early piece with deep chisel-stamped and repoussé central forms flanked by airy, stamped scroll-like designs. With the limitations of the simple tools at their disposal, it is all the more remarkable that the silversmiths were able to make a piece as visually exciting as this bowguard. Circa 1880s.

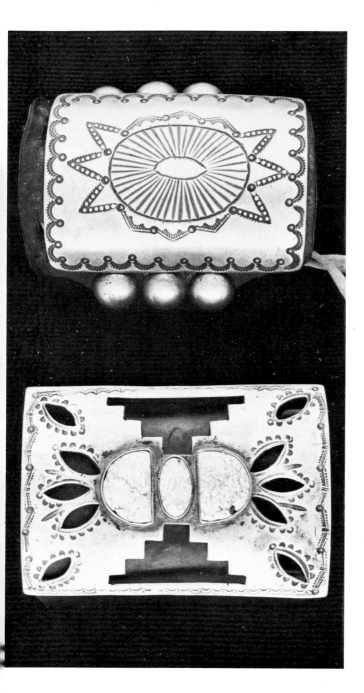

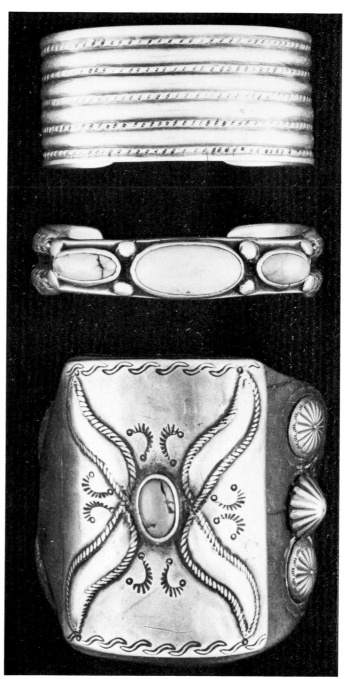

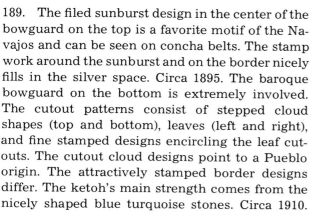

189. The filed sunburst design in the center of the bowguard on the top is a favorite motif of the Navajos and can be seen on concha belts. The stamp work around the sunburst and on the border nicely fills in the silver space. Circa 1895. The baroque bowguard on the bottom is extremely involved. The cutout patterns consist of stepped cloud shapes (top and bottom), leaves (left and right), and fine stamped designs encircling the leaf cutouts. The cutout cloud designs point to a Pueblo origin. The attractively stamped border designs differ. The ketoh's main strength comes from the nicely shaped blue turquoise stones. Circa 1910.

190. The well-worn silver bracelet at the top has alternating ridges of simulated twisted wire or rope work effect. There have been many copies of this popular style. Circa 1890s. The middle bracelet with the oval stones separated by pairs of silver studs has its ends formed out of one piece of silver almost divided in two. Circa 1920s. The well-worn child's ketoh has an unusual crisscrossed, twisted wire effect pattern forming the edges of the four-petal design. The stamp work around the green oval stone and on the edges further enhances the ketoh. Circa early 1900s.

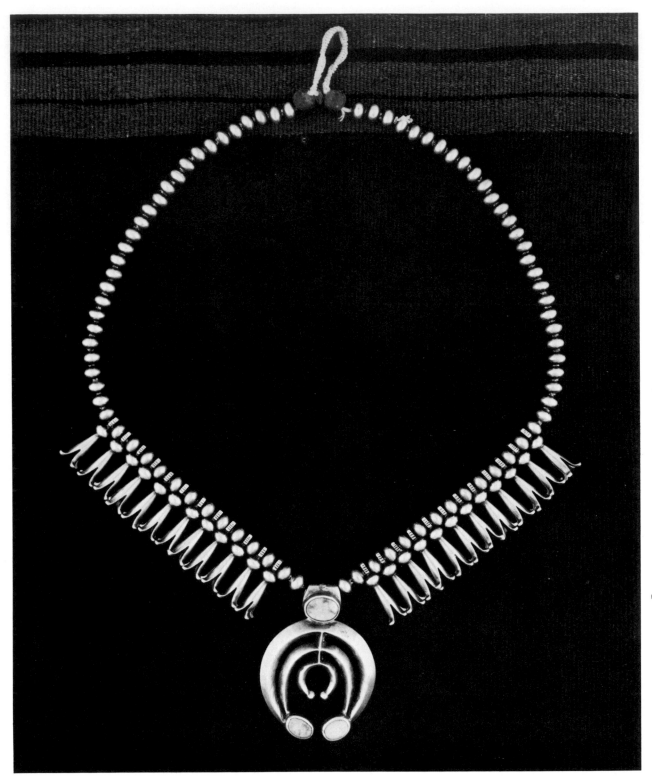

191. This refined squash blossom necklace is nicely balanced between the delicate silver beads and squashes and the handsome, imposing naja. The sandcast naja consists of two crescents joined together at the terminals by two oval green stones and a dainty inner, small crescent with silver knobs as terminals. The small silver beads complement the small, graceful, closely placed squashes with notched and filed stems. The loop with the round stone is one piece with the naja. Collected by Mary C. Wheelwright at Grand Canyon, Arizona. Circa 1920.

192. This old style, graceful sandcast naja has no hands, knobs, or stones at the terminals. The naja is tapered and slightly raised in the upper part of the crescent. The loop is soldered onto the naja. The piece has been restrung at a later date. Circa 1880s.

193. The Pubelo Indian silver cross necklace came from San Juan Pueblo in northern New Mexico and dates from the 1890s. The refined crosses all match except those on the ends. The well-worn double-barred cross pendant is rocker-engraved and stamped and at its base is a heart-shaped form. It is earlier, circa 1870. The shortness of the necklace shows that many of the beads have been lost. The small Zuni Pueblo jar, dating around 1900, is presented for comparison. At the bottom of the jar is a dragonfly that is double-barred (or winged) and has a bloblike shape at the bottom (see cross pendants in Figure 7), corresponding to the heart-like form. It is hard to determine whether the naja seen here (and in general) is a version of a Christian cross or a modified dragonfly in the Plains and Pueblo Indian cultures. On the jar above the dragonfly is a butterfly; both figures are symbols for water, particularly at Zuni.

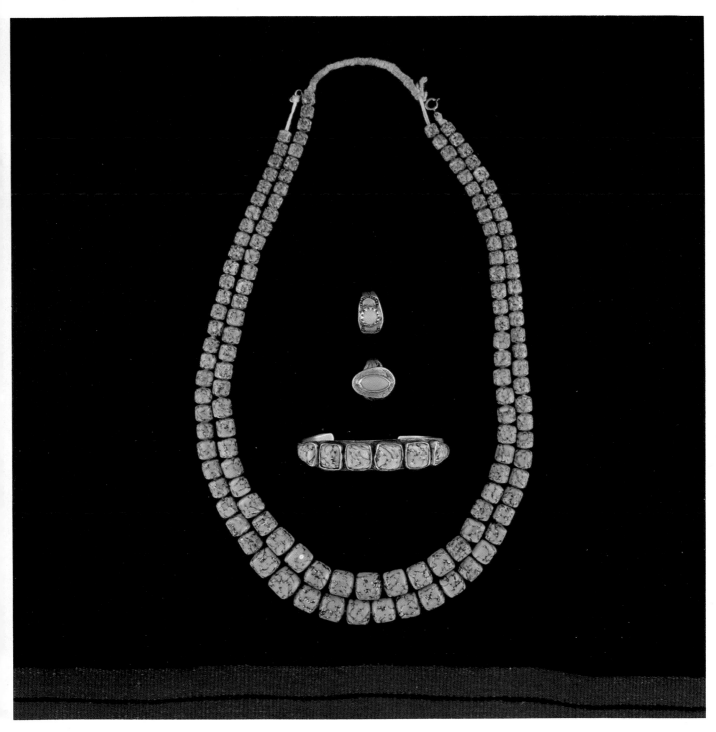

194. The use of glass to replace stones in jewelry-making was a common custom in the Southwest, particularly between 1890 and 1900. The bracelet is set with Hubbel trade beads imported from Czechoslovakia and the two-strand necklace is composed of the same beads. Although not cherished as much as the native turquoise, Hubbel glass trade beads had the advantage of being consistently vivid blue streaked with black, much like spider turquoise. The beads were introduced into the Southwest around 1900 by Lorenzo Hubbel who operated the Hubbel Trading Post in Arizona and had an important influence among the Indians at the turn of the century. Both rings have blue glass instead of turquoise stones. The upper ring is gracefully stamped on the sides. The other, made from a silver fork or spoon, is stamped, "Rodgers," the name of a manufacturer of silver tableware.

195. The squash blossoms here are unusually shaped: long, thick and not flared out as are the traditional ones of a later date. Their small, round, wirelike loops replace the normal flat silver stems, indicating good age. The beads are well worn and have become unsoldered at the ends. One squash blossom to the right is of the old short, plump variety like those made by the Mexicans. The sandcast naja is simple, with primitive hands as terminals. There is some stamping on the loop connecting the two crescents. The loop is one piece with the naja. Circa 1880.

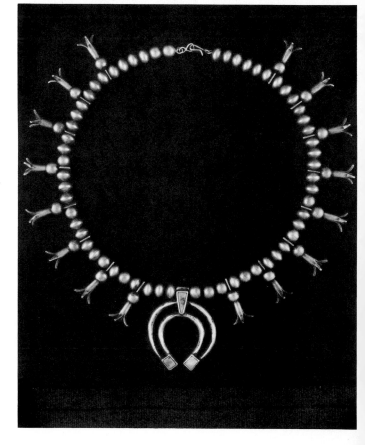

196. This simple two-crescent naja is dominated by the blue triangular turquoise stone on the soldered loop and the two square blue stones serving as terminals for the two crescents. The small silver beads and squash blossoms give this necklace a dainty aspect. This necklace has been restrung as shown by the squash blossoms of two different shapes. Circa 1915.

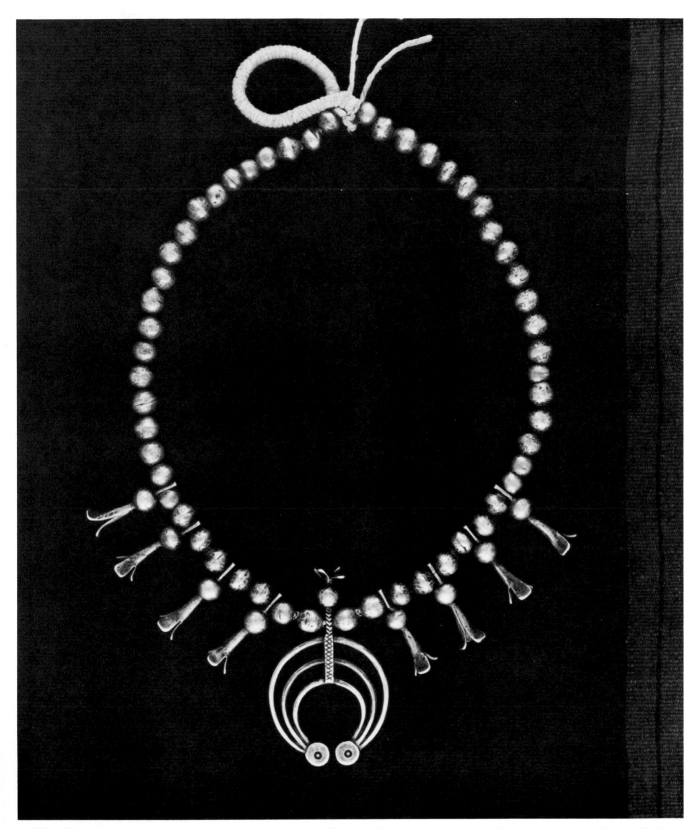

197. The three crescents forming the naja are well arranged, all ending in terminals that consist of round flat silver disks soldered onto the crescents. The soldered bar that connects the crescents to-gether and serves as the loop is attractively filed as well as being crowned by a squash blossom. The stems of the squashes are only notched on top (not visible). Circa 1900.

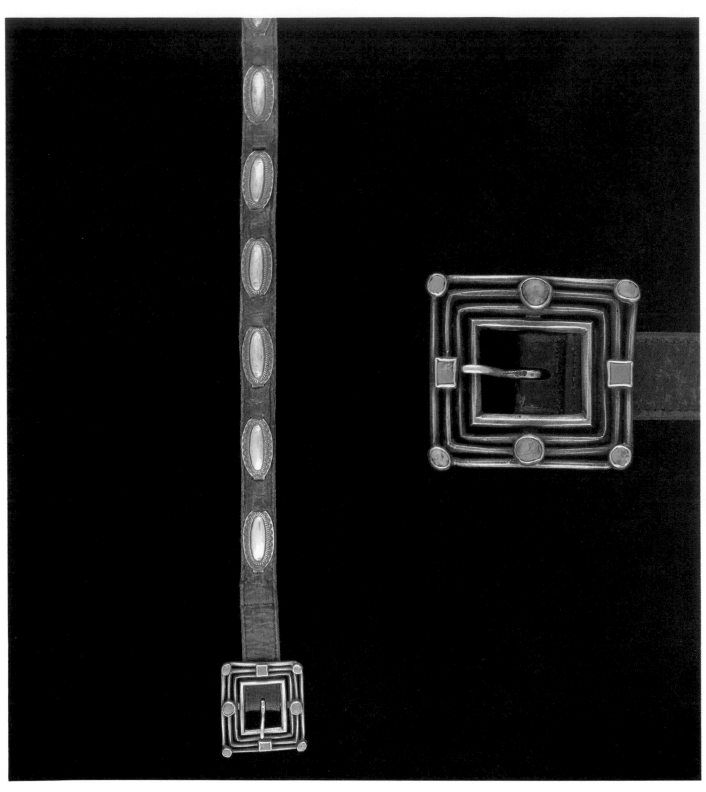

198. The refined and unusual concha belt is backed by old leather into which the small, nicely stamped conchas are inserted by their ends (see the similarly fashioned ketoh in Figure 77). This is in contrast to the usual copper or brass loops fastened on back of the concha and through which the belt slides. The conchas are delicately stamped on the borders leaving a plain silver oval form in the center without designs. The superb buckle of four silver squares is handsomely mounted with light green round and square turquoise stones. Circa 1900.

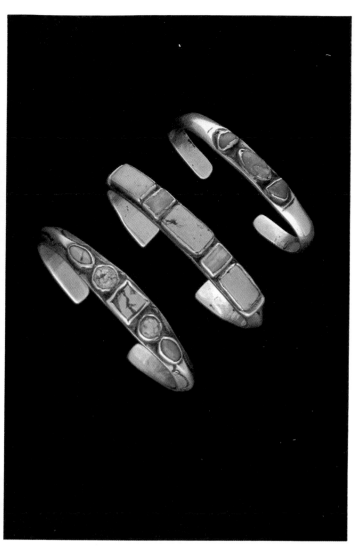

199. The upper green turquoise stone bracelet and the lower blue stone one (having one green stone that is possibly a replacement) are examples of early and charmingly crude pieces that show much wear. The first bracelet is the earliest with little stamp work (at each end of the stones) and dates circa 1890s. The lower bracelet is more fully stamped and dates around 1900. The Pueblo Indians, before their exposure to the trading posts, used turquoise stones that were often flawed or that contained matrix or were chipped. Furthermore, the stones were not necessarily matched. The beauty of a piece consisted more in the simplicity and natural qualities of the components and the silversmithing rather than perfect symmetry. The middle bracelet has three blue rectangular turquoise stones and two square "stones" made out of an orange-colored shell. The orange "stones" are most pleasing. The bracelet was found in one of the Northern Rio Grande Pueblos in New Mexico and was most probably made there. Circa 1900.

200. The enormous silver bracelet with a huge, green flat turquoise stone could serve well as a ketoh. Whether it was worn more as a display piece at social occasions rather than for everyday use is not known, but its large size shows that it was a man's bracelet. Flanking the stone on each side are three silver studs and below them the three silver bands show stamp work. Circa 1920.

201. The fine belt buckle with a handsome variety of repoussé petal and elliptical forms and tiny stamped arrows would also make a splendid ketoh design. The stamped arrows have most probably been added later. The stamp work around the center slot opening, at the edges, and at the edges of the leaf forms serves as a unifying motif. The heavy conchas with repoussé central flower-shaped forms, slightly punched in their centers, are the type of powerful, massive first phase work the Navajos were known for. The expanse of silver surrounding the center is well hammered. The dainty twisted wire effect and pleasing border design balance the otherwise crudely strong piece. Circa 1885.

202. The sandcast bracelet on the top is a nicely executed later sandcast version of the upper bracelet in Figure 236. It represents one end of the spectrum of possibilities inherent in the sandcast process in that it is graceful and refined rather than blunt and massive (compare the bracelets in Figure 92). Serrated bezels around the oval turquoise stones and punched and filed branching finials all add to its charm. Circa early 1900s. The "butterfly" ring to the left and the earring with a wire frame around airy stone-inset dangles could almost be Zuni but each object is a simpler, cruder version of the Zuni cluster style. Circa early 1900s. The lower heavy bracelet has two nicely shaped turquoise "earbob" stones with serrated bezels separated by two silver studs. Circa early 1900s. Collection of Mr. and Mrs. Stanley Pepper.

203. The two middle silver bands on the upper bracelet, raised and alternating with the plain silver areas, make this an attractive piece. The filed and stamped designs on this bracelet are an interesting variation on those of the top bracelet in Figure 190. Circa 1890. The excellent repoussé and stamped design and fine execution of the lower bracelet come brilliantly together. The central sunburst design focuses on a large green turquoise stone with a thick bezel. The elegant stamped design on the sides incorporates the traditional elliptical forms. Circa 1890.

204. This wide German silver bracelet with a rocker-engraved design of thirteen stars was found in 1969 at Cubero, an abandoned Pueblo near Laguna Pueblo in New Mexico. It was most probably made by the Plains Indians and acquired by the Pueblos. Plains Indian contact extended deep into Pueblo Indian and Navajo regions. Circa 1870. Compare the star design on the silver belt decoration in Figure 223.

205. The Mexican iron cinch buckle with two different stamps and filed designs on its edges is the type of ironwork the Mexicans manufactured for their own use and for trade in the eighteenth and ninteenth centuries. The stamped and scalloped edges are similar to the borders of Navajo Indian silver conchas. The actual tools and techniques that are shown in this piece were used by the Mexican blacksmiths and transmitted to the Navajo Indians in the 1850s. The individual elements and the total design relate to first phase silver jewelrymaking.

206. The early-nineteenth-century wooden chest has an iron strap with decoration done by file, a stamp, and a punch. The overall effect shows the heritage of technique and design that led to the Navajo first phase concha belt. This plus the form and shape from Plains Indian hair plates (Figure 13) produced the Navajo concha belt. See early conchas on the bridle in Figure 79 and the conchas in Figure 41. Photo courtesy Millard J. Holbrook II.

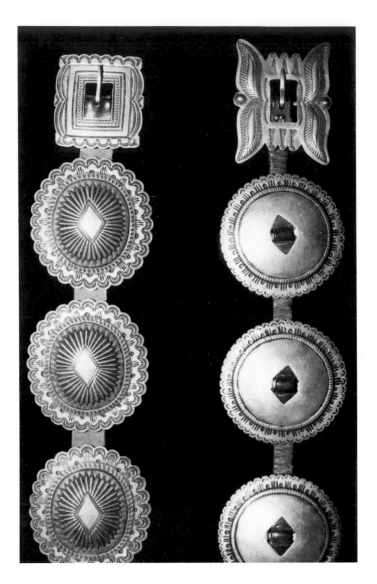

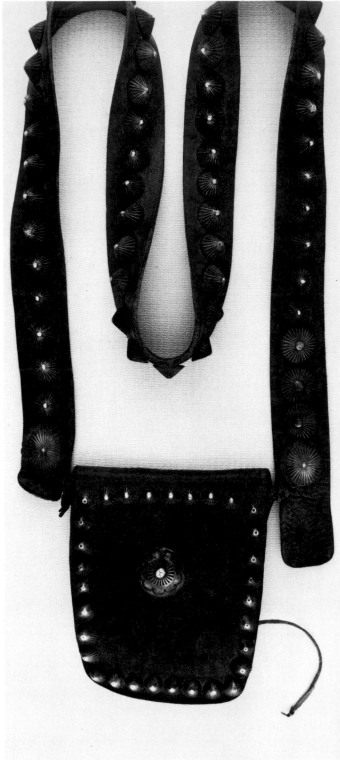

207. The round silver conchas on the first phase belt to the right date from the 1870s. The belt buckle is stamped, filed, and domed, and dates around 1900. The closed center silver concha belt on the left with the solid diamond-shaped centers contrasts nicely with the open center slot belt. This is another early example of a closed center style with fine file work, cold-chisel and regular stamping, dating around 1885.

208. The almost square leather bandolier pouch carries a large number of embossed buttons filed on the edges and a center button with a turquoise stone. The buttons on the strap are of heavy, embossed silver with a stamped, then filed, design. Circa 1900.

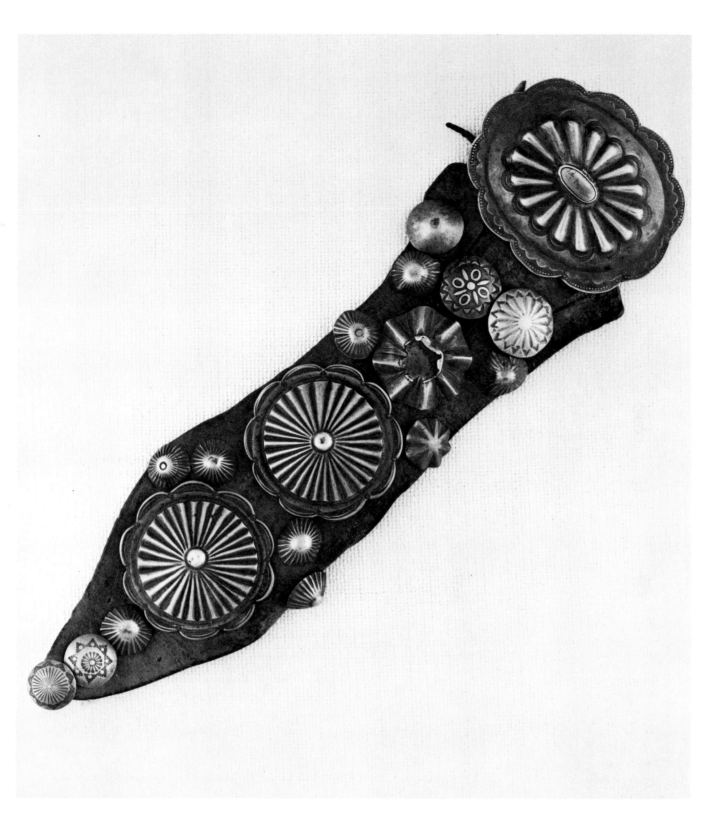

209. Belt decorations were worn at the end of the period when leather bandolier bags were beginning to be used primarily as decorative items instead of actual containers to carry personal items in lieu of pockets; around 1900. The decoration was worn on the belt and dangled downward; a leather belt once slid into the leather loop in back of the largest button. Many types of silver buttons adorn this decoration covering a period of at least ten years, 1900–1910.

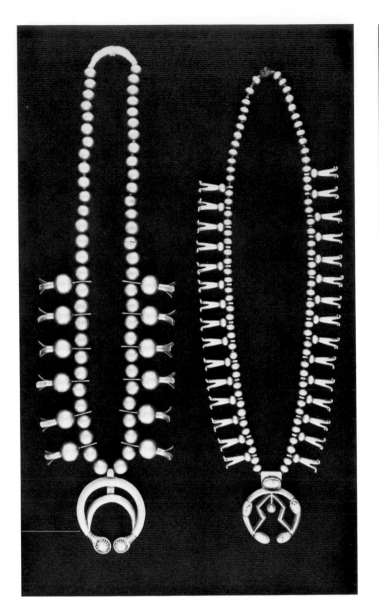

210. A Hopi Indian silver squash blossom neck-lace is on the left. Hopi traits include the large size of the round silver bead part of the squash blossoms as well as the thin silver stems through which the buckskin was strung. The double-crescent naja has embossed terminals with button-type designs, and above the terminals are chisel-stamped decorations. Circa 1890s. The ornate sandcast naja to the right with zigzag silver bars, five oval turquoise stones, and delicate silver beads and squash blossoms dates from the 1920s.

211. The Pueblo Indian–style necklace has small sandcast silver crosses and a sandcast double-barred cross pendant. A cold-chisel stamp was applied directly to the tufa cast crosses. The "X" in the center of the crosses is typical of Mexican work of the eighteenth and nineteenth centuries and is still in use today. The necklace is strung with coral beads and a few silver ones. Circa 1900.

212. The handsome silver bowguard to the left exhibits ten repoussé elliptical shapes forming a clear, crisp pattern. The guard has been mostly cold-chiseled with one stamp mark. One can see the marks left by the stone-polishing. Circa 1875. The other ketoh has a sunburst with no border design and has been decorated with cold-chisel and file work. The wider rays to the four corners correspond to the floral designs normally found in repoussé on traditional ketohs (see Figure 213). Twisted wire encircles the turquoise stone, and silver buttons decorate the leather. Circa 1925.

213. A sandcast ketoh to the left (circa 1900) is contrasted to a wrought silver one to the right (circa 1910). Both use floral petal designs for decoration. The repoussé, stamped, and filed ketoh to the right was made by a Navajo for a man in Santo Domingo Pueblo around 1910. Navajo silversmiths were in great demand until the Pueblos developed their own professional craftsmen. The turquoise stones, used previously as earbobs, came locally from the Pueblos and were often traded to the Navajos for Navajo silverwork.

214. The two oval convex silver disks on either side of the center piece with a design of a bull are quite distinctive in this headstall. The naja is of a much later date. The bridle still retains a nice old silver buckle with cold-chisel stamped decoration. Repoussé, stamp, and file work are evident throughout. Circa 1900.

215. With the look, almost, of an Egyptian necklace, this heavy Navajo squash blossom necklace makes a timeless statement. The sandcast naja is perfectly proportioned. The silver knobs on the end of each crescent, forming the terminals, are symmetrically pleasing. The bead sections of the closely spaced squashes are the same size as the silver beads themselves. The stems of the squashes are filed. The soldered loop has a blue stone set in it and the entire necklace is strung on buckskin. Circa 1915. Collected by Millicent Rogers in the 1940s.

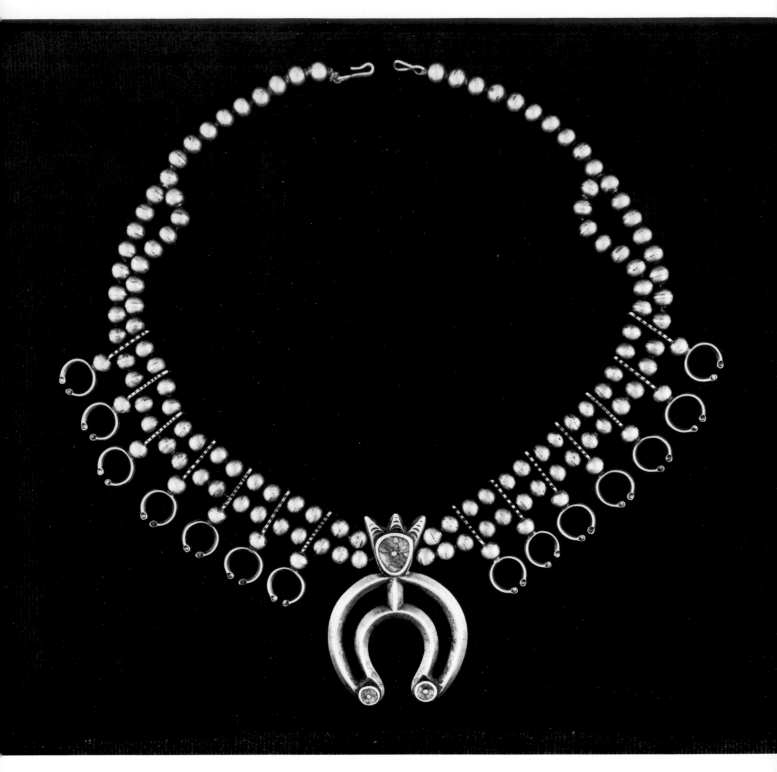

216. This regal and beautiful squash blossom necklace once adorned a Navajo as part of her dress. The two crescents of the sandcast naja are joined together by two blue stone terminals pierced by silver pins. The loop connecting the upper part of the naja is one piece with the naja. It is inset with a blue stone with a silver pin in it and topped by a stamped, three-point form. The double strand of small beads matches the bead part of the unusual "squash blossoms." The "squash blossoms" have long, notched stems, thin and small, finely made triangular-constructed najas and punched knobs as terminals. Circa 1910.

217. An old, heavy, sandcast squash blossom dominates this string of old, worn beads. The elaborate loop which is one piece with the naja has a triangular green turquoise stone set in a thick serrated bezel crowned by a five-prong top piece. The terminals, the area just below the stone, and four of the prongs are punched. Interestingly, the smaller crescent deviates markedly from the outer one, causing some tension within the piece. Collected by Mrs. Gerson Gusdorf around 1920, circa 1890.

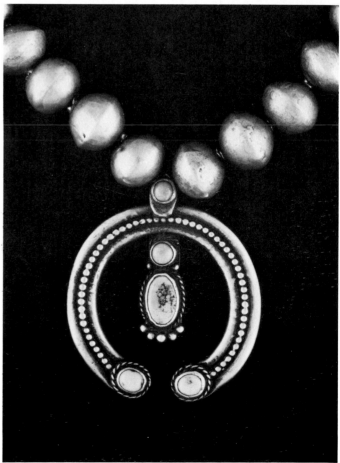

218. The small, dainty naja shows much wear. It has a simulated silver dot effect between the two crescents of the naja. The delicate two-stone drop is edged by tiny silver dots and simulated twisted wire. The terminals consisting of fancy bezels and two turquoise stones and a stone inset into the loop (which is one piece with the naja) make this a most ornate naja. Circa 1910. Collected by Ralph Meyer around 1930.

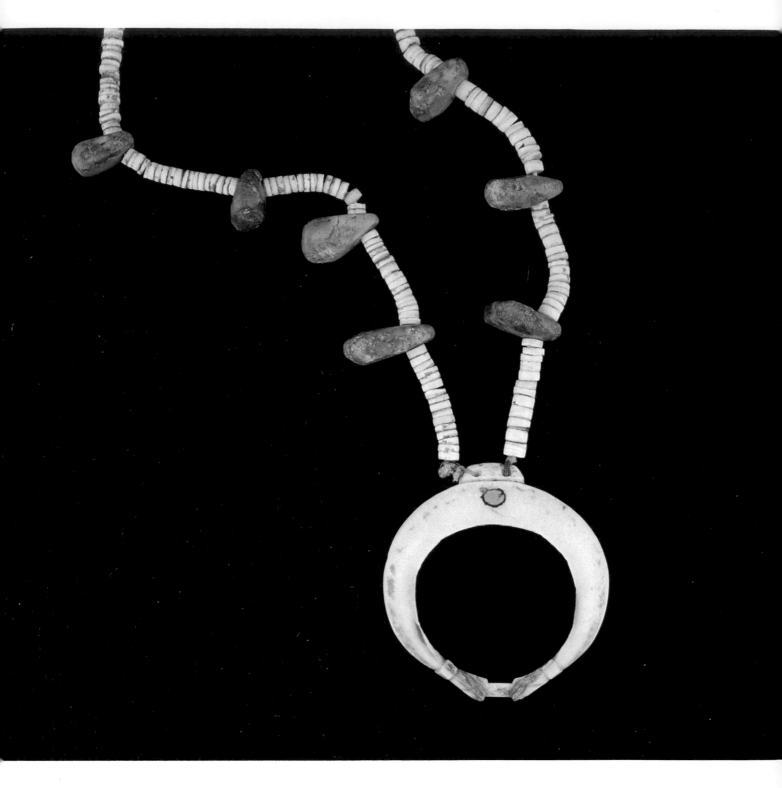

219. The old Zuni Pueblo white shell naja with hands forming the terminals relates to the early silver najas that the Navajos were making in the 1870s and 1880s. The naja conforms to those prototypes: the primitive hands with delineated fingers; a "cuff" above each hand (on silver najas these would be filed); a definite loop piece above the naja; just below the loop, an inset turquoise green stone which corresponds to the stones inset into the upper parts or loop pieces of silver najas. The naja dates circa 1880s; the heishe (strings of drilled discoidal beads made of shell) and turquoise beads might have been added later.

220. The necklace of black, faceted glass beads, one small silver cross, and an elaborate double-barred silver cross with a distinctive cutout heart at its base once hung on the neck of a New Mexican santo made in the 1880s. The fact that it is impossible to tell whether the silverwork was done by an Indian, New Mexican, or Mexican silversmith emphasizes the common heritage of the silver cross form. The glass seed beads are strung on leather and are crowned by brass filigree work (see Figure 221). The tiny seed beads were used by the Plains Indians along with the larger, faceted glass beads and, as mentioned before, the Pueblo double-barred cross was at one time the Pueblo and Plains Indian "dragonfly" symbol (see Figure 193). This is obviously a Christianized version. The filigree work and the faceted beads are most probably of Spanish origin. Circa 1880s.

The other necklace shows a different makeup and use of Indian jewelry. Collected in the Taos Indian Pueblo and owned by an old man, this necklace was assembled to be used as a ceremonial dance piece. The brownish-yellow grizzly bear claw pendant was traded to the Pueblo Indians and has several holes drilled into it, indicating that it was worn for different purposes at different times. The silver crosses and beads strung on buckskin are normal attributes to Pueblo Indian necklaces but, combined with the Plains Indian bear claw pendant, this necklace takes on a new and powerful aspect befitting a religious ceremonial dance. The crosses and bear claw pendant seem to be older than the silver beads.

221. This is a detail of the left-hand piece in Figure 220.

222. The commanding hands in the double-crescent silver naja are most expressive. Perhaps the tiny stamped circles represent the knuckles of the hands and the filed bands represent "cuffs" (see Figure 23 for a similar necklace showing the inside of the hand). Circa 1880. The origin of the hands is unknown. One idea is that the Arabic religious concept of the "hands of Fatima" proliferated through the non-Christian Moors to the Spanish colonists and was adapted by the Navajos. The question is whether the hands motif was transmitted directly to the Navajos by the Spanish or indirectly through the Plains Indians (see Figure 179 for a najalike crescent with hands). Concurrently, the various crescent forms hailing from the eastern United States in the seventeenth and eighteenth centuries, such as silver gorgets and pectoral ornaments, were made by silversmiths in the English colonies, England, and France and were traded to the Eastern Indians. This material began reaching the Plains Indians in the beginning of the nineteenth century. Whether the Plains Indians who inherited the European silver jewelry tradition came in contact with the Spanish and "borrowed" the hands motif from them is another question, but items such as Figure 179 show that the Plains Indians had incorporated into their real and German silver crescents the hands motif by the 1860s.

223. The unique belt decoration of five bold, graduated, cold-chiseled and filed silver conchas with star designs is similar to the round silver hair plate ornaments used by the Plains Indians. The Plains Indians also used belt ornaments extending from the belt and dropping down the side (see woman to the right in Figure 14). The example of a German silver bracelet (Figure 204) found buried at an Indian site and attributed to the Plains Indians has a very similar star design. The pieces have been remounted on newer leather. Circa 1895.

224. This early and exquisite bandolier leather pouch was found in one of the Northern Pueblos in New Mexico although it is clearly Navajo in origin. The leather strap has old, stamped, filed, and punched domed buttons which are of exceptionally fine quality. The domed central silver button, striking against the leather surface with much patina, matches in style the domed silver buttons on the strap and also resembles early first phase conchas in its twisted wire effect and scalloped border. The fine silver buttons at the bottom of the bag give it a pleasing effect and relate to the buttons on the strap. Circa 1885.

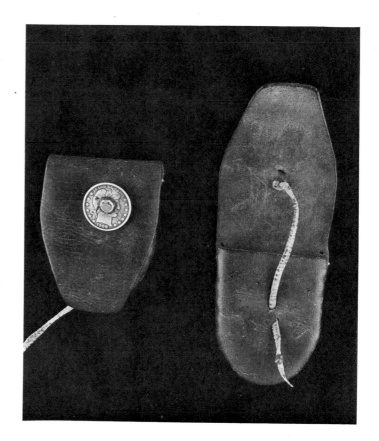

225. This small leather pouch is made exactly as the preceding larger bandolier pouch but it no longer has a shoulder strap. The reverse side shows the method used to open and close the flap; a leather drawstring pulls down and secures the flap. A 1908 United States fifty-cent piece inset with a turquoise stone is the only ornament. The little pouch was used to carry personal effects. Circa early 1900s.

226. The first phase oval concha belt has an attractive stamped design around its diamond-shape center slot opening. File and cold chisel were used to produce the tight twisted wire effect and scalloped border designs. The silver buckle in the shape of a horseshoe with the early stamped arrows did not appear until the 1890s and the conchas are most probably contemporary. The old leather backing, fitting the concha exactly, is revealed. It was a standard method of keeping conchas from slipping on their leather strap and protecting both the silver and the wearer.

227. A bridle, if properly considered, is a piece of hanging sculpture with its varied forms and appendages. This handsome bridle has a combination of file, cold-chisel, punch, stamp and repoussé work. The central design on the silver center piece is an elliptical sunburst which matches the shape of the two pleasing pieces under the large conchas. The conchas have a domed center with a stamped button-type design and strong, radiating grooved lines, notched and bursting at their ends into fine twisted wire effect and a scalloped border. The najas have been added later, but the bridle has its original leather and an excellent old silver buckle. Circa 1885.

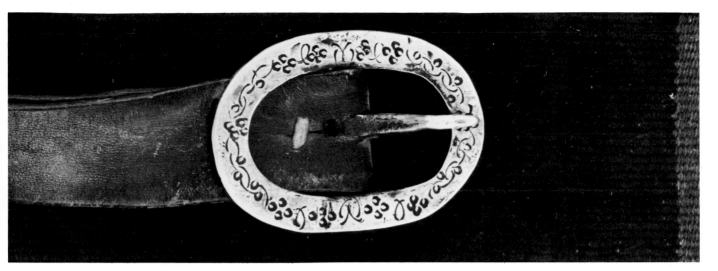

228. Here is a closer look at the silver buckle shown in Figure 227. It has fine and unusual stamped designs reminiscent of rocker-engraved work. Circa 1885.

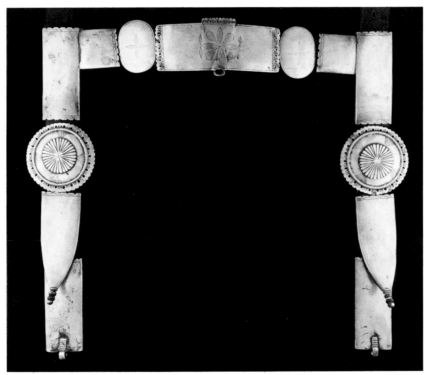

229. This headstall is not quite as old as those in the Museum of the American Indian (Figure 79) and the Laboratory of Anthropology (Figure 116). It shows some file and chisel stamp work in the conchas while the other headstalls are rocker-engraved predominantly, if not completely. On the conchas there are rocker-engraved triangles between the raised sunburst and the simulated rope work pattern; this space is normally left undecorated. The filed and chiseled sunburst designs have been made on separate silver plates and riveted onto the conchas. This is an early technique used in lieu of solder. The unique emphasis of the rocker-engraved designs on the center piece and oval pieces (notice the engraved edges) show this early headstall to be influenced by Plains Indian styles and techniques. The silver is thin which is a typical characteristic of the old styles and reminiscent of German silverwork. The border designs of the center piece have scalloped edges with punched holes — designs similar to those of silver conchas which reflect the Spanish blacksmith's influence. The naja is missing. Circa 1875. Collection of Tom Mudd.

230. The Navajo hand-forged iron bit is also from Figure 227 and shows a delicate tracery effect. The Navajos were taught by Mexican blacksmiths to make iron bits and although they did not need such elaborate dangles, they found them pleasing and reproduced them in all their complexity. Circa 1885.

231. Here is another variation on a hand-forged iron bit copied from the Spanish. Found with a Ute Indian beaded halter, it was traded to the Utes by the Navajos. The Navajos were known to trade the Utes fine first and second phase blankets. The braided leather reins are decorated with tiny green glass beads and strips of stroud cloth (to the left), common decorative material among the Plains Indians. The decoration hanging below the bit has five horizontal bars of small brass beads, also a Plains Indian decorative item. The flat tin dangling tabs are unusual and possibly of Plains Indian origin. Circa 1880s.

232. The silver conchas on the belt to the left are the size of large buttons. Their elongated oval forms have inset turquoise stones surrounded by miniature sunburst designs, a twisted wire effect, and scalloped borders. The scalloped silver belt buckle has four repoussé oval forms surrounded by stamp work and flanked by sets of petals. Stamp work is also apparent within the scalloped edges and outside the triangular center slot opening. Circa 1915. The older belt has a fine sandcast buckle with minimal stamp work and four green turquoise stones at the corners. The oval silver conchas are miniatures of large center-filled concha belts shown elsewhere (see Figures 147, 171, and 233). The charming size, so scaled-down, reveals the more subtle and delicate qualities inherent in old conchas. Circa 1885.

233. This closed center concha belt, circa 1900, is hammered, filed, and stamped. What would have been normally a twisted wire border decoration outside of the plain silver central area has a design similar to that of scouring rushes. The heavy plain silver buckle made by stamp and chisel work shows evidence that an attempt has been made to put a bezel into the two oval areas.

234. This photograph depicts three views of a striking silver bit. The two birds form the "shanks" of the bit, which is shown in the center in a frontal view. Above the birds are two large stamped button forms with turquoise stones in their centers and below the birds' feet are two silver forms stamped with leaf designs. Below the mouthpiece is a stamped horizontal silver bar held together by a silver disk repeated at both ends. Circa 1920.

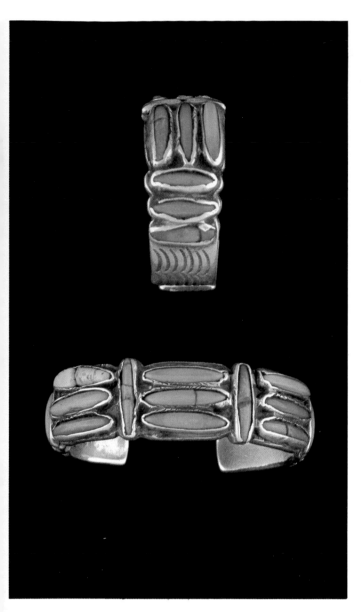

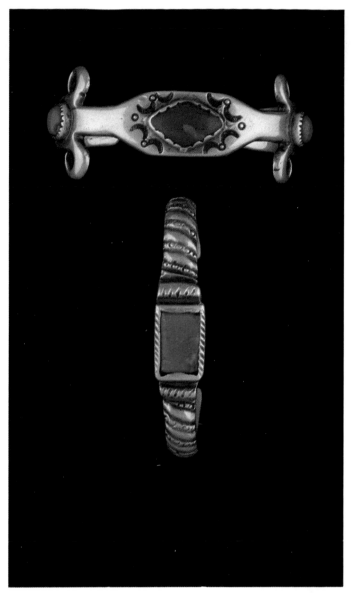

235. It is difficult to identify early Zuni Pueblo silverwork since it hardly differs from the Navajo work of the same period. Although this bracelet was collected in 1934 on the Navajo Reservation near Tohatchi, New Mexico by Marie Chabot, it might be an early Zuni piece. The bracelet consists of seventeen green, elliptically shaped turquoise stones. The stones are the bracelet; the thick silver bezels and minimal stamping on the ends only show off the profusion of dark green stones (half of one is blue and was replaced in a primitive manner). Even the subtle stamp work on the central and related bezels emphasizes the rich stones. Admittedly, the bracelet is crude by later Zuni silversmithing standards, but compared to Navajo work of the time it has a lighter, freer quality, which is the trademark of Zuni silverwork. Circa 1900.

236. The superlative upper sandcast silver bracelet is one of the early examples with turquoise stones. The central diamond-shaped green turquoise and the two round stones on the sides all have serrated bezels. The stamp work around the center stone is simple and attractive. The bracelet was first cast in ingot form and then the scroll-like forms were cut free with a cold chisel and bent to form the lovely curves, a classic blacksmithing technique. Circa 1885. The other bracelet has delightfully stamped tiny circles alternating on the cold-chiseled, filed ridges on both sides of the rectangular green stone. The circles are made by the same tool used to punch the border holes through first phase conchas. The stone with a thick, stamped bezel is inset into a deep enclosure of silver. This is another early example with turquoise. Circa 1890s.

237. Four silver bracelets with turquoise stones are seen here with their reverse sides. Starting from the left, the first, second, and fourth bracelets have the same stamped tiny circle or line designs on their sides, alternating between the filed ridges, as does the bottom bracelet in Figure 236. The third bracelet has a different side design (which is cold-chiseled) and three oval stones separated by pairs of silver studs. Both the second and fourth bracelets have stones with serrated bezels, and the terminals of the second bracelet are inset with two square green stones. The first bracelet has an un-usually long, elliptical central stone and silver knobs as terminals. All of the bracelets date from 1895 to the early 1900s.

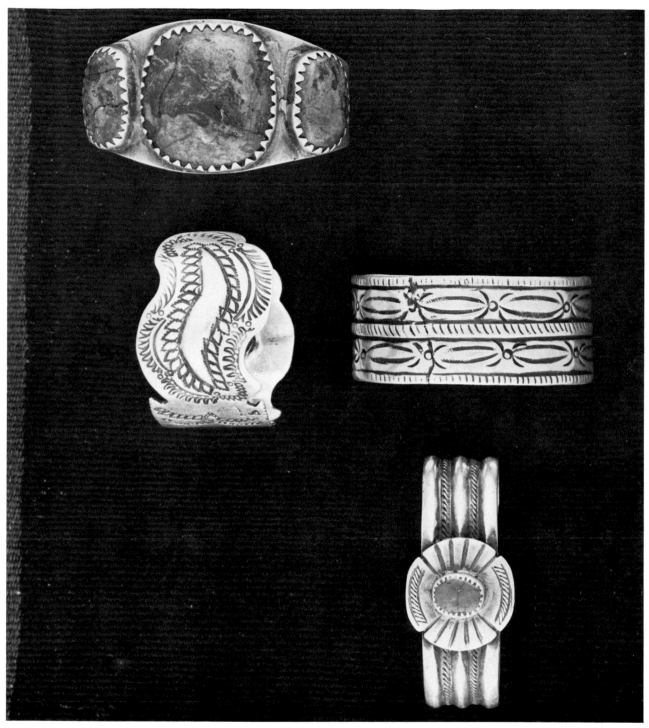

238. The early bracelet at top with three large, green turquoise stones dates around 1890. The serrated bezels surrounding the old stones are an integral part of the bracelet's design. The ends have early stamp work. Directly below is the type of bracelet made after Fred Harvey started to furnish manufactured silver to the silversmiths. The silver is thinner, the bracelet is scalloped, and what ordinarily would have been a flower-petal motif is now overly ornate. There is a certain Spanish busyness about the bracelet. Circa 1905. To the right is another well-worn silver bracelet with simple stamp work and a clearly visible crack which has been mended on the reverse side. Circa 1900. At bottom, the filed and cold-chiseled bracelet has a silver plate soldered onto a three-ridge band with a simulated twisted wire effect. The green turquoise has a serrated bezel. Circa 1910.

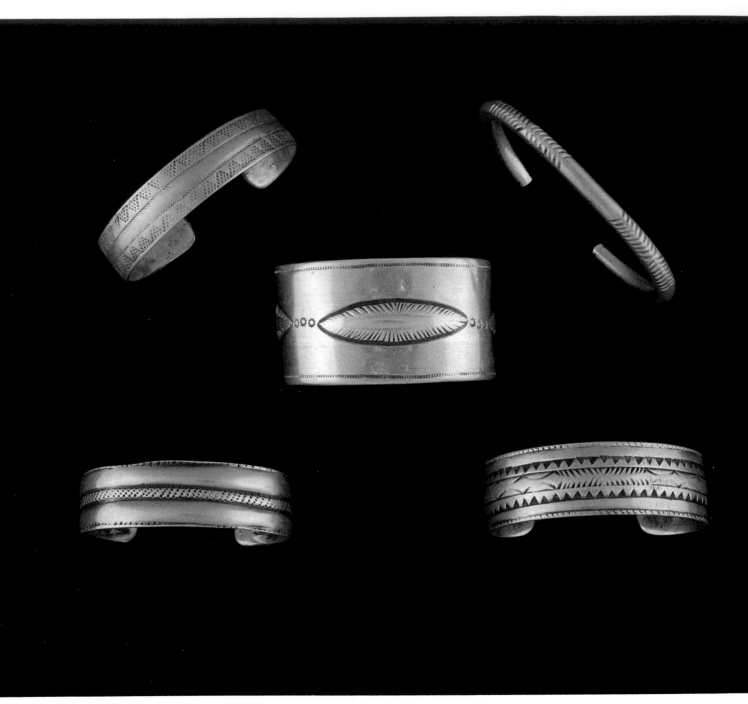

239.   The gleaming patina on the five silver bracelets is apparent. The upper left one, made of thin silver, was collected at Chamisal, a Spanish village in northern New Mexico, and dates around 1885 as does the bracelet below it, collected by Millicent Rogers in the 1940s. Both of the well-worn bracelets are delicately stamped with the emphasis of the design distributed on the edges of the upper one and in the center of the one at bottom left. In the middle, the well-worn bracelet with the wide center is an early example of the tastefully wrought jewelry that has made the Navajo silversmith famous. Fine stamping, file, and repoussé work are evident. The central elliptical form has repoussé work and the same forms are repeated at each end. The tiny stars and the fine border designs add subtle touches. Circa 1880s. The upper right stamped and filed silver bangle is one of the earliest forms of Navajo jewelry. Circa 1870. The well-worn lower right bracelet has more involved stamp work and dates around 1890. Its middle band has a separate design pattern.

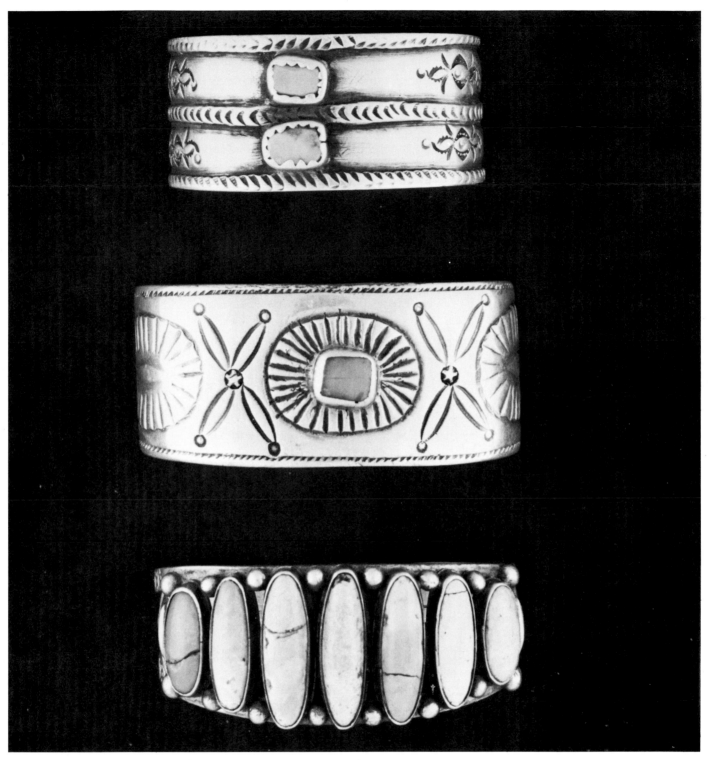

240. The bracelet with the two blue turquoise stones in serrated bezels has an interesting, stamped floral design unequally spaced from the stones. Stamped and filed designs are visible on the edges and are repeated in the middle of the bracelet. Circa 1890s. Only one green turquoise centers the three sunburst designs on the middle bracelet. Two stamped flower designs with internal starforms add to the patina of this well-worn bracelet. Circa 1885. The stone may well have been added ten years later. At bottom, graduated, elliptical, light blue stones dominate this stunning old-style bracelet that dates around 1920. The ends have simple stamp work (not visible).

241. This extraordinary cast and forged silver bar bracelet, shown from top and from underside, dates around 1900. An interesting effect is achieved by the manner in which the ridges have been filed away in order to give the rectangular turquoise an extra visual dimension and also a firmer setting. The terminals consist of four early hand-cut triangular stones which once were part of a necklace (except one) and have silver pins filling the drilled holes. For the most part bracelets with irregular and unmatched turquoise stones indicate a relatively late date of manufacture.

242. Navajo silversmiths also made silver jewelry for the children of the Indian Southwest. The stamped silver ring with turquoise and the stamped thin silver bracelet below it could have been worn only by a baby. The other two stamped bracelets were also worn by youngsters. All date around 1900.

243. Tightly twisted square silver wire forming an attractive band design produces a fine, delicate effect here. Except for the different arrangement of green turquoise stones and the small, filed bar between the two stones in the lower bracelet, the bracelets could be a matched pair. Notice that the two wires were twisted in opposite directions, forming this pleasing effect. Circa 1900. Collection of Mrs. Armand Bartos.

244. Another type of manta pin exists which utilizes a brass or copper stick pin rather than the usual loops soldered onto the reverse side, as seen with the previous manta decorations. The stunning pin with the sunburst design centered with a small turquoise stone inset into a diamond-shaped area has deep grooving on its convex silver reverse side which cannot be seen. Circa 1895. The use of silver U.S. coins was common practice as the pins themselves could always be converted into money with which to buy goods. Sometimes the units of coin are mixed, such as a dime being placed next to a quarter (bottom pin). The pins with coins date circa 1920s. The upper pin with turquoise stones in serrated bezels in the form of an arrow is later and dates around the 1920s.

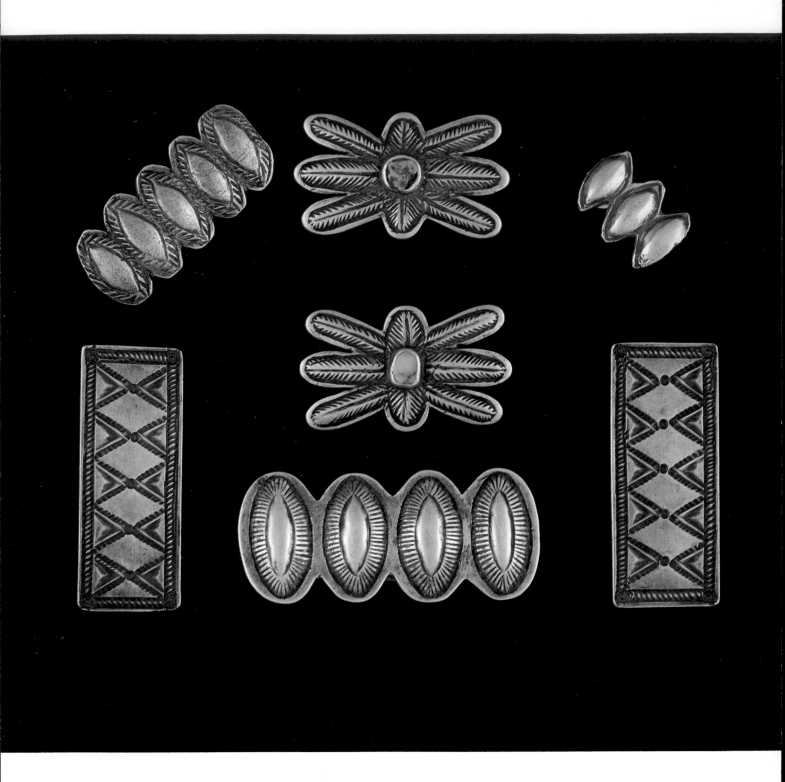

245. Jewelry accessories like these superb stamped and filed manta decorations are some of the striking personal silver adornments worn by the Indians of the Southwest. The unusual pair of long, rectangular manta pins were executed in somewhat varied designs — the V shapes of the right-hand pin do not quite meet. At center, the striking pair of pins with turquoise stones resemble intricate leaf patterns. The three pins with a series of oval forms are typical examples. All of these manta decorations have a rich silver effect and date around the 1880s and 1890s.

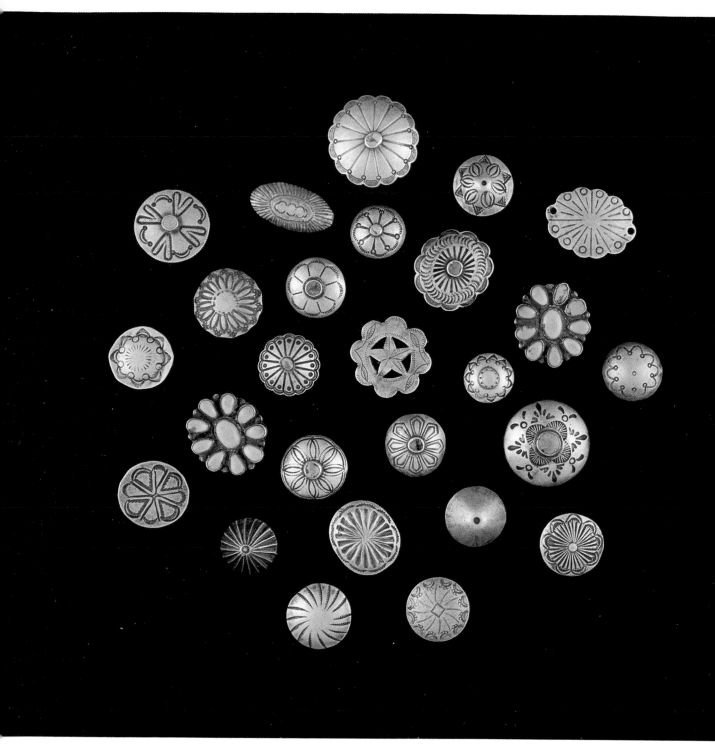

246. This array of mostly early silver buttons testifies to the remarkable imaginative design vocabulary the silversmith used on relatively simple forms. The center, cutout button is made of German silver and is rocker-engraved, relating to the Plains Indians. The oddly shaped elliptical button (upper left) resembles the pair of oval pieces on the Navajo bridle with the iron bit (Figure 227) and the hair ornament-like conchas in the Millicent Rogers Collection (Figure 154). There is an early plain silver button with only one punch mark in its center (lower right). A pair of later buttons with a cluster of green stones and a thin twisted wire around the central stone borders on being Zuni Pueblo work. The buttons date from the 1880s to the 1920s.

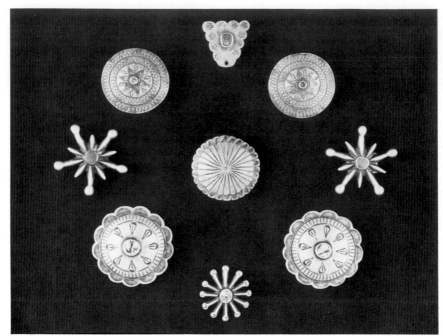

247. Silver buttons are also little artistic gems wrought by the silversmiths. Each button reveals a total design, sometimes as complex as on any other type of jewelry, especially the upper pair of stamped buttons centered with tiny stones. Circa 1900. The bottom pair with stones is later, and in general buttons set with turquoise came later than stamped and punched buttons like the one in the center (circa 1900). The pair of large sandcast star-shaped buttons (circa 1910) are earlier than the bottom sandcast button, circa 1930. The pendant on the top dates from the early 1900s.

248. These are all high-domed buttons and many date as early as the 1880s. Some look like miniature versions of early conchas with their twisted wire effect and scalloped border designs. The dark button (upper left) between the two large bright ones might be the oldest. The buttons are chiseled, stamped, repoussé and filed.

249. The ketoh has a round chrysocolla stone surrounded by tiny silver beads on a stamped square area embellished by more stamped forms. On each side are three petal designs with twisted wire effect borders. On the side of the leather is a tooled star design. On the underside of the silver plate the leather has been gouged to effect a crude undulating surface (not visible). Circa early 1900s. The early silver belt buckle with six square turquoise stones flanking a design of simulated twisted wire was found in Hopi Pueblo and had been in use for many years. The grooved end forms are a part of a sunburst design. Circa 1900. The superb manta pin below has six repoussé elliptical designs centered by a large dark green turquoise stone (probably added later) set in an elliptically serrated bezel. Circa 1880s.

250. Earrings have marvelous shapes like pieces of sculpture as well as engrossing designs. The earliest silver styles shown here are the two pieces with silver loops and silver balls, near the top. Circa 1870s and 1880s. Next in chronological order are the four silver loops with scalloped edges and no turquoise in the center row. Circa 1880s to 1890s. The two scalloped versions in the row to the left are later, circa early 1900s. The special single earbob in the middle right row has a turquoise stone with an early bezel and thick silver studs; circa 1890. The center pair with triangular stones and the bottom pair with green stones of the same triangular shape were common in the early 1900s. The red stone pair in the center row is perhaps from Hopi Pueblo and dates well before the turn of the century. The latest items (top center row), of Zuni manufacture, are a pair of elaborate earrings with nine stones in each and a number of silver dangles, circa 1930. An early fluted squash blossom occupies the lower right row, circa 1880s.

251. The design on this Spanish Colonial hand-made wooden chest from northern New Mexico reveals two flowering pomegranates (one not visible here). The pomegranate or squash blossom motif was prevalent in the Spanish frontier colony of New Mexico considerably before the actual Navajo silver version of it appeared in the latter half of the nineteenth century. The chest dates from the early 1800s. Silver "squash blossom" ornaments were worn on Spanish and Mexican capes, jackets, and trousers but this is a special indication of the popularity of the motif in New Mexico and Spanish areas bordering the Navajo Reservation.

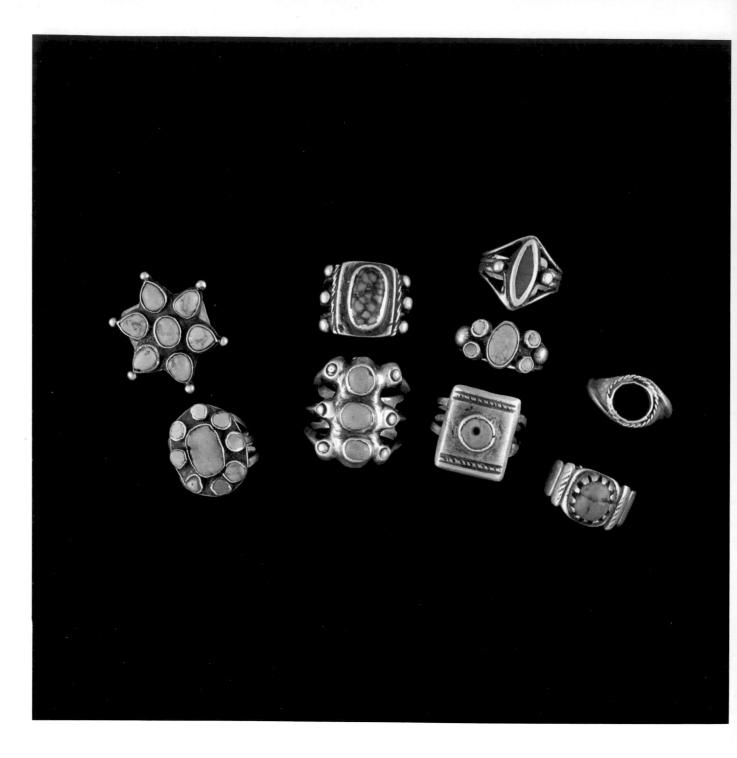

252. All of these are early rings except the top left one which is not a ring at all but an elaborate button, circa 1920s. The rings show great design and sculptural qualities. The top right twisted silver ring has a black jet stone which comes from fossilized coal. Circa 1930. The bottom right ring has a green turquoise stone with a serrated bezel and worn stamped designs, circa 1900. To its left, a pierced turquoise bead has been inset onto a stamped sandcast silver plate soldered onto the ring, circa 1880s. Left of it is a boldly designed ring with a set of punched designs flanking the three roundish green stones, circa 1900. The ring to the uppermost right is bounded by a triangular silver shape. It and the cluster ring below it are circa 1910. To its left is a ring with an old spider turquoise stone, circa 1910. The ring at lower left dates around 1920.

253. The two rings left of center have been termed "butterfly" rings because, as is the case with the ring on the top, the shape resembles that of the butterfly and, more subtly and abstractly, the middle section representing the butterfly's body is of a different color than the outside stones. In this case both rings qualify — the middle sections are green and the outside parts are blue and, in the one below, the stones in the middle row are circular, not tear-shaped. The two right rings are unusual; both look like early Zuni work and the one on the bottom (circa 1915) uses the early channel-setting technique in setting the stones, which are almost all green. The topmost ring has wrought silver wire scroll work flanking a green turquoise stone. The latest ring (bottom left), a coiled green snake with eyes, was most probably made by Leekya, a prominent Zuni silversmith, in the 1930s. The other rings make effective use of dark green oval turquoise stones.

Anneal To soften silver by heating to a dull red glow and quenching in water.

Anvil A hard surface to hammer on. During the first phase smooth rocks, a short section of railroad rail, or the end of a wedge, sledgehammer, or large bolt were used.

Bandolier pouch A leather pouch usually decorated with silver buttons. Carried by men, this pouch hung from a strap that passed over the shoulder.

Bangle Early style bracelet, often a piece of heavy wire decorated with file work or stamping.

Bezel A vertical wall of silver used to hold a stone in place on jewelry.

Bit The iron bar or bars put in the mouths of horses to control and direct them.

Bowguard A wristlet worn on the left arm to protect it from the snap of a bow string. Often decorated with a large silver plaque and worn purely for decorative purposes. Also called wristguard. *See ketoh.*

Buttons Used for fastening garments but among the Southwest Indians primarily for decorating trousers, moccasins, blouses, and leather pouches.

Cabochon A popular shape for turquoise — flat on the bottom and with a rounded top. The outline is often oval but can be round, square, or free form.

Channel setting A mosaic with metal on two sides and stone on stone on the other two sides. A Zuni technique.

Closed center A concha with a solid center; fastened to the belt by loops soldered to the back.

Coin silver Metal used to make jewelry, obtained by melting down silver coins.

Cold chisel A hardened steel tool with a 1/2-inch to 3/4-inch straight cutting edge. This was the primary cutting tool during first phase metal work.

Concha Also called concho at this time. A silver plaque of round or oval form used in groups to decorate belts.

Crucible A small container to melt silver in.

Die A steel tool used to raise or lower the surface of silver for decoration. Sometimes used in pairs or a male and female set.

Diamond slot An early style of concha that is held to the belt by means of a bar with triangular holes at either side that the leather passes through. The shape formed by the two triangular holes is a diamond.

Double-barred cross An early form of pendant with a vertical member crossed by two horizontal pieces. This design may be a Christian symbol or a stylized dragonfly design — symbol for water among the Southwest Indians.

Draw plate A piece of metal or bone with graduated and tapered holes drilled in it to draw down or reduce the diameter of wire.

End-of-a-file stamp A stamp decorated by striking the softened end against the face of a file.

File work Decoration on silver work, usually in the form of notches and grooves but also including filing away material to leave areas in high relief.

First phase period. 1868 to 1900.

Flux A chemical, usually boric acid, used to prevent silver from oxidizing during the soldering process.

Forge To alter the shape of metal by hammering.

Forge soldering Heating the parts to be joined in a forge using charcoal and bellows to provide the heat.

German silver An alloy of nickel and copper. This metal was used extensively by the Plains Indians and only rarely by the Southwest groups. Also called white brass.

Granular solder Early handmade solder, predating commercially available solder. "Granular" refers to the surface texture after melting.

Gunpowder charger A metal scoop used to measure powder for muzzle-loading weapons. A popular item of production by silversmiths during the 1870s and 1880s.

Hand-cut stones Stones ground by hand against a coarse-grained sandstone, basalt, or other rock.

Hard solder Solder using a silver alloy that melts at a relatively high temperature.

Headstall The strapping of a bridle that holds the bit in a horse's mouth.

Housing An Indian term for bezel.

Ingot A piece of silver formed by casting.

Iron Metallic material with very little carbon in it. Used by Southwest Indians for bits and female dies.

Jacklas A small loop of turquoise beads that hangs from the bottom of a chunk turquoise necklace. They used to be worn separately as earrings.

Ketoh Navajo word for bowguard. Pronounced "gato."

Lead solder A solder that melts at a low temperature. Used extensively by the Plains Indians and not at all in the Southwest.

Machine-cut stones Turquoise and other materials ground to shape with the use of motor-driven lapidary machines.

Manta pin A fastener used to hold the early style of dress together.

Miniature canteen See Tobacco flask.

Naja Navajo word for the crescent-shaped pendant.

Punch Another word for stamp.

Repoussé Raising the surface of metal by hammering out from behind and then refining the design on the front by further hammering and file work.

Ring shank The silver band that holds the top of the ring on a finger.

Rocker-engraving Decoration applied to metal by rocking a very short bladed chisel from corner to corner while at the same time pushing it forward.

Sandcast Cast in stone molds. This term may have resulted from the early use of sandstone for molds.

Scratch engraving Decoration on metal by scratching with a needle or steel awl.

Silver solder A solder that melts at a high temperature and has silver in it.

Squash blossom The shape found on necklace side pendants, said to resemble the flower of a squash or pumpkin. The design probably is derived from Spanish or Mexican prototypes and if anything represents a pomegranate flower.

Stamp A tool with a design on the end that is used to impress a pattern on metal work and leather.

Stamp blank A piece of carbon steel from which a stamp was fashioned.

Steel Iron with carbon added, which enables it to take a temper and be used for tools such as stamps and cold chisels.

Sterling silver An alloy of 925 parts silver to 75 parts copper.

Temper To harden steel.

Tobacco flask A small container made by Southwest Indians primarily for sale to soldiers as a novelty item. Also called miniature canteen.

Transitional period 1900 to 1930.

Tufa stone A stone of compacted volcanic ash used for casting molds.

White brass An alloy of nickel and copper. Also called German silver.

Wire A metal rod, often round but also found in other shapes such as triangular and square.

Construction

Hand-drawn and forged wire	1868–1900
Chisel cutting	1868–1920
Silver forged from cast ingots	1868–1930
Plain dome buttons	1875–1900
Forge soldering	1875–1910
Direct design casting (openwork)	1875–present
Heavy overlapping bezel setting	1880–1900
Hand-ground stones	1880–1920
Blowtorch soldering	1900–1930
Stamped and domed buttons	1900–present
Thin bezel setting	1900–present
Machine-cut stones	1900–present
Commercial solder	1900–present
Machine-processed silver (sheet, wire, beaded wire, etc.)	1900–present
Saw cutting	1920–present

Decoration

Scratch engraving	1868–1875
Rocker-engraving	1868–1875
Chisel stamping	1868–1880
File decoration	1868–1900
Garnets for settings	1880–1885
End-of-a-file stamp	1880–1900
Repoussé	1880–1915
Hand-cut turquoise settings	1880–1920
Stamps with leatherworkers' designs	1880–present
Swastika and arrow stamps	1900–1930

◇ Selective Bibliography

Adair, John. *The Navajo and Pueblo Silversmiths*. Norman: University of Oklahoma Press, 1944.

Bedenger, Margery. *Indian Silver*. Albuquerque: University of New Mexico Press, 1973.

Belous, Russell E., and Weinstein, Robert A. *Will Soule, Indian Photographer at Fort Sill, Oklahoma 1869-74*. Pasadena: The Ward Ritchie Press, 1973.

Cushing, Frank Hamilton. "Primitive Copper Working: An Experimental Study," *The American Anthropologist*, Vol. VII, January 1894, p. 93.

Feder, Norman. "Plains Indian Metal Working," *American Indian Tradition*, Vol. VII, Nos. 2 and 3, 1962, pp. 55-77 and 93-112, respectively.

Hegemann, Elizabeth Compton. *Navajo Silver*. Southwest Museum Leaflets, No. 29, Los Angeles, 1962.

Hunt, W. Ben. *Indian Silver*. New York: Collier Books, 1960.

Jenkins, Myra Ellen, and Schroeder, Albert H. *A Brief History of New Mexico*. Albuquerque: University of New Mexico Press, 1974.

Jones, Oakah L., Jr. *Pueblo Warriors and Spanish Conquest*. Norman: University of Oklahoma Press, 1966.

Matthews, Washington. "Navajo Silversmiths," *Second Annual Report of the Bureau of American Ethnology, 1880-81*. Washington, D.C.: Government Printing Office, 1883, pp. 167-178.

Mera, Harry P. *Indian Silverwork of the Southwest Illustrated*, Vol. 1. Tucson: Dale Stuart King, 1960.

Neumann, David L. "Navajo Silversmithing," *El Palacio*, Vol. 77, No. 2, 1971, pp. 13-32.

Newhall, Beaumont, and Edkins, Diana E. *William H. Jackson*. A Morgan and Morgan Monograph. Fort Worth: Amon Carter Museum, 1974.

Wheat, Joe Ben, letter, July 14, 1977.

Woodward, Arthur. *Brief History of Navajo Silversmithing*, Northern Arizona Society of Science and Art, 1938.

General

Dockstader, Frederick J. *Indian Art in America*. Greenwich, Conn.: New York Graphic Society, 1966.

Feder, Norman. *American Indian Art*. New York: Harry N. Abrams, 1970.

Frank, Larry, and Harlow, Francis. *Historic Pottery of the Pueblo Indians, 1600-1880*. Boston: New York Graphic Society, 1974.

◇ List of Illustrations by Object

◇ Accession Numbers

For readers who wish to do further research, the following list of museum accession numbers will aid in the identification of objects. Unless otherwise stated, the numbers are given in the order that the objects are discussed within the captions. Not every object has an accession number.

The Terrible Night at

RORKE'S DRIFT

by

James W Bancroft

SPELLMOUNT LTD
Tunbridge Wells, UK

HIPPOCRENE BOOKS INC
New York, USA

BOK BOOKS INTERNATIONAL
Durban, RSA

RORKE'S DRIFT

by

James W Bancroft

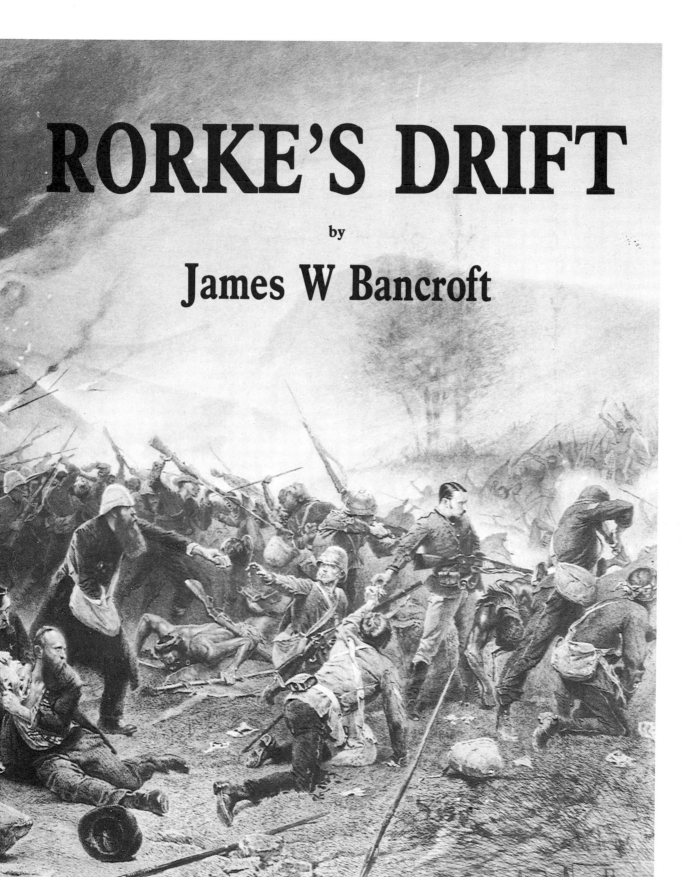

In the Spellmount Military list:

The Territorial Battalions – A pictorial history
The Yeomanry Regiments – A pictorial history
Over the Rhine – The Last Days of War in Europe
History of the Cambridge University OTC
Yeoman Service
The Fighting Troops of the Austro-Hungarian Army
Intelligence Officer in the Peninsula
The Scottish Regiments – A pictorial history
The Royal Marines – A pictorial history
The Royal Tank Regiment – A pictorial history
The Irish Regiments – A pictorial history
British Sieges of the Peninsular War
Victoria's Victories
Napoleon's Military Machine

In the Nautical list:

Sea of Memories
*Evolution of Engineering in the Royal Navy Vol 1
1827-1939*

In the Aviation list:

Diary of a Bomb Aimer

First published in the UK in 1988 by
Spellmount Ltd,
12 Dene Way, Speldhurst,
Tunbridge Wells, Kent TN3 0NX
ISBN 0-946771-48-0 (UK)

First published in the USA in 1988 by
Hippocrene Books Inc,
171 Madison Avenue,
New York NY10016
ISBN 0-87052-571-9 (USA)

First published in the RSA in 1988 by
Bok Books International
PO Box 20194
Durban North 4016
ISBN 0-947027-95-5

British Library Cataloguing in Publication Data
Bancroft, James W.
   Rorke's Drift – (Military pictorial history series)
   1. Zulu War, 1879
   I. Title   II. Series
   968.04   DT777
   ISBN 0-946771-48-0

© James W. Bancroft 1988

Design and picture research by Ravelin Ltd, Stamford, Lincs.
Figure artworks by Richard Scollins.
Typeset by Vitaset, Paddock Wood, Kent.
Printed in Great Britain by Anchor Brendon Ltd, Tiptree, Essex.

The Terrible Night at
RORKE'S DRIFT
The Zulu War, 1879

To
Remind us
Always, that
Courage and
Endurance
Yield success

CHAPTER ONE:
Zulu Defiance

*'It is the habit of every
aggressor nation to claim that
it is acting on the defensive.'*
Jawaharial Nehru

For most of the nineteenth century South Africa was disturbed by continuous friction between its mixed population. After British troops had twice seized the Cape from the Dutch at the turn of the century, settlers began to arrive in 1820, and as they expanded the frontier, there were many disputes over land boundaries between Cape Colonists and African Bantu tribes, which kept the British army on constant alert. These disagreements on occasions led to confrontations that became known as the Kaffir, or Frontier, Wars.

Soon after the British Government had abolished slavery in 1833, Boer farmers who were of Dutch origin, began to push northwards into the interior, to search for land where they could settle independently from British administration at the Cape. These 'Treks' met with resistance from the natives, especially the Zulu, who, because of a series of bloody battles and subsequent reprisals, became their bitter

In this scene of life in a military kraal, Mpande has called forward his finest warriors to perform a ceremonial dance during his review of the troops. They will then take part in a display of combat skills set by the king.

enemies. The Boers continued to push over the Drakensburg mountains, and the British moved across the Great Kei river, which formed the north-east border of Cape Colony, until by the middle of the century the Zulus found their kingdom bordered on the west by The Orange Free State and The Transvaal Republic, both of which had been founded by the Boers, and in the south by the British province of Natal.

Early in the century the Zulus had been disciplined by a great military-minded chief named Shaka. Shaka had been born the illegitimate son of Sezangakona, chief of the Zulus, and a woman called

Boer farmers struggle to negotiate a dangerous ridge on the Drakensburg Mountains during their legendary 'Great Trek' across the interior veld to establish independence from British domination at the Cape.

Nandi from a neighbouring tribe. At that time the Zulus were only one of a number of small Nguni tribes, which also included the Swazi, the Xhosa and the Mthethwa. They lived in the area between the Drakensburg mountains and the south-east coast. Because of the circumstances of his birth, Shaka and his mother led difficult lives as outcasts, and this had a lasting effect on him.

At an early age he began to show great courage and skill with weapons which at that time consisted of a throwing spear and a long, knobble-ended mace, called a *knobkerrie* used for clubbing an opponent. Tales abounded concerning Shaka's prowess. As a herdboy he fought and killed a fierce leopard that had come to attack his cattle. There was also the saga of a mad giant who lived on a hilltop in Shaka's district and for years this warrior would come down to terrorise and plunder the local natives. But one day he chose to approach the herd of cattle

that was in Shaka's care. The madman was confronted by the 6 feet 3 inch muscular young man who had, by now, become a proficient fighter. After a duel that was still talked about among the Zulus a hundred years later, Shaka triumphed. He became a fearless warrior, and his skill in battle soon attracted the attention of Dingiswayo, a Mthethwa chieftain with great military talent. Dingiswayo initiated the promising young man into one of his regiments, and in 1818 he was instrumental in making him ruler of the Zulus.

Shaka learned the advantages of an organised regimental system from Dingiswayo. As soon as

Shaka was a tall, powerful figure, who ruled his people with an iron fist. His dreaded army slaughtered thousands of Bantu tribesmen during the Zulu rise to greatness. But he sealed his fate when he began to exterminate his own subjects.

young Zulus reached their teens they were put into age-regiments, led by chiefs, or *inDunas*, chosen by Shaka. Regiments of old warriors and regiments made up of young warriors were combined to form a Corps, thus enabling the new recruits to learn from the experiences of the older men, and eventually to take their place. Each regiment had its own distinctive style of war regalia, and the warriors lived in military stockades, segregated from the domestic settlements. Shaka assured aggression in his warriors by depriving them of female companionship for long periods. And the fact that warriors who had been defeated in battle were put to death on their return, also considerably enhanced their determination for victory. Killing became a custom of the Zulu nation, and 'To Conquer Or To Die' became their motto. The warriors were not allowed to marry without the permission of the king, and this was not given until they had fought in battle and 'washed their spears' in human blood. The regiments who had proved themselves and had been allowed to marry, carried light-coloured shields, and wore a head-ring, or *isiCoco*, woven into the hair at the crown of their heads.

Shaka also made revolutionary improvements to their weaponry. He was an expert with the throwing spear, but he was not impressed by its effectiveness. He had noticed in battles that no real harm was done to an enemy until his warriors had closed on them. And the spears could be picked up by an opponent and thrown back. So he rearmed his regiments with short, broad-bladed stabbing spears called *assegai*s. These required very close combat, so swiftness of foot was important. Shaka believed that bare feet could move more surely across the hard rocky ground, so he ordered his warriors to discard their sandals. Some men disapproved, because the terrain was also very thorny. Shaka solved this problem by ordering them to prepare beds of thorns on the ground, and to harden their feet by repeatedly marching over them.

Tribal warfare had always, until then, been fought without any basic organisation. But Shaka introduced a tactical fighting formation based on an old hunting technique. His army, known as an *impi*, was divided into four groups. The bulk of the warriors formed a central group – the chest – that first engaged the enemy. Then two groups – the horns – swiftly moved round on each side to attack the flanks and rear, and encircle them. A reserve force – the loins – was kept at the rear, ready to be used if

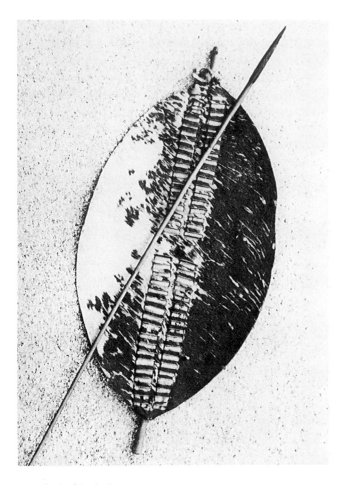

Left: *A throwing spear and the small cowhide shield adopted in the mid-1850's. The shield was designed to allow the warrior more mobility, while still providing protection in battle.*

Right: *The exotic bird plumes and feather, with otterskin headband and loincloth incorporated in this warrior's war regalia makes him distinguishable to his regiment. His dress blends with his surroundings, although he may have discarded some of the regalia when he went into combat.*

Below: *The assegai was grasped by the hand grip and thrust forward in an underarm movement. When carrying the knobkerrie mace in addition to the simple but effective weapons shown on this page, the Zulu warrior was a formidable foe in tribal warfare.*

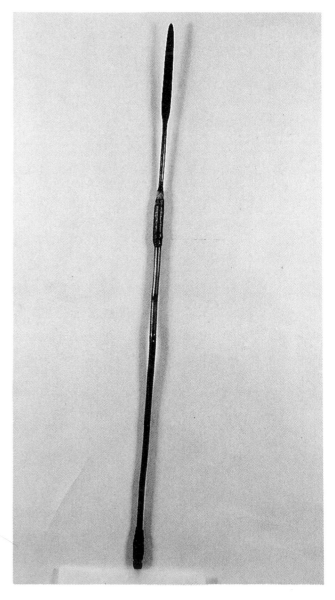

needed. Shaka's tough and bold warriors were well drilled with their weapons, and disciplined in battle. They slept naked on military expeditions, whatever the weather. The King revenged himself on those who had treated his mother badly, and one by one the Bantu tribes were crushed. The Zulu took possession of all conquered land. Any courageous warriors lucky enough to survive a battle were incorporated into the Zulu regiments. Within four years the land of the *amaZulu* – 'The children of the heavens' – covered over 20,000 square miles!

Shaka led the Zulus to greatness, but eventually his rule became one of terror. With no tribes remaining prepared to urge war against his superior forces, he had no means by which to relieve his aggressive feelings. He began to commit needless atrocities on his own people. He executed four hundred women on suspicion of witchcraft, and any shield-bearer who allowed a ray of sunlight to fall on him while he was shading him from its glare, was killed. And yet there was no shortage of men willing to take over the honour of shading the royal head. There was security in having a feared king, and the Zulu people were prepared to put up with their precari-

King Mpande was a weak ruler by Zulu standards, but he upheld some of the harsh traditions passed down the generations. He is seen here sitting in state outside his harem. He is protected from the sun by his shield bearer, whose own future was not bright if he allowed a ray of sunlight to shine on the royal head.

ous existence, so long as they knew that Shaka commanded the reputation of a powerful leader. But after his mother Nandi died in 1827, he brooded, and even began to lose the respect that he had built up for himself. He executed anyone who did not show continual grief at her death, and subjected his people to long periods of fasting. Sex was banned for a year, and the meaningless slaughters went on. He put to death anyone who sneezed while he was eating, and cut open a hundred pregnant women during a fad he had for embryology. At last the Zulu could stand it no longer, and in 1826 some of his own family, including his successor Dingane, conspired to stab him to death.

It was during Dingane's reign that the Zulus had started to resist the expansionist Boer republics. But he and his successor Mpande, who came to the throne in 1840, relaxed the strict military traditions. Mpande had not been king long before his family were squabbling about who would succeed him. Eventually Cetshwayo and Mbalini were the two men who emerged as the main rivals for the throne. The dispute was decided in 1856, when Cetshwayo's 20,000 Usuthu warriors pursued Mbalini's isiGqoza faction of about 30,000 men, women and children, including five more of Mpande's sons, until they trapped them at the river near the Ndondakuaka kraal. What followed was one of the most shocking massacres in Zulu history.

Mpande died in 1872, and Cetshwayo was crowned king of Zululand in the following year. He was a cunningly prudent leader. He hated the way his father had allowed the Zulu to lose their military reputation, and loved to hear stories of the great Shaka period. Under his leadership the Zulu army again became great. He added new regiments, and by 1878 these numbered thirty-three.

Although the main structure of Zulu life was built on military lines, Cetshwayo did not keep a standing army as Shaka had done. Except for his personal bodyguard, most of his warriors enjoyed a comfortable life farming the fertile coastal land, that with a fine sub-tropical climate endorsed with a regular rainfall, was perfect for agriculture and grazing sheep and cattle. They lived in circular homesteads called kraals, with dome-shaped thatched huts, each kraal being governed domestically by an inDuna. The king had become mainly a figurehead to whom the inDunas usually stayed loyal.

The women spent their day repairing basketwork for the huts, or preparing food. Some also boiled millet to make beer, or picked leaves to make pipe tobacco or snuff. When the men were not working the land they were kept in shape by regular military exercises, which now included learning to use the firearms that Cetshwayo acquired from white traders. But a Zulu warrior still prided himself on his ability to fight in close-combat, and was always restless to gain military honour. They saw themselves as invincible, and among the local native tribes they were. Cetshwayo had as many as 40,000 of these efficient warriors at his disposal, and this threat naturally caused great unease among his European neighbours.

Cetshwayo ka Mpande patterned his mode of rule on that of Shaka, being more intelligent and at times equally ruthless. He strengthened his army to retain independence for the Zulu, but when his kingdom became the main obstacle to confederation, the British invaded.

While it was a great honour for a young Zulu to reach the age when he could join a regiment, a Briton took the Queen's shilling as a last resort, usually when he could not find work. Redcoats were mostly looked upon as social outcasts, and usually came from the lower classes. Many were unskilled factory workers, farm labourers, or petty criminals, who joined at the police courts to save themselves from being thrown into jail.

In 1879 the British army included over a hundred numbered line-regiments, made up of eight companies lettered from A to H. The first twenty-five had two battalions. In 1871-72 the Secretary of State for War, Lord Cardwell, introduced a number of reforms. The branding of deserters was stopped in 1871, and commission by purchase was abolished in 1872. He introduced the retirement of officers, and the short service system, whereby a soldier could serve for three years with the colours, and then transfer to the army reserve for another five, giving married men the opportunity to spend more time close to home. But the soldier still had to serve for twenty-one years to qualify for a pension. The building of new depots and the introduction of cookhouses made life healthier for the rank and file. But army life was still tough and disciplined. Scrawny lads from city slums found themselves developing more respect for their personal cleanliness and domestic hygiene. The army made them into men. Each company lived, ate, and slept in the same barrack room, and they became a closely-knit unit. Their day was filled with drill on the parade ground, fatigues, such as scrubbing out the barrack block, and guard duty. A soldier caught napping on duty could still be severely flogged. Wages were a shilling a day, with half deducted for luxuries such as extra rations and laundry. The rest was usually spent on recreation, such as drinking heavily, picking up loose women in the nearest town, and ending the evening brawling with members of a rival regiment. In some cases battalions of the same regiment could not be trusted together.

There were fine traditions and staunch loyalties and, overall, officers had complete faith in the steadfastness of the British soldier. But ideas had changed little since Waterloo, and methods of training and tactics had become outdated. The professional British army owed its existence to the Empire, and it guarded it well. The 'British square' where ranks of soldiers stood shoulder to shoulder and maintained a continuous fire, was effective against a

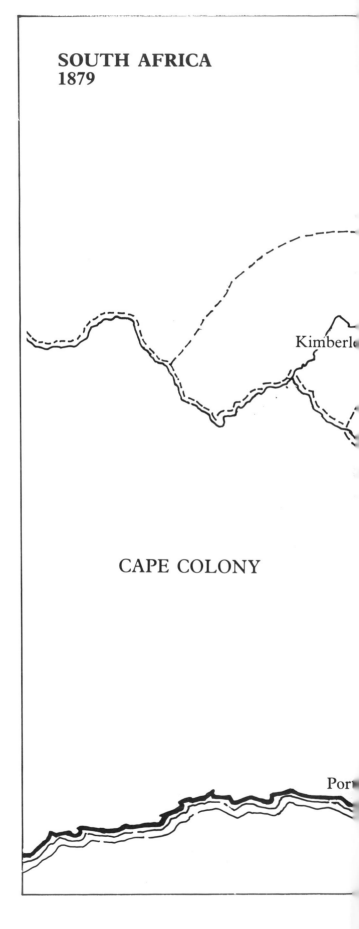

SOUTH AFRICA
1879

Kimberl

CAPE COLONY

Por

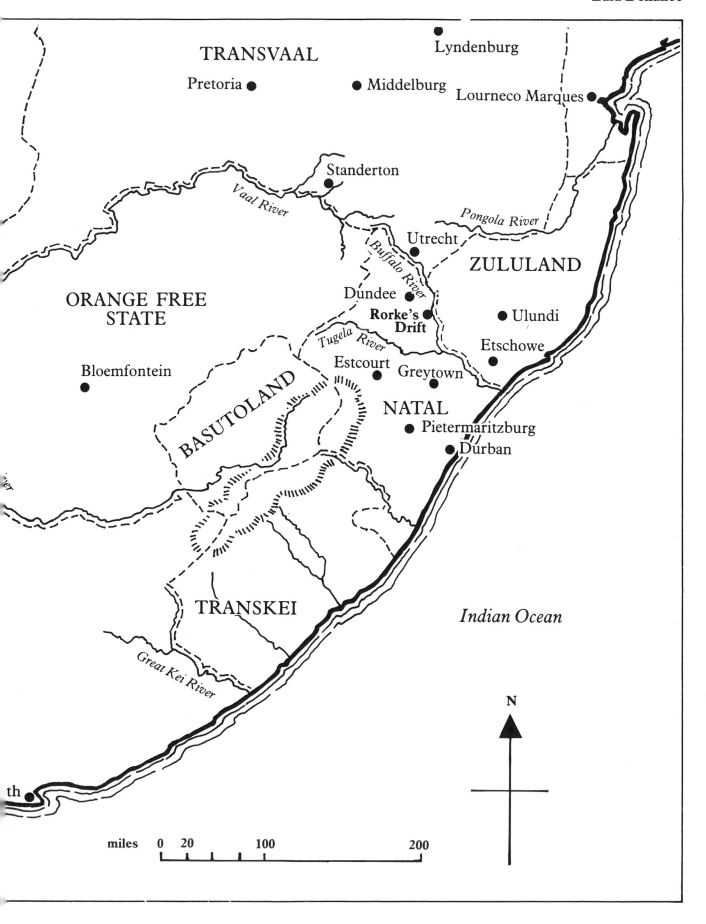

TRANSVAAL

Lyndenburg

Pretoria

Middelburg

Lourneco Marques

Standerton

Vaal River

Pongola River

Utrecht

Buffalo River

ZULULAND

ORANGE FREE
STATE

Dundee

**Rorke's
Drift**

Ulundi

Tugela River

Etschowe

Bloemfontein

Estcourt

Greytown

BASUTOLAND

NATAL

Pietermaritzburg

Durban

TRANSKEI

Indian Ocean

Great Kei River

th

N

miles   0   20   100   200

charging enemy armed with the relatively primitive weapons from 60 years before. But modern European armies had begun to introduce tactical stratagems such as using small, detached units, making use of cover. Successive British governments were reluctant to spend money on the army, and even more so in South Africa, once the Suez Canal opened in 1869 and shortened the passage to India.

British administration in South Africa, after years of endless squabbles and requests for the protection of the crown, tried to put in motion an idea that it had been considering for years, a plan to bring all the races together into one confederation under British rule. Most of the European colonists disliked the idea. Cape colonists had no desire to take on their less fortunate squabbling neighbours, and the Boers had no intention of losing the independence for which they had fought and died. To add to this, there were still many territorial disputes that would have to be settled before any form of legislation could be implemented. One such dispute between the Transvaal Boers and Sekukuni, chief of the Bpedi tribe, centred on an area near the Blood river. Sekukuni claimed the land and in 1876 his warriors repulsed a Boer force, and then took refuge in a stronghold in the Transvaal mountains. From there he sent out raiding parties to plunder the area.

In 1877 the reluctant, but bankrupt, Boer state was annexed to Britain, and the Sekukuni problem became the responsibility of the Crown. But he continued to resist all efforts to force him out. Sekukuni was known to be an ally of Cetshwayo, and there were all the signs that other native clans were going to rebel. The British suspected that Cetshwayo was encouraging their defiance. Zulu power would have to be dealt with. The desire for a Confederation of states, including Zululand, and the wishes of the restless Zulu warriors to wash their spears meant that some kind of conflict was inevitable.

In February 1878, the 2nd Bn, 24th (2nd Warwickshire) Regt, received orders to move from Chatham to Plymouth, where they were to board the troop-ship *Himalaya*, and sail to South Africa. There they would join their 1st Bn for active service in the 9th Frontier War at the Cape.

The battalion was first organised in Sheffield in 1858, and presented with colours the following year. Its first tour of overseas duty was on the sugar island of Mauritius in the Indian Ocean, from 1860 until 1865, and it had then served in Burma until it arrived back in the new depot at Brecon in 1873. Since then it had been at home, but the 1st Bn had been at the Cape since 1874. It had served in Griqualand in 1875, and had been involved in several other disturbances. But many of the soldiers of the 2nd Bn were young men fresh from the farms and factories of Britain.

The month long voyage to the Cape in cramped conditions was wearisome. After drill and kit inspection, the soldiers spent their time playing table games, or just staring out to sea with thoughts of family and girlfriends. In the evening it was impossible to move about freely on the troop-deck, because of the vast number of low-swinging hammocks and sleeping bodies on the floor.

HMS Himalaya served the British army for many years. It was used to sail troops to the Crimea and transported the 2/24th Regiment to South Africa.

After their arrival at the Cape, the troops were transported to King William's Town in the north-eastern Cape, the most advanced post in the area of unrest where the Gaika and Gcaleka tribes were causing problems. The campaign followed the usual pattern of kaffir disturbances: the rebels used the bushy terrain for refuge and extended lines of troops entered the scrub to flush them out. By June, Sindali, chief of the Gaikas had been killed, and the Gcaleka chief, Kreli, had been captured. The rebels lost heart, and the uprising was over. These sweeping skirmishes in the Perie Bush gave the 2nd Bn their first experience of active service.

Lt-Gen Sir Frederic Thesiger, soon to become the 2nd Baron Chelmsford, was Commander-in-Chief of the British forces in South Africa. He now turned his attentions to the 'arrogant' Cetshwayo and the Zulu problem. A coastal mail-steamer took the 24th Regt to Natal and on to Fort Napier, Pietermaritzburg to prepare for war.

A series of incidents then occurred. Cetshwayo had little understanding of the principles of European law and simply thought that if he did not show hostility towards the British they would have no reason to quarrel with him. A number of aggressive outbursts in defence of his opinions provoked the British. Zulus were marauding across the northern border into Swaziland, and there were signs that

The border commission present Sir Henry Bartle-Frere's fateful ultimatum to Cetshwayo's representatives beneath the shadow of a tree on the banks of the Lower Tugela River.

the *impis* were growing restless. There were reports that they had actually begun to fight amongst themselves. On the 28th July 1878, a dispute within the family of an InDuna called Sihayo kaXonga, chief of the Qungebe tribe, whose kraal was only four miles from the border with Natal, resulted in what was considered to be the unlawful killing of two of his adulterous wives, and violations of British territory by the family factions.

The governor of the Cape, Sir Henry Bartle-Frere prepared an ultimatum, that was deliberately unworkably harsh. On the 11th December Zulu emissaries came to the border to hear the results of a boundary commission which found that the Zulu claim was justified. But the ultimatum was also put to them. It requested the turning over of Sihayo's sons, who were the culprits, and a large fine in livestock. It also contained various extra clauses, including demands that the Zulu army must be disbanded, and the warriors made free to marry. This was to be answered before the first day of 1879.

Cetshwayo and his councillors were divided in their opinions of how to react to the ultimatum. The offenders of the border incursion had fled to the north, and Sihayo refused to betray them. So Cetshwayo began to gather livestock to send on his behalf. However, he knew that to accept the terms would mean the loss of Zulu independence, and the ultimate breakdown of Zulu society.

No reply to the ultimatum was received from the Zulu king after twenty days, so a further ten days' grace was allowed. This expired at midnight on Friday, 10th January, 1879.

CHAPTER TWO:
The Wild Frontier

*'If our time is come, let us die
manfully for our brethren's sake,
and not have cause of reproach
against our glory.'*

1. Macc. ix. 10.

British troops gradually made their way towards the border, and Zulu scouts warned Cetshwayo of the build-up of forces along the frontier. The total number of men under Lord Chelmsford's command was 5,400 Imperial soldiers, 1,200 colonial volunteers and 10,000 Natal natives. He also had a thousand transport vehicles at his disposal. To enter Zululand along the narrow tracks with such a convoy of men and wagons would be impossible. So he decided to divide his troops into five sections. His plan of action was almost the same tactic as the chest and horns formation used by the Zulus. Three main columns were to enter Zululand at different points along the border, and advance towards the royal kraal at Ulundi, about seventy-five miles away by the tracks. Two reserve forces would stay on the near side of the river to watch the frontier. This, he believed, would tie-down all the Zulu regi-

A view across the Buffalo River from the area around Rorke's Drift, which would have been the scene of the central column advance into Zululand. Isandhlwana Hill is visible in the distance.

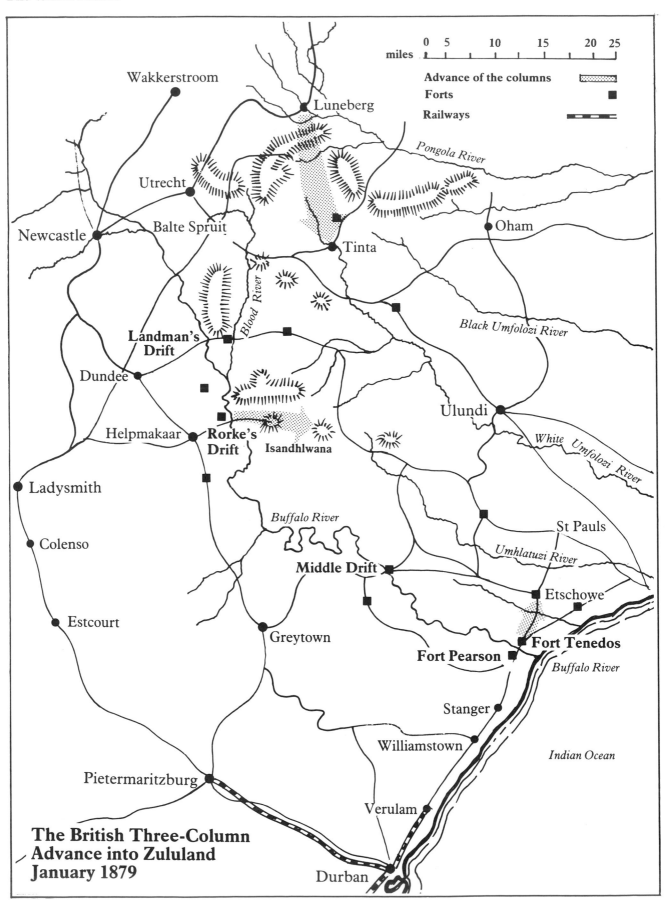

The British Three-Column
Advance into Zululand
January 1879

ments, and thus prevent any counter-strike into British territory.

Col Charles Pearson, 3rd Buffs, was to command a column that was to cross the border near the mouth of the Tugela river, and camp at a Norwegian mission-station near the town of Eshowe, in southern Zululand. He was to wait for a progress report on the other two columns before advancing further. Col Evelyn Wood VC, 90th Light Infantry, would advance his column from Utrecht in the Transvaal, across the Blood river, and move towards Ulundi via Khambula Hill, twenty miles from the border. He was to keep in contact as much as possible with Lord Chelmsford, who had attached himself to the Central, or 3rd Column, commanded by Lt-Col Richard Glyn, CB of the 24th Regt, which was to cross the Buffalo river at a place called Rorke's Drift. Col Anthony Durnford, RE kept a force of mounted volunteers, and colonial natives at the middle-drift of the Tugela, with orders to stay on the south side of the river. Another reserve section under Col Hugh Rowlands VC, 41st Regt, was camped at Luneberg in the Transvaal, to keep an eye on Sekukuni, and any possibility of a Boer extremist uprising while the British troops were preoccupied in Zululand.

It was considered that all three main columns were strong enough to withstand anything that Cetshwayo could send against them. But an army marches on its stomach, and Lord Chelmsford's problems were with the marshalling of transport and supplies, another factor that had dictated his need to split the troops. The transport consisted of Cape wagons that were eighteen feet long and were awkward and heavy when loaded. Even with eighteen oxen to pull just one of them, they could be stopped by the slightest ridge or soggy patch of track. Zululand was a maze of *dongas* (steep-sided water courses), with sudden high ridges and unpredictable marshlands, that could be a muddy quagmire after a morning downpour, becoming hard and dusty under the sweltering mid-afternoon sun. The tracks were rough and bumpy, and the sudden, heavy thunderstorms could swell a river and make the crossing treacherous if not impossible.

With all these points in mind, the British could hardly chase after an army as mobile as the Zulus who were capable of running from the capital to the border in less than two days, and could go for days without food. The only safe way of moving the columns was to establish several base camps during the

Above: *Lt-Col Glyn of the 24th Regiment, who commanded the 3rd column, was known to be a grouchy, quarrelsome man, and may have resented the Commander-in-Chief's presence with the forces under his command.*

Below: *A colonial covered ox-wagon typical of those used by the British invasion force. With an average unladen weight of nearly thirty hundredweight, it took between sixteen and twenty oxen to pull it when loaded.*

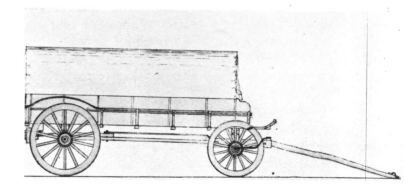

advance, and build up supplies by relaying teams of ox-wagons backwards and forwards. He needed to keep the bulk of the troops in each column together, and hoped that the Zulu warriors, armed with their primitive weapons, would attack the steady lines of British infantrymen, armed with the man-stopping Martini-Henry breach-loading rifle, capable of firing twelve rounds every minute. Faced with this sustained fire, he hoped that the morale of the Zulu *impis* could be smashed, and he could then end the war by capturing the king. He estimated that the campaign would take about six weeks.

The thump of drums filled the air as the 24th Regt began to move northwards from Pietermaritzburg, at the start of their 125 mile march through the wilderness. The Regimental band strained to the tunes of 'All Honour to the Noble Twenty-Fourth, of Glorious Renown', and 'Men of Harlech', as they reached Greytown. One company of the 2nd Bn was left to garrison the town, as they moved up to the little frontier outpost of Helpmakaar, where the column began to take shape.

Two companies of the 1st Bn were temporarily to garrison the outpost, which left thirteen companies of the 24th Regt to proceed to the border. Lord Chelmsford had received no cavalry units from England, so they formed a squadron of a hundred mounted infantry from the various Imperial companies. The mounted volunteers were made up of The Royal Natal Carbineers – who were not issued with carbines – The Newcastle Mounted Rifles and The Buffalo Border Guard. The Natal Mounted Police, under Major John Dartnell, had been on the border since November. Twenty-five recruits had come out from England in August 1878, and their strength was now two hundred. But because of a mishap with their horses they joined the column late. 'N' Battery, 5th Brigade, Royal Artillery, under Lt-Col Arthur Harness, had six 7-pounder field guns. The engineering work would be in the hands of Lt Nolan, and his ten men of the Natal Pioneers, who were joined later by Lt Francis McDowell with four Royal Engineer sappers. The 3rd Regt of the Natal Native Contingent was divided into two battalions. The 1st Bn was commanded by George Hamilton-Browne, and overall command was given to Rupert Lonsdale. Each Company was under European officers. The native troops wore a red rag around their heads, to distinguish them from Zulu warriors. They were badly trained and sullen. Neither the Imperial soldiers nor their own

At the start of the British campaign against the Zulu in January 1879, a typical bustling column of troops, wagons and ox-teams pushes on through broken country along one of the few tracks that were capable of carrying such a convoy.

officers had any respect for them, and they were known to be afraid of Zulu *assegais*. The total strength of the column was 1,700 regulars, 250 mounted volunteers, and 2,500 Natal natives. The transport consisted of 220 wagons, 82 carts, 1,500 oxen, and 70 mules. There was an English journalist with the column. His name was Charles Norris-Newman, or 'Noggs' as he was known. He was special correspondent to the London Evening Standard. There was also several colonial contractors. One of these was a large, rowdy man called Robert Hall, who was to provide bullocks for meat rations among the colonial troops.

On the 9th January the column moved twelve miles due east, across rolling lowlands, and skirting

The Rev George Smith came from East Anglia, and was stationed at St John's Parish, Estcourt. He was well known in the area. This sketch of him dressed in an alpaca frock was drawn by Lt John North Crealock, Lord Chelmsford's military secretary.

the terraced mountains towards the frontier. As the track came over a high ridge and sloped down to the river, it passed a five-hundred feet high mountain known as the 'Itchian' or 'Eyebrow', to the local natives, a quarter of a mile before it reached the Buffalo. On a ledge between the mountain and the track stood two thatched buildings and a cattle kraal, all built mainly of stone. They were the property of a Swedish missionary called Otto Witt, who lived there with his wife and three young children.

Witt had been in South Africa for three years, two of which he had spent learning to speak Zulu. The original owner of the land had been an Irish farmer and trader called James Rorke, who had died about four years earlier. Witt had built the kraal, and had personally re-named the mountain 'The Oscarberg' after the king of Norway and Sweden. He had turned the larger of the two buildings into a school chapel, where he taught the local natives a basic education and the Christian faith.

However, the army had commandeered the homestead, and he had sent his family to the Gordon Memorial mission-house at Umsinga, about twenty miles away across the border. He had stayed behind to keep an eye on his property, and intended to make himself useful by acting as an interpreter between the medical men and their kaffir orderlies. He was joined by George Smith,[1] a tall English missionary, who sported a great red beard. He was vicar of Estcourt mission, but he had been appointed acting chaplain to the volunteers. Most of the natives had gone to Umsinga, but as the once peaceful location began to bustle with activity, a tall copper-coloured teenager watched in awe as the red soldiers came in. His name was Umkwelnantaba – a direct cousin of the Zulu king.

The Wild Frontier

The ponts at the crossing of the Buffalo River at Rorke's Drift in 1879, showing the engineer's tent on the right. It was at this place that the main column of British troops crossed into Zululand on the 11th January, and the Zulu War began.

The Buffalo river at Rorke's Drift is wide. But there is an island about half-way across. It is dangerous and rocky in some places, and the recent heavy rains had swollen it, making the current strong and treacherous. Jim Rorke had cut the banks away to make it safer for transport, and the engineers began to assemble two ponts for the crossing. One was a raft on big barrels, and the other was a pontoon supported on boats. These floating bridges were large enough to carry one Cape wagon, or about eighty men at a time.

Officers bellowed their orders, as detachments of troops came in and pitched their bell-tents. And drivers yelled and cracked their whips as the heavily laden ox-wagons rumbled back and forth. A sprawling military camp was quickly built up around the mission-station.

At that time the Commissariat and Transport Department, although they were considered to be civilians, actually officered by men of the Army Service Corps. Assistant Commissariat Officer Walter Dunne[2] had served in the 9th Frontier War, and had been involved in the operations against Sekukuni, but after an exhausting ride of a hundred miles from the Transvaal to Helpmakaar, he had moved up to Rorke's Drift to form a supply depot in the chapel building. It measured 80 feet by 20 feet, and he supervised the men who began the arduous task of stocking it with stores.

There were 200lb bags of corn, or mealie, wooden boxes filled with biscuits, each weighing a hundredweight, smaller wooden boxes containing 2lb tins of corned beef and wooden ammunition boxes, each containing sixty packets of ten cartridges.

Mr Dunne was joined by Acting Assistant Commissariat Officer James Dalton,[3] a tall red-haired veteran of a line regiment, who was now in his mid-forties. He had served as a volunteer in the recent frontier war, and had been mentioned in despatches for his efficient conduct as the only Commissariat Officer at Ibeka depot. He had volunteered his services for the Zulu campaign. He and Acting Storekeeper Louis Byrne, a young clerk who had been working in Pietermaritzburg, had both ridden up from the capital in torrential rain on New Year's

Day. Second Cpl Francis Attwood[4] of the ASC, had also been working as a clerk in the capital since his arrival in Natal in the previous November. But he disliked the job, and decided to join the column. Five other ASC men were with the column, but they were to move into Zululand with the troops. Some of the regular soldiers who were not fit for the task ahead would also be assigned to store duties as soon as they had organised their tents. There was also a detachment of about three hundred Natal natives, under Capt William Stephenson, 2nd/3rd NNC, who could speak Bantu, that had been attached to the ASC on fatigue duty and would stay behind when the column advanced. One company of regular soldiers would also be left behind to guard the store.

The medical teams and ambulance wagons then came in. The ambulances were ordinary Cape wagons that had been fitted with a sprung frame, which acted as a kind of suspension, to make it more comfortable for casualties in transit. As the native levies began to unload the pack wallets and tentage from the mules, Surgeon-Major Peter Shephard and Surgeon James Reynolds,[5] eyed Witt's thirty year old ramshackle house, that they and the men of the Army Hospital Corps would have to utilise as a field hospital. One Surgeon, two stretcher-bearers, and an ambulance man were assigned to each company, so Doctor Reynolds, and three men of the AHC would stay behind with the company that was to garrison the depot. Reynolds was an Irishman who had much experience of military operations in South Africa. He had served alongside the 1st/24th Regt at Griqualand in 1875, and during the Frontier War he was again with them at Impetu, when the force that was guarding the drift there was besieged by Gcaleka rebels for months.

The house measured 60 feet by 18 feet, and into it Rorke had somehow squeezed eleven poky compartments that were separated by thin partitions made from mud and bricks with slight wooden doors. Doctor Reynolds decided to use one of the rooms to store medical supplies and stretchers, and two front rooms were prepared as casualty stations.

A company of the 99th (Lanarkshire) Regt, attached to Col Pearson's column, make the first crossing of the lower Tugela River. Scenes like this became common at points along the river as the British army went to war.

A close-up of the building which in turn had been Jim Rorke's barn, Otto Witt's chapel, and the British commissariat store. On the verandah Surgeon Reynolds established a temporary casualty station after the hospital building had been evacuated.

His patients would have to be crammed into seven dismal rooms that stretched in an 'L' shape at the western end, and along the back of the building, the doors of which faced south towards the Oscarberg. Only one of the rooms had access to the interior, which meant that the doctor would have to walk around the outside of the building to attend to most of his patients. The beds were straw-stuffed mattresses on hard boards placed on bricks to elevate them off the dusty floor. Reynolds was also responsible for a water-barrel on a cart and several appliances for filtering water. The two buildings were forty paces apart, and each had a verandah facing south, away from the mountain.

No reply to the ultimatum had been received from Cetshwayo when the period of grace expired. So early in the morning of Saturday, 11th January 1879, hostilities began when British troops crossed the frontier into Zululand. Zulu scouts watched from the hills as the barrel raft, platform pont, and a few small boats began to bring the red-coated soldiers across the mist-shrouded river. The mounted men and the natives crossed lower down. The kaffirs linked hands and charged into the water, wading neck deep through the current. Many were swept away and smashed to death on the rocks or

A view of Rorke's Drift post after the defence, looking towards the Oscarberg from the north-west. A more permanent loopholed stone wall has been erected. The storehouse with bare rafters can be seen, and where the hospital stood on the left of the tree.

simply lost their footing and disappeared from the surface. How many died was not known because nobody had bothered to count exactly how many there were to begin with.

Once across and supported by the six field guns, they formed a bridgehead and camp in enemy territory. The troop crossing was completed by 06.30hrs. Progress was halted however, when it was found that the track beyond the new camp was impassable for transport. Lt McDowell and his unit were instructed to prepare the bed for a road across the swampy Bashee River Valley.

The eighty-two men of 'B' Company, 2nd/24th Regt, were the unit left behind to garrison the depot. They were commanded by a stocky, thirty-three-year-old lieutenant, Gonville Bromhead,[6] who had twelve years of service behind him and had come from a distinguished military family. But his own career had been hindered by a serious hearing problem. Some of the disgruntled men of 'B' Company were apt to blame their officer's deafness for the reason why they were regularly given such secondary tasks as guarding supply dumps. Lt Bromhead had asked for permission to fortify Rorke's Drift, but this had been put off. The 4th (King's Own Royal) Regt, and the 5th Company of Royal Engineers were moving up to the frontier, and the job was to be left to them. 'B' Company hoped to rejoin the main advance when these reinforcements arrived.

Sub-Lt Thomas Griffith, 2nd/24th Regt, had been put in charge of the four soldiers of the 1st Bn, who were assigned to store duties. They were Sgt Edward Wilson and Ptes Thomas Payton; Patrick Desmond, a notorious drunkard; and Henry Turner, who suffered from epilepsy. They were acting as issuers of stores. Six more men of the 1st Bn were in the hospital. Pte John Waters was special orderly to Surgeon Reynolds. Ptes Thomas Beckett, William Horrigan, James Jenkins, Edward Nicholson and William Roy, a malaria victim who was also having severe eye problems, were all patients.

There were already more than thirty patients in the hospital. In all twenty-two were soldiers of the 24th Regt. Of the seventeen men from the 2nd Bn, Pte Edward Savage had injured his knee. The rest were from other companies, including Pte John Connolly, 'C' Company, who had a dislocated left knee and Sgt Robert Maxfield, 'G' Company, who was tossing and turning with fever in the Witt's bed. Gunner Arthur Howard of the Royal Artillery had been Col Harness's servant, but he had been left behind in the hospital suffering with diarrhoea. Apparently he was holed up in a corner room near the toilet, along with Gunner Abraham Evans, who

A leather service belt and ammunition pouch of the type used by the 24th Regiment at the time of the Zulu War. The pouch held four paper packets each containing ten rounds of ammunition.

Otto Witt's mission-station was one of several dotted about the landscape of Natal and Zululand, where European church workers preached the gospel. Witt had made himself unpopular locally because of the exaggerated stories he told to the press.

was suffering from a similar complaint. Bombardier Thomas Lewis had been injured in a wagon accident. His thigh, and all down one leg was swollen. Troopers Robert Green and Sydney Hunter of the Natal Mounted Police[7] were stricken with rheumatic fever. And there were five Corporals of the Natal Native Contingent. Friedrich Schiess,[8] a well-built young Swiss, had arrived in South Africa in 1876. Since then his size had helped him to get work as an unskilled labourer. He had fought in the Frontier War with distinction, before joining the 2nd/3rd Regt, NNC. But he had a severely blistered foot from wearing damp ill-fitting boots. The other NCO's were Michael Anderson, William Doughty,

Carl Scammel and John Wilson. Cpl James Graham of the 90th (Perthshire) Light Infantry was also invalided. All the bowel disorders had been caused by drinking bad water.

Sihayo's kraal was close to the Bashee Valley, so, on the second day of the invasion, a force was detached to attack his strong-hold in a rocky gorge. Sihayo was at Ulundi, but some of his sons were present. His retainers put up some resistance, but after a short skirmish, thirty had been killed, including two of the chief's sons, and over a thousand head of livestock were in British hands. There were also sixteen Natal Native Contingent casualties. Two natives had been killed and an ambulance wagon brought some of the wounded back to Rorke's Drift. Among them were Lt Thomas Purvis, 1st/3rd NNC, who had received a severe wound when a Zulu bullet went through his arm, and Cpl Jessy Mayer of the same unit, who had been caught below the knee with an *assegai*. Among

the six badly wounded natives was a warrior of Mkungu's Xhosa tribe, of Weenen County, whose thigh had been split by a rifle bullet.

After the engagement, Trooper Henry Lugg of the Mounted Police, a teenager from Devon, was ordered to ride to Pietermaritzburg with despatches. He was eager not to miss the advance into Zululand, so he made a pony express-style ride, using ten horses in relays, and was back at the mission-station by the seventeenth. But his effort was in vain. As he tried to cross the river to re-join his troop, his mount lost its footing, and crushed his knee as it fell. His admission into the hospital brought the number of men on the sick list to thirty-six.

A civilian ferryman named Daniels was looking after the ox-teams at the drift. And Sgt Frederick Milne, 2nd/3rd Regt, (The Buffs), was supervising the ponts. Because of neglected maintenance and constant usage, one of the ponts had been put out of action. Lord Chelmsford was becoming agitated at the slow progress at the crossing, and the engineers

were still busy with making good the road. So he ordered another advance party of Royal Engineers to move up to the river to work on the idle pont. Because the rains had drenched the tracks, the movement of wagons was slow, and so it wasn't until the morning of Sunday, 19th January, that a light mule-wagon carrying the necessary equipment, rattled by the mission-station and down to the river. With it came a dark-bearded lieutenant called John Chard,[9] his driver and batman Edward Robson, a corporal and three sappers. Chard was a thirty-one-year-old West Country man, who had passed out at Woolwich eleven years earlier. Most of his service to date had been in southern England, and he had not yet seen action. He was feeling under the weather. His re-vaccination at Capetown had become inflamed, and his right shoulder and side were sore. They pitched their tents by the river, and the sappers set to the task of securing the rope cables that were pulled to move the points across the water.

Above: *Off Duty: The soldiers in camp normally spent their leisure time playing cards or relaxing with their pipes and tobacco. The officers occasionally went hunting for wild game. Here John Chard, wearing his medal, poses for a photograph with fellow Royal Engineers.*

Left: *Lt John Rouse Merriott Chard of the Corps of Royal Engineers was born near Plymouth in 1847. He had only recently arrived in South Africa and had no time to acclimatise when he received orders to proceed to Rorke's Drift.*

Lord Chelmsford had chosen Isipesi Hill, twenty-two miles into Zululand, as the place where the first of the main fortified camps would be constructed, and a reconnaissance party had selected a site for an intermediate, temporary camp, at the base of an isolated hill called Isandhlwana, ten miles away. The road was finally ready on Monday, 20th January, so the column broke camp by the river and a general advance was made towards Isandhlwana. The men of 'B' Company were disappointed not to be going with them, as they wished 'Good Luck' to their friends when they left. As the post settled down, it seemed detached and quiet after the events of the past ten days.

Colonel Durnford was not happy with his command over a reserve force, and Lord Chelmsford was aware of it. So when the British commander received a message from Durnford stating that he had heard a rumour that a Zulu impi was going to attack Natal by way of the Middle Drift, and he was preparing his troops to cross the frontier to meet it, Chelmsford sent a note back at once, ordering him to bring half his force to Rorke's Drift, with the threat that he would be relieved of his command if he did not obey. So during the dark hours of Tuesday morning, Durnford arrived with a strong force of colonial troops, a Royal Artillery rocket battery and a number of wagons, and took over the area that the field column had vacated.

He had 255 mounted volunteers with him, which represented the best troops the colony could offer. Lts Roberts, Charles Raw, and Richard Vause commanded fifty Ngwane natives each. They were known collectively as Sikali's Native Horse. Lt Alfred Henderson led the Hlubi troop of fifty-five BaSotho, and Lt Nathaniel Newnham-Davis of the 3rd Buffs, had the Edendale troop of fifty Kholwa natives. The soldiers in the rocket battery were drawn from the 24th Regiment.

As a temporary appointment, Major Henry Spalding DAQMG of the 104th (Bengali) Regiment, who was one of Lord Chelmsford's staff officers, had been left in charge of the area of Rorke's Drift – Helpmakaar. 'D' Company, 1st/24th Regiment, under Capt Thomas Rainforth, had been requested to move up from Helpmakaar, to form a guard over the drift. But they had not yet arrived. That afternoon Lt Chard received orders from Isandhlwana, stating that his men were to move up to the base camp. So he went to the mission-station to report this to Major Spalding.

Above: *Colonel Durnford, Royal Engineers, was a forty-eight-year-old Irishman. He had been in South Africa since 1871, during which time he had learnt to respect the Zulu and knew them well. However, he had a habit of making decisions that were contrary to his orders.*

Right: *Lord Chelmsford's Orders of the Day, which included the command that Colonel Durnford should move his troops from the Middle Drift to Rorke's Drift, and take up a position on the Zululand side of the river. The column moved on into Zululand the next day, and Durnford's contingent arrived at Rorke's Drift during the early hours of the 21 January.*

... rd R. E.

... C. ...

... Helpmakaar ...

1. You are requested to move the troops of your immediate command viz: mounted men, rocket battery, and Sikeli's men to Rourke's Drift tomorrow 20th inst; and to encamp on the left bank of the Buffalo (in Zulul...

2. No 3 Column moves tomorrow to the Isandhlana Hill.

... Major Bengough with his battalion ...
... contingent at Sand Spruit ...
... himself in readiness ...
... Buff ... ro at the shortest ...
... operate agai ...
... etc. His w... ...
... this benefi- ...

4. ...
... eserted as to ...
... for ... the above battalion ... can best cross, so as to co-operate ... th No 3 Column in clearing the country occupied by the chief Matyana.

By order

H. Yintling Major
DAAG

Camp ...
Rourke's Drift
19 . 1 . 79.

Left: Lord Chelmsford was an ex-Grenadier Guardsman, aged 51. He had seen service in the Crimea and in the latter stages of the Indian Mutiny. His administrative skills earned him the reputation of an officer with 'great ability and untiring energy.'

Chard was uncertain about the orders, because they did not seem to include him. So Spalding granted him permission to go to the camp at Isandhlwana to check the orders for himself. Spalding however told Chard that he must postpone the visit until morning, because he first wanted him to select a good place where the Company from Helpmakaar could entrench when they arrived to protect the ponts.

As the light was beginning to fade and the post was settling down for the night, Sub-Lt Griffith arrived at the drift and requested to be ferried across. He was finding his store duties tedious and had decided to ride out to Isandhlwana in search of more exciting activity.

Even before the invasion had started, thousands of Zulus had converged on the main military kraal at Nodwengu, near Ulundi, to take part in an annual cleansing ceremony, called the *umKhosi*, the 'first fruits' ritual. For this the participants wore their war regalia, and therefore many of Cetshwayo's regiments were already prepared for military operations. Those who had remained in their kraals in readiness for the coming harvest, were told that they might soon be needed, and would have to postpone the work, or the task be taken up by the women.

But by the time the camp was forming at Isandhlwana the entire Zulu nation capable of bearing arms had assembled before the King. On Cetshwayo's instructions many of the warriors had brought cattle to exchange for firearms. When news of the British advance reached the capital, the *impis* grew impatient for action. But many of Cetshwayo's council did not want war, so he tried to hang on for a settlement. Eventually he could wait no longer. He stressed to his warriors that he had not wished for war, and that the British were the aggressors. His final instructions were that they should advance slowly to save energy, and not to attack fortified places, especially after dark. The regiments demonstrated their loyalty to the king with a cry of 'Usuthu!'. Then they streamed out across the Mahlabathini plain to defend their kingdom from the white invaders.

A sketch of the tall, lanky figure of Lord Chelmsford. The British Commander-in-Chief was a good leader and was popular among his men.

CHAPTER THREE:
'When Suddenly . . .'

'Worry is rust upon the blade.'
Henry Ward Beecher.

A drizzly rain fell during the night, and the morning of Wednesday, 22nd January 1879, was cold, damp and misty. As the camp at Rorke's Drift began to stir, Lt Horace Smith-Dorrien of the 95th (Derbyshire) Regiment, who was in charge of the transport, arrived back at the river from Isandhlwana with a message for Colonel Durnford. Zulus had been sighted ahead of the camp, and Lord Chelmsford had taken more than half his force forward to meet them. Everyone was expecting action soon. Durnford was to advance his troops to reinforce the base camp. However he had set off towards Helpmakaar with the Edendale men, and had to be sent for when the lieutenant delivered the message.

There was some transport business to attend to at the depot, so Smith-Dorrien crossed the river, where Lt Chard and his men having finished breakfast, were squelching about in the heavy mud on the Natal bank, preparing to move up to Isandhlwana. The party of Royal Engineers crossed into Zululand at about 08.00hrs, which was just after Colonel

Zulu chiefs, with total knowledge of their ground, lead their impis *at great speed, though this may be doubted by the warrior on the right whose belly is, no doubt, the result of a main staple diet of maize and a weakness for millet beer.*

Durnford and his troops set off. Smith-Dorrien went to breakfast with Lt Bromhead. He told him what news there was from Isandhlwana and borrowed eleven cartridges and was on his way back to the base camp by 09.00hrs.

The muddy tracks slowed the progress of the wagons, so Chard rode on ahead, and reached Isandhlwana before Durnford. The camp was set out at the eastern base of the mountain, which was an unusual looking flat-topped feature, whose shape resembled a crouching lion. Lt Chard went to the Headquarters tent, and found that his duties at Rorke's Drift were strictly on the Natal side of the river, keeping the ponts in working order, and maintaining the track back to Helpmakaar. Through a field glass he could see groups of Zulus moving about on the distant hills to his left. They moved in a westerly direction, until the slopes of the mountain behind the camp hid them from view. This was the direction of Rorke's Drift, and he became anxious that they might close-in and prevent him from returning, or even attempt to cut off the supply line by attacking the depot. So he set off back. He met Colonel Durnford on the way, who asked him to pass some messages back along his line of troops. Then the engineers' cart came rumbling up. Chard ordered the sappers to walk with Durnford's men, and told Robson to turn the empty wagon around and follow him back to the drift. He then encountered Lt Smith-Dorrien who was riding back to the base camp. Chard arrived at the river just in time for lunch.

There a message from Major Spalding had been left in his tent. It stated that a guard of seven regular soldiers and fifty natives was to be put on the ponts. They would be relieved when the Company – which was two days overdue – arrived from Helpmakaar. Chard rode up to see Major Spalding at the post. He told him what he had seen at Isandhlwana, and although there had been no sign of any Zulus to his right on the return trip, he pointed out that if an *impi* did attack the ponts, it would be impossible to defend them successfully with the troops allocated to him.

Major Spalding acknowledged this and decided to go to Helpmakaar personally, to see what was delaying the reinforcements. He checked the army

A Zulu chief, similar to the one who appeared on the Oscarberg. The headgear and cowtail streamers enabled him to remain well camouflaged in the bush.

On receiving his orders, Lt Chard rode out of the base camp. Soon afterwards Isandhlwana took its place in history, while he returned to Rorke's Drift – and immortality.

list in his tent to see who would be in charge during his absence. Engineering officers were commissioned as lieutenants straight from passing-out at Woolwich. But Bromhead had served as an ensign (2nd lieutenant) for over four years, before becoming a lieutenant. So although Bromhead had entered the army fifteen months before Chard, Chard had been a full lieutenant for more than three years longer, and was therefore the senior officer. Surgeon Reynolds was a non-combatant, and although Captain Stephenson's rank was the highest, he was not eligible to command regular troops because his appointment was only a temporary colonial one. Major Spalding informed Lt Chard of this, and then set off for Helpmakaar, intending to be back before dark.

Chard was not too alarmed at the situation. There was a large force between the depot and the Zulus, and so he ordered no particular precautions taken. He returned to the river, gave out orders to Lance-Sgt Thomas Williams and his detail, and prepared for lunch. The flies were a nuisance when the men were eating, and the day had become humid and hot, so he decided that it would be more comfortable to eat in his tent. After lunch he lit his pipe and decided to write a letter home. He was interrupted by the natives going back to the depot to be relieved, but apart from that he was able to get on with his correspondence.

Colour-Sgt Frank Bourne[1] and his four sergeants were walking in the hills behind the post when they heard the pounding of artillery coming from the direction of Isandhlwana. They could see clouds of smoke, but the mountain was five miles distant and it was difficult to see clearly with the naked eye. The hills also muffled the sound from the men in the post for whom all was normal, as Lt 'Gonny' Broomhead had allowed most of his men to idle near their tents. Some were entertaining themselves in gaming schools, while others were writing letters home. Many men could hardly read or write, and they were waiting for Colour-Sgt Bourne to return, so that he could help them with their spelling.

A few men were going about their duties as usual. Pte Charles Mason was on guard duty. The hills around Rorke's Drift were still, and there was nothing of importance to report. But he was having problems with the flies that kept landing on him and making him itch. Pte Harry Hook[2] was hospital cook that day, and he was at the cookhouse ovens behind the store brewing tea for the sick. Pte Waters was busy with his hospital orderly duties. Pte Frederick Hitch[3], a tall Londoner, was also at the ovens, preparing food for the Company. Lt Bromhead and Mr Dunne were relaxing smoking their pipes under a tarpaulin which they had propped up with tent poles to shield them from the sun.

Otto Witt and Surgeon Reynolds were preparing their horses to pay a visit to a local missionary. But when the Colour-Sgt returned and reported to the post what he had heard, word reached them, and they decided to go up the Oscarberg with Chaplain Smith, hoping to get a better look at what was happening. When they arrived at the summit they were disappointed to find that the slopes of Isandhlwana blocked their view. They heard three more artillery shots at fifteen minute intervals and at about 13.00hrs the sky went dark, as there was a partial

Lt Adendorff and five Non-Commissioned Officers of the Natal Native Contingent were among the defenders when the Zulu offensive began. This NNC officer wears an infantry officer's style patrol jacket and buff, cord riding breeches. The slouch hat has a red rag – or puggree – *around the crown.*

RICK · SCOLLINS

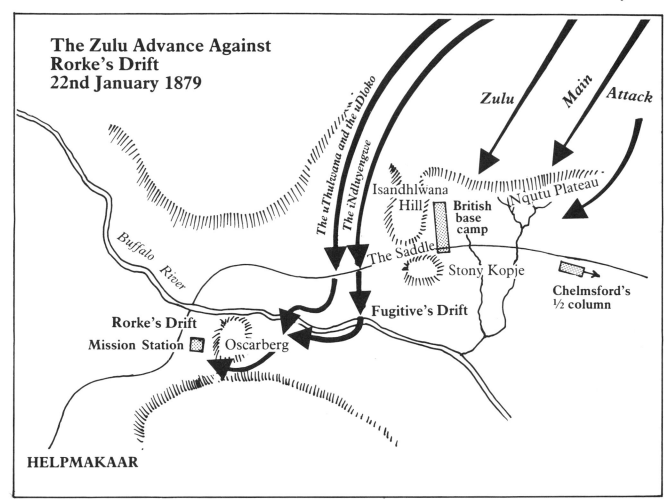

The Zulu Advance Against
Rorke's Drift
22nd January 1879

Zulu Main Attack

The uThulwana and the uDloko

The iNdluyengwe

Buffalo River

Isandhlwana
Hill

British
base
camp

Nqutu Plateau

The Saddle

Stony Kopje

Fugitive's Drift

Chelmsford's
½ column

Rorke's Drift

Mission Station

Oscarberg

HELPMAKAAR

eclipse of the sun. At 13.30hrs a large body of natives could be seen moving around Isandhlwana. They were in good order, and therefore the observers took them to be a detachment of the Natal Native Contingent. They were moving in the direction of Rorke's Drift, but the men on the Oscarberg lost sight of them as they descended into low ground, presumably to search the area for fugitive Zulu warriors.

Just after 15.00hrs Lt Bromhead and Mr Dunne noticed a commotion among the natives across the river. They started to go down to see what the problem was, but they were stopped when Pte Frederick Evans of 'H' Company, who had been attached to the mounted infantry, came galloping into the post. The men in the depot looked at each other apprehensively, suspecting that something was wrong. Evans was in his shirt sleeves and he had no helmet on and he was panic-stricken. They listened with horror as he gasped out the news that the camp at Isandhlwana had been taken by the Zulus and most of the men in it had been wiped out.

They were stunned and the shocking report

made it difficult for Lt Bromhead to think straight. But he regained his composure and sent a man down to the river to warn Chard. Nobody could grasp the full significance of the situation at first and they did not know quite what to do.

From the top of the mountain Surgeon Reynolds had seen four colonials riding towards the depot from Isandhlwana on the Natal side of the river. He thought that they might need his assistance, so he rode back down the hill, and got back just as they came pounding into the post. They were visibly frightened, and to Reynolds' surprise, one of them was on Surgeon-Major Shephard's horse. They delivered to Bromhead a pencilled note that had reached them through the combined efforts of three officers who had got out of the camp at Isandhlwana. The note confirmed the previous report, but a look of urgency came onto Bromhead's face when he read that, with the army in disarray, a large Zulu *impi* was at that moment making its way towards Rorke's Drift. This he was to hold at all costs. The fugitives tried to make them realise that the Zulus

41

were in overwhelming numbers, and their only chance was to retreat, which they themselves promptly did, leaving the men to realise the implications of the serious disaster that had happened.

The officers realised the dire position they were in and that there were some quick decisions to be made. There was a feeling among the ranks that the safest thing to do was to try to reach the troops at Helpmakaar[4]. But if they took the decision to retreat, could they get to Helpmakaar before a fast-moving *impi* caught up with them? They had no idea of the size of the *impi*, and they had done nothing to put the post in a state of defence. The depot was open to attack from all sides, and if the Zulus came upon them as it stood, they would not have a chance. But if Lord Chelmsford's advanced force was trying to fight its way back to the river, they could be desperately short of supplies and ammunition. Rorke's Drift depot was their only lifeline. Could they throw up a barricade in time?

When Commissariat Officer Dalton joined them he took the initiative by suggesting without doubt that they should make a defence. He strengthened his opinion by bringing to mind the good supply of building material they had in the store. Mr Dalton and Mr Dunne began to trace a line of fortification as Bromhead ordered the men to fall in. He quickly explained the situation to them, and told them that they were going to stand and fight. If they must die, they would do so with honour.

The tents were pulled down, and the Commissaries, with the help of Sgt Joseph Windridge and the men of the 1st Bn on store duties, began to empty the store of anything that could be used to build a temporary barricade. They piled everything in front of the store, and all ranks worked together to construct the defensive wall and loophole the buildings. There were many young men in the garrison, but they went about the task with efficiency and determination. Even Captain Stephenson's native levies were doing good service. Colour-Sgt Bourne posted look-outs, and selected six men to be posted inside the hospital building to guard the sick as soon as it had been barricaded. He then organised, and took out, a line of skirmishers.

At 15.15hrs, Lt Chard's attention was brought to two men galloping towards the Drift from the east. When they reached the makeshift jetty on the far bank of the river they called out anxiously. Chard could not hear them properly, but he was concerned at their almost hysterical behaviour. He quickly

sent the pont across to fetch them. One of them was a Natal Carbineer in his shirt sleeves, and the other was Lt James Adendorff[5] of the 1st/3rd N.N.C. When they reached the Natal bank Adendorff quickly dismounted, took Chard out of earshot of the men and told him that the camp at Isandhlwana was in the hands of the Zulus, with all the men in it massacred. His companion confirmed his report, then rode off to take the news to Helpmakaar. They had left the base camp before any mass rout had begun, and were unaware of the oncoming *impi*.

Lt Chard could hardly believe his ears, but he tried to keep calm and had his horse saddled. He was suggesting to Adendorff that perhaps he had left the scene too early to be sure of what really did happen, when Bromhead's messenger arrived asking him to go up to the post as quickly as possible. He gave orders to load the wagon and prepare the oxen, then posted his men in a good position from where they could watch the ferry, and ordered them to wait until he got back. He then made his best speed up to the mission-station.

He arrived to find the construction of the barricade well under way, and an anxious Bromhead handed him the note. Chard read it, and after learning of the advancing *impi*, had a hurried discussion with the other officers, and agreed with all the decisions that had been taken in his absence. He added his knowledge of field fortification, and the wall was built to include the two buildings and the cattle kraal, while at the same time taking advantage of all the natural defensive features.

The hospital formed the western end of the perimeter. Some of the patients were fit enough to help with the work, and most of the men who were left inside the building were able to use a rifle. Gunner Howard had borrowed Sgt Maxfield's rifle, and Trooper Lugg was hastily tying a piece of strapping around the broken stock of his Swinburn-Henri carbine, preparing to man a loophole in the kitchen extension. The men who were posted to defend the hospital occupied three of the rooms, two of which had access to another. The windows were blocked up with mattresses, and the doors buttressed with mealie-bags and furniture. The interiors were ruined as the men knocked bricks out of the side walls and loopholed the stone end-walls with pickaxes.

A barricade of bags and boxes was begun, to connect the back of the hospital with the front of the storehouse. To save time, two transport wagons were

'*Stand and Fight*': *Sgt Windridge puts his back into it as the men in the garrison are detailed to empty the storehouse of bags, boxes and anything else that could be used to build a defensive wall. The men worked with a sense of urgency, being fully aware that their lives would depend on their efforts to complete the perimeter before the* impi *came down on them.*

RICHARD SCOLLINS

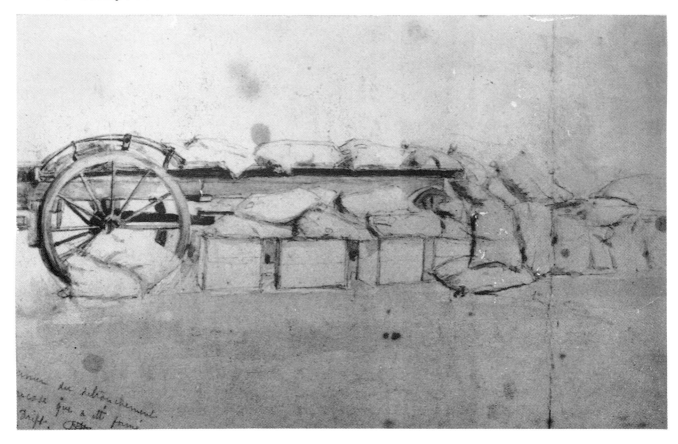

lifted onto the two-foot wide ledge of rocks that ran a natural course across the front of the post, and were wheeled into place at the store-end of this south barricade. The gaps under the wagons were filled with bags and boxes and bags were piled on top to give extra height and to form embrasures between them through which the men could fire. The high solid back wall of the storehouse completed the south section of the perimeter. Sgt Windridge organised the loopholing and barricading of the gate and windows on the outside of the compound, and men were placed in position to defend them.

The walls of the kraal were only chest high, and were too narrow to stack bags on to gain extra height. But it was very close to the eastern end of the storehouse verandah, and had to be included in the perimeter. The opening between the store and the kraal was filled with mealie bags.

Mealie bags and biscuit boxes were stacked three or more high, all along the top of the ledge, from the north-west corner of the kraal to the western end of the hospital verandah. This formed a breastwork of convenient height to fire over, while at the same time presenting a six feet obstacle to an assailant. However, in front of the verandah the rocky ledge veered outwards, and the rampart continued in a straight

Lt-Col Henry Degacher, who commanded the 2nd Battalion, 24th Regt at the start of the invasion, was a competent artist and drew this detailed picture of one of the wagons incorporated in the south barricade. It was here that the British sharpshooters were posted to keep down the Zulu sniper fire from the Oscarberg.

line along the top of a slope, before curving inwards to meet the far corner of the building. This left a step that the Zulus could use to get to the same height as the defenders. And there was an area here where only a plank, ten feet long, filled the gap. This place in the northern breastwork was very vulnerable. The length of the improvised wall facing north was over a hundred yards, and the whole perimeter measured about four hundred yards.

When Lt Chard was satisfied that everything was under control he left his fellow officers to supervise the work, and rode back to the river. The fatigue party there was ready to move. The hawsers and cables had been sunk, and the ponts had been moored in midstream. Sgt Milne, Mr Daniels and the detail of men offered to man the ponts and defend them from the decks. This was a gallant request, and Chard was heartened by their courage.

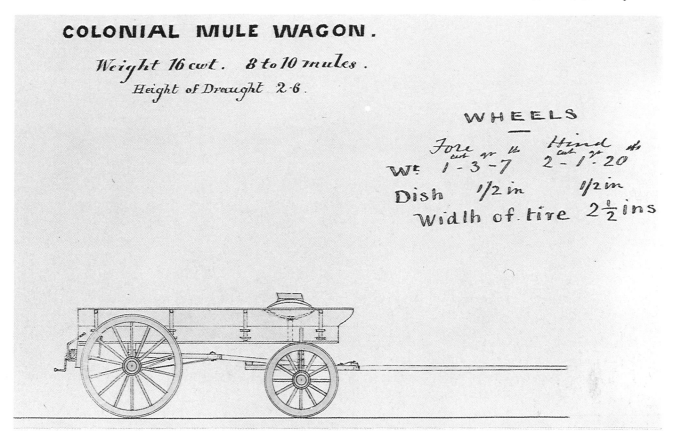

COLONIAL MULE WAGON.

Weight 16 cwt. 8 to 10 mules.
Height of Draught 2-6.

WHEELS

Fore   Hind
Wt 1-3-7   2-1-20
Dish 1/2 in   1/2 in
Width of tire 2½ ins

But such an endeavour would be both risky and pointless. They would be better deployed at the post. If the stores depot fell into Zulu hands it would not matter to the column if they destroyed the ferries. They all made their way up to the post.

The fortification was quickly taking shape. Chard went around the fort suggesting improvements, one of which was that the men should make some kind of communication through the hospital building, though this was not done. He also told Sgt Windridge to select a man to guard two casks of rum that were in the store, with strict orders to shoot without question any man who tried to touch them. Windridge ordered Sgt Milne to take up this task.

As the sweating soldiers humped the heavy bags and boxes around, they were all the time wondering, 'How close was the *impi*? At any moment they might come rushing around the Oscarberg, or screaming up from the river. They might be watching them as they worked, and could attack before they had secured the whole perimeter.

Several more fugitives arrived from Isandhlwana, and the NCOs had to break up little knots of men as they gathered around them to hear their stories. A Natal Carbineer named Fletcher rode by leading a spare horse and Ptes Grant and Johnson of the 1st

The distance between the commissariat store and the field hospital was about 45 yards, so the inclusion of two colonial mule wagons in the south barricade, each one being twelve feet long, saved the defenders valuable time and energy. The wagons were sturdy, and the gaps below were filled with bags and boxes.

Bn, who had been with the rocket battery that had that morning gone to reinforce the base camp with Colonel Durnford, came in and made a report. Two mounted policemen named Shannon and Doig also spurred by. As they passed the rear of the hospital they shouted an hysterical warning and rode on. All these men were without their full equipment and their morale had been shattered. They tried to make the men in the garrison realise the danger, and expressed their opinions that they had no chance, before they all galloped on to Helpmakaar. Rorke's Drift was no place for faint hearts, and the garrison was better off without them.

Each time a fresh, gruesome story was told the natives began to mutter to each other in Bantu, and several would then leave the camp in fright. The number remaining to help with the work was dwindling. Then an encouraging reinforcement arrived. Lt Henderson led a mixture of mounted men of the

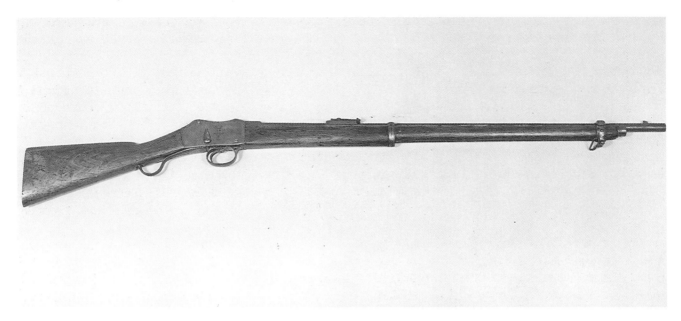

The Martini-Henry breech-loading rifle was adopted by the British Army in 1871. It was a single-shot weapon, weighing just over nine pounds, and the barrel was nearly three feet in length. If not handled correctly the kick-back was severe enough to break a man's collar bone. It was nevertheless considered the best rifle of its day.

The breech-loading mechanism: The lever behind the trigger guard was depressed to uncover the breech and eject the used cartridge. A fresh round was then inserted in the chamber and raising the lever closed the breech for firing. It fired a .45 bullet, and was most effective at about four hundred yards.

Hlubi and Edendale troops totalling about a hundred men up to the depot. Bob Hall was also with them. Lt Chard asked Henderson to send a detachment down to the river to watch over the Drift, and another to reconnoitre behind the Oscarberg to check the enemy's advance, so as to hold them back as much as possible to give his men more time to finish the fort. When forced to retire, they were to assist in the defence of the store and hospital. Mr Dalton also asked Henderson and Hall to try to rally the edgy kaffirs to stop them from sneaking off until the work was done.

Otto Witt and Chaplain Smith had watched several of the fugitives returning. Although it crossed their minds that the column could be falling back, they were reassured by the fact that none of them were redcoats. Suddenly, they noticed several natives involved in a skirmish around a farm building on the Natal side of the river, at a drift about a mile away. Flames and thick smoke began to rise from an isolated barn. Shortly afterwards, large numbers of natives came into view to their left, moving slowly up from the river. They formed in a mass and squatted down to take snuff. It was another thirty minutes before they rose and continued their advance towards the Oscarberg. The two clerics were deceived by their leisurely approach, but their suspicions were aroused when they saw that they were not wearing the red rag of the Natal Natives. The increasing force was within rifle range before they noticed that the two men on grey horses, who were leading them, were not Europeans. They were struck with terror when they suddenly realised that the oncoming force was a Zulu *impi*. They hastily made their way down the hill.

When they got back they found the garrison already alerted. Witt became angry at the sight of what had been done to his property, and cried out in broken English that he was concerned for his family at Umsinga. So he, Umkwelnantaba, and Lt Purvis, whose arm was too badly injured for him to be of any use, rode away. Chaplain Smith decided that in such a situation the presence of a man of God was never more needed, and so he elected to remain. The departure of Lt Purvis left thirty-five sick men in the camp, of which thirteen were able to assist their comrades at the barricade. This left twenty-two still in the hospital, along with the orderly, Pte Waters and the six men who had been told off to defend the building. Nine of the patients were bed-ridden.

Mr Dalton requested Lt Henderson and Bob Hall to scout beyond the shoulder of the Oscarberg, to check on the mounted men, and to bring back a report on the *impi*. As they rode out towards the hill, the defenders were told to stop work, and the officers saw to it that every man was allocated a position on the perimeter to defend. It was important to give them a breather before the attack began. The hospital water-cart was already within the enclosure, ammunition had been issued, and the opened boxes of reloads had been put in convenient places close to the men. There were two piles of bags in front of the store and stacks of wooden boxes inside.

Lt Chard knew that his weapons were far superior to those carried by the Zulus. Even if they had acquired firearms, good marksmanship was not one of their qualities. He could also gain comfort from the fact that the reputation of bravery attributed to Zulu warriors could be matched by the tradition of coolness and gallantry of the British infantryman. Whether or not they survived depended on the strength of the defences, and how heavily outnumbered they were.

Pte Hitch had been trying to get the tea ready before the Zulus attacked. He had just brought the last of four kettles into the compound, when Lt Bromhead told him to get onto the roof of the storehouse to keep a look-out. This gave him a good vantage point to over-look the area. There were several features around the position that the Zulus could use to their advantage. The heights of the Oscarberg loomed over the post about four hundred yards to the south, while there were some deep *dongas* on the approach from the south-west and from the east towards the river. To the south of the store stood the shed that had been used as a cookhouse, and beside it were two round stone ovens. There were also two shallow drainage ditches, one running away from the store, and the other running, at about twenty paces away, virtually parallel with the wagons in the south barricade. To the southeast the tents of the 24th Regt littered the ground. To the north, thick bushes grew right up to the ledge of rocks, and there had been no time to cut them down. Some thirty paces away from the hospital verandah there was a wall about five feet high, running parallel with the ledge. Just beyond the wall were two tall poplar trees, to which some horses had been tied, while a rutted track ran by on the other side of the wall. Beyond that there was a fenced garden. To the west there was rising ground

47

and a hay-stack and the toilet stood in this vicinity. To the east the ground sloped down towards the river, where there was an additional rough stone kraal close to the well built one, with the engineers' wagon standing just beyond it.

At about 16.20hrs, the sound of rifle fire could be heard from behind the Oscarberg, and this triggered a mass colonial desertion. The detachment of Durnford's Horse could now be seen retreating towards Helpmakaar. Chard's *vorlooper* lad stole a horse and went with them, while his kaffir wagon driver scampered off to find a cave to hide in on the hill. The hundred or so nervous natives that were left also took to their heels, and Captain Stephenson followed on his horse. Cpl Anderson had left the hospital to fight at the wall, but he lost his nerve and fled after them. The angry men behind the defences called after him to come back, but he ignored them. Tempers flared, and a rifle bullet brought him down.

The number of men in the garrison was by now reduced to 139, all ranks. Of these 104 were fit, but only eighty were combatants. At first they were demoralised by the flight of so many men though it was decided that the reliability of the natives had always been suspect, and it was fortunate that they had shown their weakness before the attack. Chard however now felt that the line of defence was too extended, and therefore ordered the non-combatants to begin the construction of a row of biscuit boxes, extending from the north-west corner of the store to a point about seventy feet away at the northern breastwork. This would provide an entrenchment that would be of great value if the defenders were forced to fall back from the original perimeter.

The sound of pounding hoofs and raised voices then caught everyone's attention. It was Henderson and Hall galloping hell for leather towards the post. As they moved around the position, Henderson reined in and reported that he had not been able to get his men to obey orders. Hall yelled a warning that the Zulus 'as black as hell and as thick as grass'[6] would soon be upon them. They rode around the outside of the post beyond the store, and eventually made off towards Helpmakaar.

It was past 16.30hrs now. Only ninety minutes

Private William Roy, 1st/24th Regiment was a patient in the hospital when news of the Isandhlwana massacre reached the mission-station. He was suffering from malaria, and a disease which was affecting his vision.

had elapsed since the calm had been broken at Rorke's Drift. The non-combatants were still working on the second layer of biscuit boxes that would make the reserve defence line waist high. All round there was a clicking noise as the ranks of men in single-breasted red tunics, dark trousers and low-brimmed tropical helmets, fixed their twenty-four inch bayonets to their rifles. The bayonets glistened in the bright sunshine. Some of the men at the perimeter were dismounted colonials, wearing dark corduroy uniforms and the slouch hat.

The feeling of isolation was terrifying, particularly in the face of an as yet unseen enemy, who were about to attack them and would literally try to cut them to pieces. Stories about the Zulus' blood-thirsty atrocities were rife among the colonials, and had been passed on to the British regulars. It would be useless to run because there was no safe refuge. And it was known that the Zulus took no prisoners. Some men made pacts to kill each other when all was lost, to save themselves from the horror of Zulu ritual savagery. Hearts began to pound. They could now only put their faith in their tense and nervous comrades beside them and their trained skills with rifle and bayonet.

1: *Frank Bourne – see p138*
2: *Harry Hook – see p140*
3: *Frederick Hitch – see p144*
4: *Helpmakaar – see p146*
5: *James Adendorff – see p147*
6: *Experiences of Combat – see p148*

CHAPTER FOUR:
'Here they come!'

For how can man die better,
Than facing fearful odds
For the ashes of his fathers
And the temples of his gods.
                    Thomas Macauley.

A cry of 'Stand to!' echoed around the post, and as Colour-Sgt Bourne and his skirmishers ran in and took their places at the barricade, all eyes turned to the western flank of the Oscarberg, where about fifty Zulus had come into view. They extended in open order and began cautiously to edge forward, prancing about as they did so. Their intention was to provoke the men in the garrison to open fire, so that the single Zulu who had appeared on the crest of the Oscarberg could count the guns. Nervous fingers began to ease pressure on the triggers, but the warriors were some distance away and again a command rang out, ordering them to hold their fire.

Pte Hitch called down to Lt Bromhead that he could see the main body of the *impi* behind this advance guard, and he caused a flurry of mixed remarks when he estimated their numbers as four

The Zulu impi *plunges into the fast-flowing water and the warriors surge neck-deep across the Buffalo River to the Natal bank. Frustrated at having been held back at Isandhlwana, despite orders, they decided to '. . . go and have a fight at Jim's.'*

thousand or more, their columns stretching right across the pass from the Oscarberg to another hill. He reported that several hundred were preparing for attack, in a long curved line. He could also see scores of warriors creeping along the lower terraces of the Oscarberg, where they were taking cover in caves and settling down behind rocks. These Zulus carried some of the firearms that had been captured from the action at Isandhlwana, and as Hitch took a prone position below the apex of the roof, they exchanged a few shots. Hitch also took a pot shot at the dark coloured figure standing out against the bright blue sky on top of the hill. But his target was out of range.

The reconnoitering Zulu on the Oscarberg then waved a signal, and a stout, mounted inDuna brought forward a mass of warriors about six hundred strong over the rise, and into full view of the post.

These were from the inDlu-yengwe regiment, known to be about a thousand strong, and comprising unmarried thirty-three-year-olds. Their original inDuna, Usibebu, one of Cetshwayo's fiercest rivals, had been wounded at Isandhlwana. The overall leader of the *impi* that was massing at the Oscarberg was Dabulamanzi, Cetshwayo's ambitious thirty-five-year-old brother. His *impi* had acted mainly as

reserves at Isandhlwana, and resenting not having taken any major part in the battle, had been driven on to kwa jimi – 'Jim's Place' – by their desire to prove themselves. Dabulamanzi was fully aware that he was disobeying his royal brother's order not to attack fortified places, and he knew that it would be dark in two hours. But the defenders in the fort seemed very few, and his warriors were spoiling for a fight. He felt sure that he could take the post quickly. Although the new inDuna had not had time to assert his authority, Dabulamanzi decided to give the young regiment the opportunity to wash their spears.

Their war regalia was designed to give them a ferocious appearance. They wore loin cloths with horse-hair fringes and animal tails streaming from their elbows and knees. Many wore cow-tail necklaces and beadwork ornaments. They carried black shields with a white splash and their deadly stabbing *assegais*. A few had rifles. After one loud chant of their war-cry 'Usuthu! Usuthu! Inkomo ka baba!' they bagan to advance at a steady trot. They

Prince Dabulamanzi, who commanded the Zulus at Rorke's Drift, was Cetshwayo's brother, and was an ambitious man.

Dabulamanzi on horseback. Having made the decision to move swiftly on Rorke's Drift, he expected the battle to be an easy one.

swerved to the right, and without a sound made a mad rush at the south barricade.

At about six hundred yards the defenders' rifles thundered the first volleys and clouds of black smoke rose from the barricade. Chamber levers clicked back, and used cartridge cases tinkled onto the rocky ground. The first shots were wild, but at about four hundred and fifty yards the firing steadied, and a bullet from Pte James Dunbar's rifle brought the inDuna crashing from his horse. The firing quickly gained momentum, and as the lead slugs smashed into the attackers, who were so thick that it was almost impossible to miss, the force of impact lifted them off their feet before they fell, tumbling and rolling, or sprawling over each other. The sight of this gave the soldiers confidence, but their fire was failing to stop them. The warriors in the rear leaped over those who were falling before them, and stooped forward as they ran, trying to make a more difficult target. Their legs made a strange whooshing noise as they pushed through the grass, and regardless of their dreadful losses and the danger to their lives, they raced forward.

The onrush was getting uncomfortably close,

and the men behind the wagons and boxes at the south barricade were bracing themselves to receive the coming black tide with their bayonets, when at about fifty paces the Zulus were caught by such heavy volleys from the south barricade and the back of the hospital, together with a tremendous cross-fire from the store that the advance was checked.

Those Zulus who were carrying rifles scattered and took cover around the cook-house and ovens, while others scrambled into ditches and took advantage of anything that would shield them from the bullets. Some ran up to the storehouse and threw themselves against the walls, but there was little cover there and they were shot down. The greater number veered to their left without stopping and rejoined the rear of the main body of the *impi*, which Dabulamanzi was leading in a wide sweep around the hospital. Some then came in to attack the corner of the defences in front of the verandah, while the rest rushed into the thick bushes and trees to the north-west and, under this cover, pushed further around the post.

The warriors who had taken cover in front of the south barricade then opened a desultory fire, and those on the Oscarberg, after waiting to see the outcome of the first attack, sent a barrage of bullets raining down onto the post. Other Zulus had taken cover at the mouth of the cave where Chard's petri-

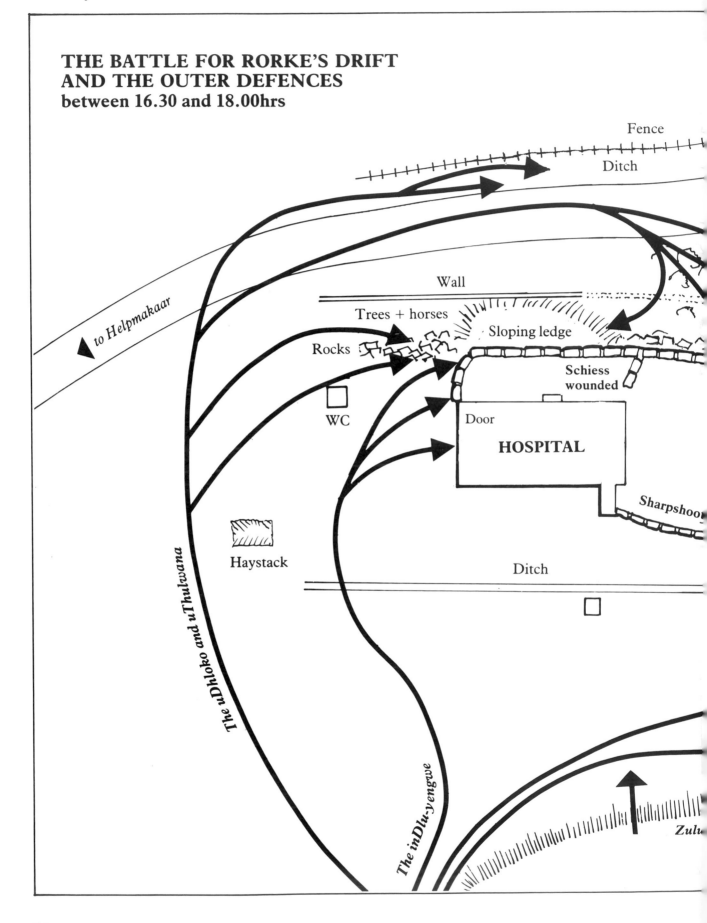

**THE BATTLE FOR RORKE'S DRIFT
AND THE OUTER DEFENCES**
between 16.30 and 18.00hrs

Fence

Ditch

Wall

to Helpmakaar

Trees + horses

Sloping ledge

Rocks

Schiess
wounded

WC

Door

HOSPITAL

Sharpshoo

Haystack

Ditch

The uDhloko and uThulwana

The inDlu-yengwe

Zulu

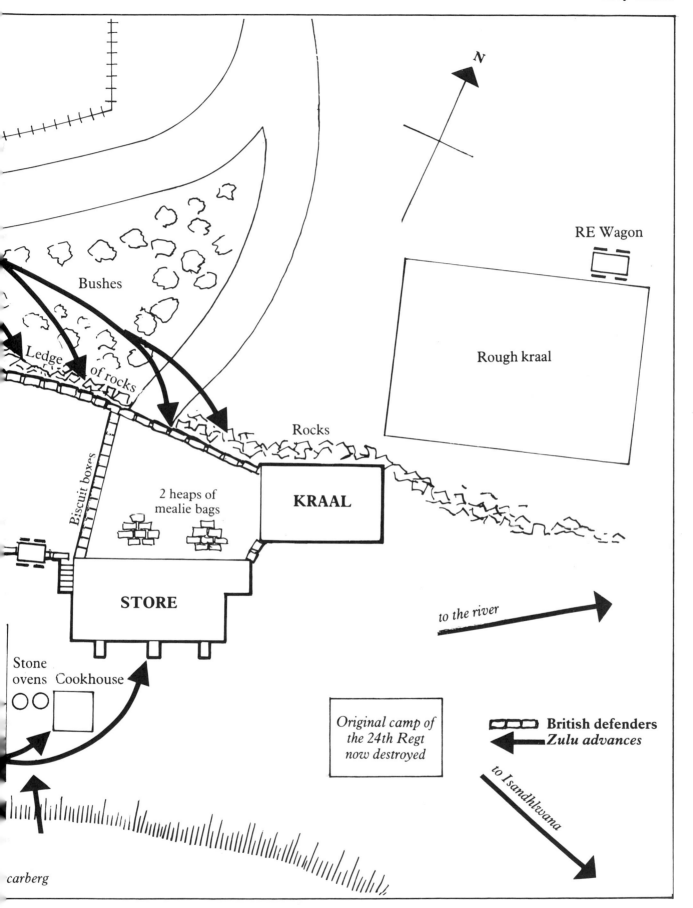

N

RE Wagon

Bushes

Rough kraal

Ledge

of rocks

Rocks

KRAAL

Biscuit boxes

2 heaps of
mealie bags

STORE

to the river

Stone
ovens Cookhouse

Original camp of
the 24th Regt
now destroyed

British defenders
Zulu advances

to Isandhlwana

carberg

fied wagon driver was hidden in the darkness. Even there they were unsafe, as British rounds came in, and one Zulu was hit.

Pte Hitch slid off the roof of the storehouse, fixed his bayonet as he ran across the compound, and took up a position behind the men in front of the hospital. They gritted their teeth as they met the rush of warriors, and there was the rattle of bayonet on shield, and the clatter of rifle barrel on *assegai*, as the Zulus threw themselves against the breastwork, and with fanatical bravery, tried to get over. There was a desperate struggle as some warriors climbed onto the bags and slashed and stabbed at the defenders in their frenzy, while others dug at the barricades in an attempt to pull them down. The defenders parried, prodded and thrust violently back at them with their bayonets, or blasted them at point blank range. Some warriors fell screaming with dreadful injuries. When necessary the butt of a rifle or even a swift left hook did the job of keeping a warrior out. The officers and non-combatants gave shouts of encouragement and warnings of danger. Some Zulus began to smash their spears on the doors at the western end of the hospital. Others grabbed at the rifle barrels of the men who were shooting at them through the loopholes.

The determined attack was pushing the defenders back from the area in front of the hospital, to a dog-leg breastwork that jutted in from the outer peri-meter. Pte Hitch shot a Zulu as he and several other warriors jumped onto the step to get at the soldiers. But before he could reload another warrior broke through, dropped his weapons, and grabbed the muzzle of Hitch's rifle trying to wrench it from him. Hitch had a firm hold of the butt and managed to hold on to it. As they struggled he managed to reload the weapon, and shot the Zulu, who held his grip for a while before falling. Lt Bromhead then lead a counter-charge, which threw back the attackers at bayonet point and gave his men renewed spirit. The tide changed, and the Zulus were forced to scramble back out of the fort, and take refuge in the bushes. But within moments a second wave of warriors attacked the position.

The whole place was now alive with Zulus. The main body had moved around the post, using the thick bushes as cover. Many were crouching behind Witt's wall, and they had also occupied the ditches, the garden and the hollow in which ran the track. The defenders could not see them, but they could hear them, and some fired into the bushes in the hope of scoring an unseen hit. The Zulu crept right

A view of Rorke's Drift post from the Oscarberg, where Zulu snipers were positioned to fire down on the garrison. It was also from this direction that the impi *first attacked the post. The monument and cemetery can be seen in the foreground.*

A young warrior of the inDlu-yengwe regiment who appeared on the neck of the Oscarberg. The leopardskin headband is the only item of ceremonial dress he has retained. He is carrying the small war shield bearing the colours of an unmarried regiment.

RICHARD SCOLLINS

up to the ledge of rocks extending as far to their left as the bushes reached, where they surprised the soldiers as they rose up and attacked the breastwork.

These were mostly warriors of the uDhloko, about two thousand forty-one-year-olds, and the uThulwana, the regiment that Cetshwayo had once belonged to, which totalled about a thousand forty-five-year-olds. The inDlu-yengwe and the uThulwana were known collectively as the uNdi Corps.

The men in the garrison did not know at the time, that a fourth regiment called the iNdlondlo had set off towards Rorke's Drift, but they had turned back. Some carried white shields and others ruddy shields with light spots, and most wore the head-

Lt Chard's panoramic sketch of the mission-station and the area around Rorke's Drift post, viewed from the north. Chard has indicated the direction from which the Zulu impi first appeared. This sketch, and the diagrams in this work, which are based on his official scale plan, should give the reader an accurate picture of the garrison's defences.

ring of the battle-experienced married regiments. They wore monkey-skin earflaps, plumes of exotic birds such as the crane and ostrich, otterskin headbands and ornaments of beadwork. Snuff boxes dangled from their ear-lobes, and ivory snuff-spoons were fastened to their heads.

Once again the fighting became fierce, as

Bromhead and his men drove them out of the compound near the hospital. Weapons clashed as the Zulus kept one side of the breastwork while the defenders held their ground on the other. Each time the Zulus were driven back into the bushes they would shout their war-cry 'Usuthu', clash their *assegais* against their shields, then spring up and again rush at the breastwork. The defenders replied with defiant shouts, and each onslaught was met with rapid fire. As the defenders stabbed with their bayonets the Zulus grabbed at them and some were wrenched from the rifles. But they were continually driven back into the bushes. There were acts of bravery on both sides, as they were locked in the fierce brutality of war. Cpl Schiess had been strong enough to help at the breastwork, and on several occasions he had climbed over the bags and got amongst the Zulus on the rock step, smashing them off with the butt of his rifle, and thrusting his bayonet at them as they pounced forward and grabbed at him. The men fighting near him were impressed at his bold conduct, and were alarmed when he was shot in the foot of his already injured leg. But it boosted their morale when, after flinching at the initial stab of pain, he simply ignored the wound and kept at his post.

The backs of the men defending this area were completely exposed to the rifle-fire of the Zulus on the Oscarberg terraces. Pte Thomas 'old king' Cole had been one of the men posted inside the hospital, but he ran out of the building to join the men at the breastwork. They were almost immediately showered with his blood and brain tissue, when a Zulu slug went straight through his head, and then hit Pte James Bushe on the bridge of his nose, splattering his face with blood. Pte Nicholson and Pte Roy had left the hospital to help. But Nicholson also had his brains scattered by enemy fire, while Pte William Tasker and several other men were slightly wounded.

Surgeon Reynolds was by them at once, putting cold water on the injury, and applying a cold compress to stop the bleeding. He was looking after a terrier dog called Pip, which belonged to an officer who had moved up with the 3rd Column. The excited animal bounded along at his feet barking at the Zulus. The Rev Smith spent his time moving along the perimeter with his native servant handing out cartridges from his hat, as well as reproving curses and stopping to give spiritual consolation to the wounded. Birds were darting through the smoke overhead, disturbed and confused by the cries and turmoil. Higher in the sky vultures were hovering as they waited in scavenging anticipation.

After some time a cloud of dust could be seen rising from behind the hills on the track from Helpmakaar. Some men said that they had caught a glimpse of red now and then, and they were given new heart when they thought that the two companies of the 1st Bn were coming to their aid. But the dust dispersed and they waited in vain.

The sharp shooters at the south barricade were concentrating their fire power towards the Zulus on the Oscarberg, who were sending bullets whizzing over their heads. Some slugs rattled into the wagons and wooden boxes, thumped into the mealie bags, or went pinging off the walls of the store and hospital. Cpls William Allan[1], Alfred Saxty[2], and John Lyons were among these men, exposing themselves over the barricade to get a more accurate aim. Many warriors were being hit, and Pte Dunbar received a few complimentary remarks when he brought down eight Zulus with as many consecutive shots.

Suddenly there was panic all around when thick smoke began to rise from the far end of the hospital roof. The Zulus had set light to the thatch. Fortunately for the garrison the grass was tightly packed and only smouldered at first. To add to this crisis the soldiers were once again being pushed back from the area in front of the verandah, and the breastwork was beginning to sag inwards from the sheer weight of Zulu numbers.

Surgeon Reynolds and the AHC men realised that they would soon have to abandon the medical supplies. So they had to move quickly to try to save some of them. He and his two privates, Thomas Luddington and Michael McMahon dashed to the dispensary, while his corporal, Robert Miller, and Mr Dalton covered them with their rifles. As they were grabbing as much as they could, a Zulu sprang forward and pulled Cpl Miller towards him by the muzzle of his rifle and was about to thrust his *assegai* into his stomach when Dalton shot the warrior and saved the corporal's life. They all then burst through the Zulus and ran to the entrenchment.

As Cpl Scammel was putting his rifle to good use from behind the front rank of soldiers, he cried out in pain as a bullet ripped into his shoulder and he dropped to the ground. He crawled to Lt Chard and handed him his cartridges. He then asked for a drink of water and Mr Byrne quickly brought him one. But while Byrne was helping the distraught corporal he himself was shot through the head and fell dead.

James Reynolds was a thirty-four-year-old Irishman, who was taking part in his third campaign in South Africa. He had been appointed Surgeon in 1873.

Scammel was taken to the doctor, who was now using the storehouse verandah, calmly busying himself with organising and attending to his casualties and seemingly unconcerned about the violence going on all around.

To the east of the defences a number of warriors had begun to creep up to the wall of the kraal to assault it, while others were running in on the storehouse with burning torches in an effort to set fire to the roof. Sgt Windridge and Cpl Attwood were among the men defending the upper windows, and Lt Adendorff was manning a loophole in the side of the building, which gave him a clear aim at any Zulus who were creeping along the outside of the south barricade, or at those who had moved around to the back of the hospital. A warrior escaped the line of fire from the windows and reached the back wall of the store. He began to climb the wall with a tuft of blazing grass, and stretched up to make con-tact with the thatch. Lt Adendorff saw him just in time and shot him down.

Lt Chard could see that the post was now in great danger from all sides, so he gave the order that the two heaps of bags in front of the store should be converted into a high redoubt, to give them a second line of defence. This would also be the place where they could make a last stand. Mr Dunne and a few men at once began to pull sacks from the tops of the piles and stack them in two parallel lines between the heaps, leaving a hollow in the middle where the wounded could be safely put.

It was now beginning to get dark, and as the light faded they began to realise that they might be over-run by the Zulus under cover of darkness. But the smoking roof, which they had considered to be a catastrophe when it first occurred, became their saviour when it burst into flames and lit up the whole area. They would now be able to see the warriors as they attacked.

In their endeavour to keep the Zulus out, most of the defenders at the breastwork had concentrated their efforts at the north-west corner, and had left the perimeter between the cattle kraal and the place where the biscuit boxes met the breastwork danger-ously undermanned. Lt Chard was giving a helping hand with the redoubt when he noticed that the Zulus were preparing to break through at that point. Lt Bromhead had just led the sixth bayonet charge to force the Zulus back from the verandah when Chard brought his attention to the serious situation behind them. Bromhead quickly called out half a dozen names and they all ran back to strengthen the section.

It was time for Lt Chard to look around the post and check the situation. Bromhead had secured the position near the kraal once again, but now the men in the hospital were hard pressed. If he decided to abandon the outer perimeter the men inside the hospital would be in great peril. But a large body of Zulus were pushing forward again and he could see that the men would not be able to hold the position much longer. He had no choice but to call all the men in the firing line back to the biscuit box en-trenchment. As they retired the warriors occupied the verandah, and many more ran in on the outer perimeter and used it as cover from which to fire. The hospital building was now completely isolated.

1: *William Allan – see p149*
2: *Alfred Saxty – see p150*

RICHARD SCOLLINS

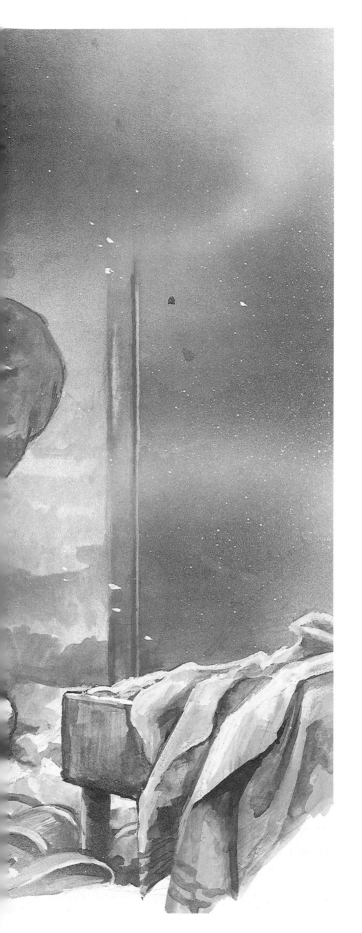

CHAPTER FIVE:
The Hospital Siege

*'No one can guarantee success in war,
but only deserve it.'*
Winston Churchill

All this time the men inside the hospital[1] were engaged in a desperate struggle, both with the Zulus who were swarming all around the building, and the fire that was beginning to blaze above them and send dense choking smoke into the rooms.

Pte Waters was in an inner front room defending a window which opened out on to the verandah. Gunners Howard and Evans were defending their north-west corner room, which also had access to the verandah, and a window from which they could fire at the Zulus who were massing at the front of the building. Behind this was the middle end room where the Zulus were fiercely assaulting the outer door, and from which there was no communication with the interior. Ptes John Williams and Joseph Williams were defending this room. They had left factories in South Wales to join the army at the same time, but they were not related. John had joined the army in a false name, his real name being Fielding[2]. There were four patients in the room.

'Struggle For Survival': A dazed and anxious patient is assisted through the escape hole into a room filled with smoke fumes from the blazing hospital roof. And the ordeal is not yet over.

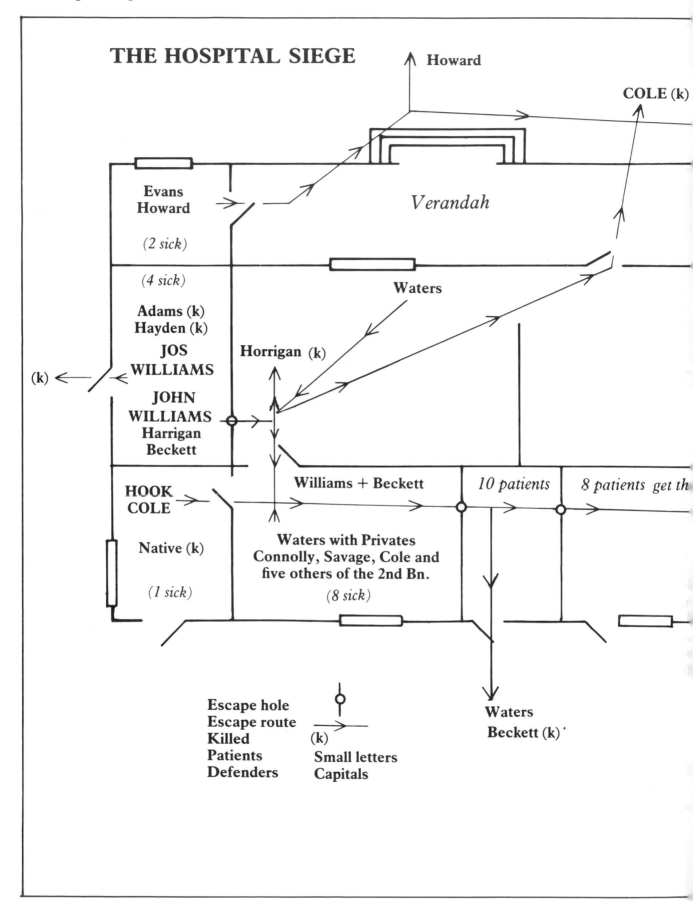

THE HOSPITAL SIEGE

Howard

COLE (k)

Evans
Howard

(2 sick)

Verandah

(4 sick)

Adams (k)
Hayden (k)
JOS
WILLIAMS

Waters

Horrigan (k)

JOHN
WILLIAMS
Harrigan
Beckett

(k) ←

Williams + Beckett

10 patients

8 patients get th

HOOK
COLE

Native (k)

Waters with Privates
Connolly, Savage, Cole and
five others of the 2nd Bn.

(1 sick)

(8 sick)

Waters
Beckett (k)

Escape hole
Escape route
Killed
Patients
Defenders

(k)
Small letters
Capitals

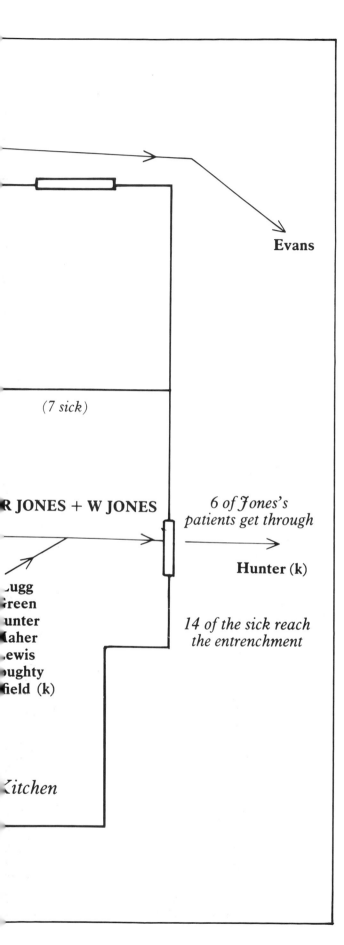

Evans

(7 sick)

R JONES + W JONES

6 of Jones's
patients get through

Hunter (k)

14 of the sick reach
the entrenchment

Lugg
reen
unter
Maher
ewis
oughty
field (k)

Kitchen

Pte Horrigan was able to offer assistance, but Pte Beckett was ill, and the other two were bedridden.

Joseph had pushed several bricks out of the wall to form a loophole the size of a small window to gain a wider line of fire. He was shooting at the warriors who were running in, throwing their weight against the door, and smashing their *assegais* at the panels trying to break it down. The patients were becoming anxious and the defenders more desperate as they realised that the door was beginning to give way. They would all be killed if they did not get out.

As soon as he had fired his last cartridge John Williams began to smash at the back partition with his bayonet, while Joseph Williams started to stab at the Zulus through the splintering door. John hacked away at the blocks to make a hole large enough to get through. By the time he had succeeded Joseph Williams had run out of bullets, and frenzied black hands were grabbing at him through the door. He fought hard to hold them back, but as John Williams and Horrigan struggled to get Pte Beckett out through the hole the Zulus forced their way in. The gallant defender was seized by the arms and legs, and Ptes Garrett Hayden and Robert Adams, both of 'D' Company were attacked in their beds. Williams was dragged outside, and all three were slaughtered in accordance with Zulu ritual. They were repeatedly stabbed, and their stomachs ripped open. The Zulus believed that this released the evil spirits from within, and prevented their own stomachs from swelling.

The three breathless men who got out of the room now eyed the area they had escaped to. They could not go left towards the verandah because Zulus were getting in that way. But through the thick smoke they could just make out the welcome form of Pte Waters, standing in a doorway to their right. Williams and Beckett got through the door but it was too late for Pte Morrigan. The warriors who had broken in behind them raced forward and set about him. They dragged him towards the verandah, threw him violently to the ground and began to stab and rip at his body. Pte Waters quickly closed the door as several other Zulus sprang for him.

Inside the room with Waters was Pte Hook and eight sick men. Pte Waters had been shot in the arm as he struggled to keep the Zulus at bay, and had retired through the inner door where he found

The Hospital Siege

Hook single-handedly protecting the sick from Zulus who were trying to get in by another entrance. Hook had managed to strap up his injured arm to try to stop the bleeding.

Pte Hook and Pte Cole had defended the native, who had been wounded at Sihayo's Kraal, in a small room at the south-west corner. There was an outside door facing south and an interior door that connected with the room they were all now in. But it was above this corner room that the Zulus had first set light to the thatch, and Pte Cole had run out when the tension and fumes became too much for him. Pte Hook had then fought back the Zulus for as long as he could with the Xhosa native groaning near him and

begging him for a weapon. But the struggle became hopeless. As the Zulus were breaking in he was forced to retire and escape through the interior door. The native cried out to him to help him to take off his bandages so that he could come, but there was nothing Hook could do for him. When the Zulus burst in they questioned the man, then assegaied him to death.

There were now twelve men in the room, and the

Below: *Pte Hook impales a warrior in the doorway with the point of his bayonet, as John Williams helps a patient towards the escape hole cut in the hospital wall.*

At last Williams broke through, and with sharp slicing blows he began to widen the gap. When the hole was large enough he assisted the patients as they began to wriggle through. Hook continued to hold the Zulus back until there was only Pte Connolly left. He was sitting near the opening nursing his painful knee. A Zulu pressed his weight against the door and tried to force his way in, but Hook put the muzzle of his rifle on him and fired. The blast threw the Zulu and all the warriors behind him sprawling back from the doorway. Hook then quickly grabbed hold of Connolly with both arms and dragged him out. The patient cried out in agony but he was relieved to escape the raging horde that burst into the room behind them.

Pte Hook stayed at the hole in the partition and thrust his bayonet at the warriors who tried to follow, while John Williams wasted no time and began to pick at the wall to get them into the last two rooms that had a communicating door between them, and a high window leading out into the abandoned area of the fort.

Pte William Jones[3], an old soldier sporting a black goatee beard, and Pte Robert Jones[4], who had only been born the year before his comrade and namesake had enlisted, had defended seven patients in these rooms. There was a door and window in the back wall, but Trooper Lugg had been able to get a good shot at any Zulus who came around the back of the building through a loophole in a kitchen extension. Those Zulus who had managed to dodge his fire were met at the doorway by the two Joneses, who together were bayonetting them as soon as they approached. Robert Jones had received three *assegai* wounds to the body from warriors who had sprung forward with stabbing spears in their eagerness to get past the two defenders. At the same time they were trying to help the sick up to the high window from where they could drop down into the compound. Trooper Lugg and five other patients had managed to do this, but Sgt Maxfield was delirious and the Joneses were struggling to dress him.

Cpl Allan and Pte Hitch were keeping the Zulus away from the area outside below the window by continuous rifle fire. When Dr Reynolds had no patients to attend to he was supplying them with ammunition. This post was dangerously exposed to Zulu crossfire, and on one occasion, as the doctor was running to the hospital with his arms full of cartridges, a Zulu slug hit his helmet and gave him a jolt.

Above: *Pte Robert Jones cuts down a warrior as a party of Zulus try to get at the patients. Jones received five wounds whilst in Africa.*

defenders fought desperately to keep the maddened warriors back from the two interior doors. Pte Williams quickly realised that their only path of escape was again through the partition. His bayonet had snapped from the muzzle of his rifle so he took up one of the pickaxes that had been used to make loopholes and started to hack at the far wall. *Assegai* blades kept thrusting forward as the Zulus smashed at the doors, and one of them hit Hook on the front of his helmet and caused a scalp wound. The warriors grabbed for the rifles and tried to snatch them away but the determined defenders gripped them tightly. Several times they managed to load the weapons as they wrestled for possession and shot the foremost attackers.

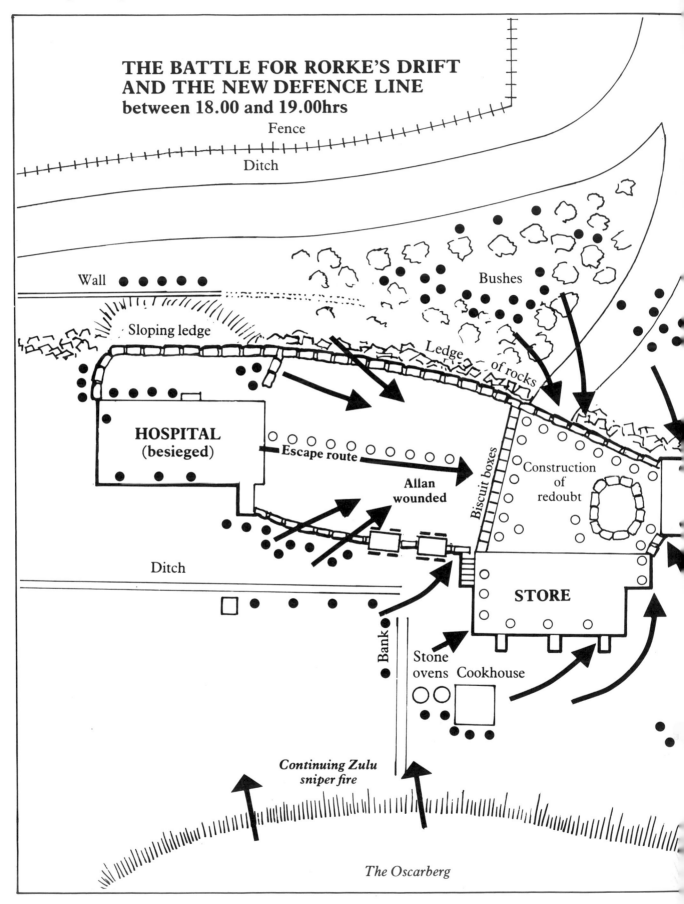

THE BATTLE FOR RORKE'S DRIFT
AND THE NEW DEFENCE LINE
between 18.00 and 19.00hrs

Fence

Ditch

Wall

Bushes

Sloping ledge

Ledge of rocks

HOSPITAL
(besieged)

Escape route

Allan wounded

Biscuit boxes

Construction of redoubt

Ditch

STORE

Bank

Stone ovens

Cookhouse

Continuing Zulu sniper fire

The Oscarberg

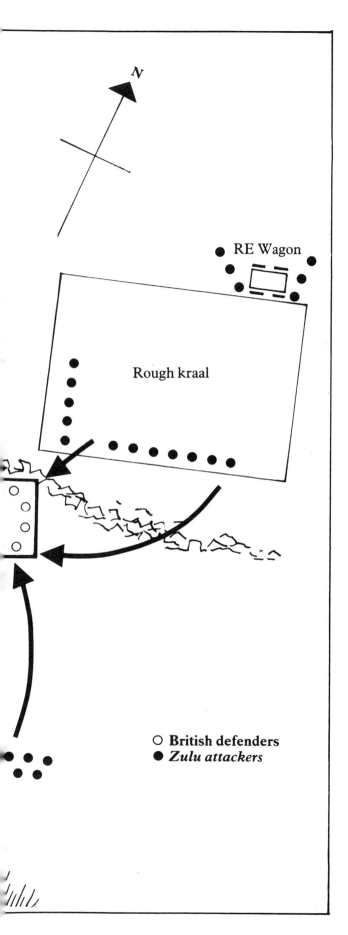

RE Wagon

Rough kraal

○ **British defenders**
● *Zulu attackers*

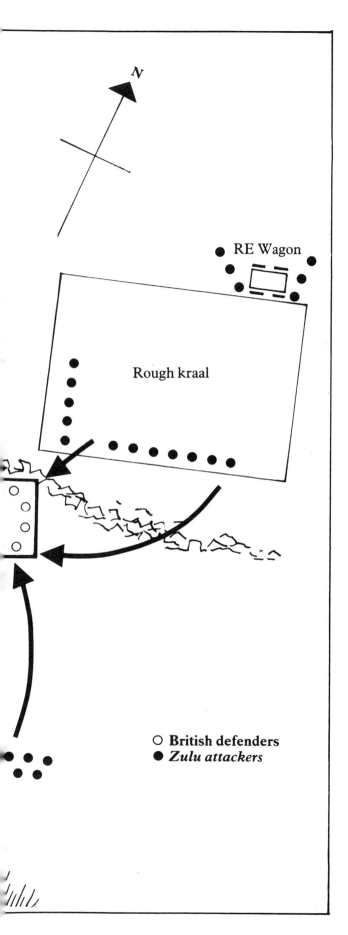

The patients dropped down from the window and began to hobble across the enclosure, or dropped to the ground and crawled frantically towards the biscuit-boxes. Gunner John Cantwell[5] ran out to assist Bombardier Lewis, while Pte Hitch levelled his rifle at his waist and shot a Zulu as he came around the hospital to attack them. Trooper Green stumbled as a piece of shrapnel hit him in the side and Trooper Lugg and Cpl Mayer were able to assist him to safety.

Trooper Hunter was dizzy from the effects of his illness, and he hesitated as he tried to get to safety. A Zulu ran up behind him, and his tall figure shielded the warrior from the aim of the rifles at the boxes. The defenders shouted to Hunter to drop to the floor so that they could get a better shot, but the deafening noise and the flashes of light confused the trooper and the warrior caught up and started to assegai him. Hunter fell dead, and the Zulu was shot immediately after.

The struggle inside the hospital was still going on. Pte Williams, his hands cut and blistered, had begun to shepherd the patients into the last room. The fire had now burned through to the rafters, and fierce flames were curling menacingly above their heads. It was unbearably hot and the patients were coughing and spluttering from the effect of smoke-fumes and dust. Eight patients got through the hole, but Pte Beckett had had enough, and Pte Waters, becoming weak from loss of blood, realised that the Zulus would be upon them before they could get out. Hook yelled at them to hurry up, but as the Zulus were getting in they took advantage of the screen of thick smoke and both climbed into a cupboard in the corner. They pulled items of clothing over themselves and hoped that they were not discovered.

The warriors piled in, and luckily for the two nervous soldiers they made for the hole in the partition without noticing the cupboard. The Zulus were again stopped in their tracks by Hook's lunging bayonet, and Williams smashed at them with the muzzle of his rifle, or swung the butt at their heads as they appeared at the hole. The Joneses had managed to dress Sgt Maxfield, but he was being difficult in his delirium and they could not get him to move. They eventually had to leave him to take over at the escape hole, while Hook and Williams pushed and heaved their eight tired patients out of the window.

Several Zulus again scaled the ramparts and ran to attack the patients as they struggled across the

A warrior of the uThulwana regiment fighting at close quarters. He carries the full war shield and stabbing spear. A single chrome feather adorns his otterskin headband, and at his neck he wears a horned snuffbox.

RICHARD SCOLLINI

compound. Pte Savage limped anxiously across the fort and scrambled over the boxes. But Pte Robert Cole, 'F' Company, was having problems and a number of Zulus were approaching him. Pte McMahon ran to help him, and Pte Hitch added his fire-power, shooting three warriors as McMahon led Cole to safety. Cpl Allan was assisting the last few men over the boxes when a Zulu slug went right through his arm.

The whole roof of the building was now a blazing inferno, and it had become extremely hazardous for anyone who stayed inside. So the four gallant defenders who had rescued the sick decided to make their own escape. As the Zulus were scrambling into the room, William Jones, Hook and Williams climbed out. But with complete disregard for his own safety Pte Robert Jones passed his Martini-Henry out of the window, and decided to make one last attempt to save Maxfield. He groped his way back into the smoke-filled room, only to find the Zulus stabbing the helpless Sergeant as he lay on his bed. There was nothing he could do, so he quickly jumped up to the window, and heaved himself out before the Zulus noticed him. He had no sooner dropped down from the window when part of roof of the building collapsed behind him.

Pte Waters had eased the door of the cupboard open slightly, and had been shooting a few individual warriors as they left the building. But when the roof fell in Pte Beckett had run out of the cupboard, and without thinking he dashed out of the doorway, finding himself in the midst of the Zulus. A warrior thrust his *assegai* into the small of his back as he went by, but the momentum of his pace kept him going for a few more strides, and he collapsed into a ditch. The Zulus did not pursue him, but he was bleeding very badly. Eventually it became too hot and suffocating for Waters, so he covered himself with a garment that had been hanging in the cupboard, and ran out into the flickering darkness. He lay down in the long grass and rubbed dirt on his face to hide his identity.

Gunner Evans had seized the opportunity to race around the front of the hospital to the safety of the entrenchment. But when Gunner Howard ran out of the building he went the wrong way. He vaulted the breastwork, rolled off the step and crawled into bush in the shadows. The Zulus were becoming maddened by their lack of success in killing the British soldiers, and the fortification was frustrating them. They began to slay anything they could get

'Onslaught!'. While the struggle continued inside the hospital, events outside were no more certain. The defenders at the entrenchment smashed and stabbed at the Zulus, who in their frenzied state were frightening in appearance. The only retreat from here would be for a last stand in the mealie bag redoubt.

their hands on. The three horses that had been left tied to the trees near Witt's garden wall were lying mutilated close by, and as the anxious gunner pulled loose grass over his legs to hide the stripes on his trousers, a pig was struck down near him and its squeals attracted attention. He lay uneasy among the Zulu corpses.

1: *Events within the Hospital – see p151*
2: *Joseph Williams (Fielding) – see p152*
3: *William Jones – see p154*
4: *Robert Jones – see p155*
5: *John Cantwell – see p155*

CHAPTER SIX:
Behind the Entrenchment

*'It is well that war is so terrible –
we shouldn't grow too fond of it.'*
Robert E. Lee

Most of the fourteen patients who reached the entrenchment were taken to be attended to by Dr Reynolds, and some were able to take up places among their comrades who were valiantly defending the inner fort. As soon as Cpl Allan had his arm bandaged he helped Rev Smith to distribute ammunition. Pte Savage lay on his side and fired his rifle through a gap in the boxes, and Trooper Lugg manned a position below the eaves of the storehouse roof.

Mr Dalton was still using his rifle well. A Zulu fell almost each time he fired it, and he continually moved along the barricade encouraging the men. He brought attention to a warrior running in at the wall, and had raised himself up to full height to fire at another when he was shot through the right side of his chest. He turned pale, but he managed to keep on his feet and handed his rifle to Lt Chard. He then asked Chard to take his remaining cartridges from his pockets, and the doctor quickly

*Darkness comes on as Rev Smith gives out
ammunition to the defenders who are desperately
trying to force the Zulus back from the entrenchment.
Lt Chard thrusts forward his sword.*

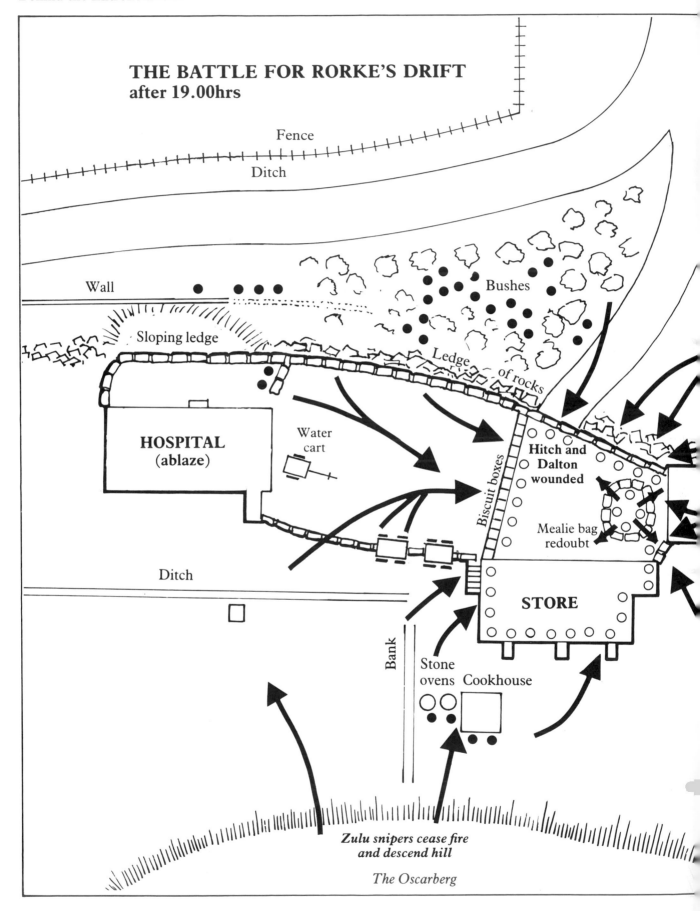

THE BATTLE FOR RORKE'S DRIFT
after 19.00hrs

Fence

Ditch

Wall

Bushes

Sloping ledge

Ledge of rocks

HOSPITAL (ablaze)

Water cart

Biscuit boxes

Hitch and Dalton wounded

Mealie bag redoubt

Ditch

STORE

Bank

Stone ovens   Cookhouse

Zulu snipers cease fire and descend hill

The Oscarberg

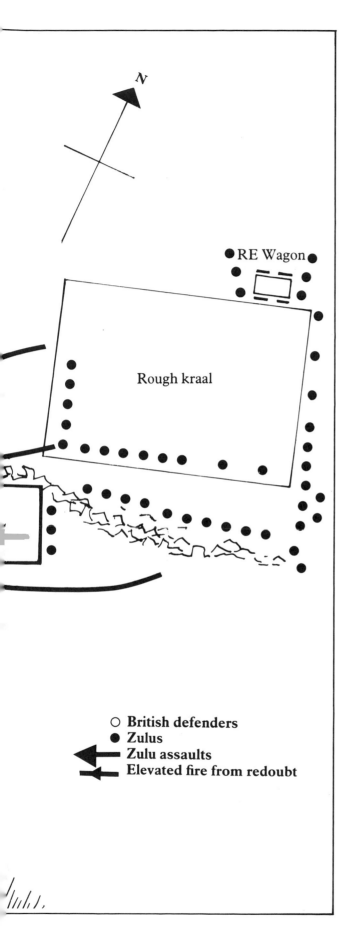

N

●RE Wagon●

Rough kraal

○ **British defenders**
● **Zulus**
◀ **Zulu assaults**
◀ **Elevated fire from redoubt**

bandaged his wound. The stretcher-bearers helped him to the redoubt, and he was made comfortable as the walls were hastily raised around him.

Mr Dunne was totally exposed to enemy fire as he stood high up on the bags directing the construction. The men toiled relentlessly until the sides were about eight feet high, and they had totally exhausted themselves. Between thirty and forty men then climbed inside and the most serious casualties were also housed there.

It was now past 19.00hrs and the tremendous Zulu assault had become general all around the perimeter. The darkness, and the storehouse buildings shielded the defenders from the aim of the Zulus on the Oscarberg, so most of them came down and took cover nearer to the wall, from where they began a harassing fire. The warriors stalked out of hiding and crept up to the wall under cover of the shadows created by the light from the burning hospital, and sprang up on to the ramparts to get at the defenders. The riflemen posted at the loopholes in the western end of the store were able to keep the warriors away from the shelter of the outside of the south barricade. But to the east of the defences the men in the kraal were being pushed back.

Driver Robson was among these men. He was concentrating his fire at the Zulus who were ransacking the wagon with the engineering equipment in it. They had wrecked the camp of the Twenty-Fourth in the darkness beyond the storehouse and because the kraal was some distance from the light of the burning hospital it was not as well lit as the rest of the fort and many warriors were able to approach the walls undetected. One warrior crawled along in the darkness and grabbed Pte Michael Minehan's leg. He prodded the straw frantically with his bayonet and killed the Zulu. Eventually, however, the defenders were pushed back to the low partition, and then to the inner wall below the mealie-bag redoubt while the Zulus occupied the abandoned walls. But the walls were an awkward height and the men on the redoubt were well elevated above them. Each time a warrior presented his rifle over the wall he was easily picked off.

Lt Bromhead and the men he had brought back from the outer perimeter were still defending the much exposed area where the biscuit-boxes met the northern breastwork. A Zulu bullet hit Lance-Sgt Williams in the left side of his chest, and he fell seriously wounded. As the stretcher-bearers were taking him to the redoubt Pte John Fagan was also hit in the chest. He fell against the biscuit boxes, but managed to keep hold of his rifle and remained at his post. Ptes James Chick 'D' Company and John Scanlon 'A' Company were shot down and killed by Zulu cross fire, and Lt Chard would also have been killed if Pte Jenkins had not shouted a warning and pulled his officer's head down just as a Zulu round whizzed over it. Jenkins himself was later killed.

Lt Bromhead was keeping an eye on the ammunition, and was continually telling his men to take careful aim and not to waste rounds. As he took steady aim at a warrior near the hospital a Zulu managed to scramble over the breastwork and came up behind him with his *assegai* raised to strike. Pte Hitch saw the warrior but his rifle was not loaded and he had lost his bayonet. He could do nothing but try to bluff the warrior by putting the muzzle of his rifle on him. The ruse worked, and the startled Zulu clambered back out of the enclosure without delivering the fatal blow.

Still more Zulus sprang up and attacked the wall and so Hitch joined the men fighting to keep them back from the northern breastwork area. A Zulu attempted to climb the bags, so he blocked him and tried to force him back. As he did so he noticed another Zulu to his left who was aiming his rifle straight at him. He reeled backwards from the wall as the Zulu shot him in the right shoulder. As he fell the Zulu moved in for the kill. Lt Bromhead had been behind Hitch providing a second line of fire, and he also saw the Zulu. He levelled his revolver and shot dead the Zulu. Hitch was bleeding badly, but got to his feet, stripped to his shirt and put his injured arm into his belt. Pte George Deacon tore the lining from the sleeve of Mr Dunne's greatcoat and tied it around his shoulder to secure it. Hitch then borrowed Bromhead's revolver for a while, but began to feel ill, and eventually decided to help with the distribution of ammunition. Mr Dalton had also recovered enough to help with the ammunition.

Pte Desmond was nicked in the fleshy part of his thumb by a slug, and another found its way through a gap in the biscuit boxes and hit Cpl Lyons in the right side of his neck. He fell sprawling over the biscuit boxes and landed outside the enclosure but the defenders dragged him back in and Dr Reynolds quickly attended to him.

The Zulus who were crouching behind the outside of the perimeter wall were causing problems with their short-range fire. Cpl Schiess was concerned by the amount of damage they were doing,

Pte Jenkins aims his Martini-Henry from a kneeling position behind the breastwork at the north rampart. During the height of the Zulu assault on the entrenchment he saved Lt Chard's life. It was acts of vigilance and comradeship such as his which undoubtedly helped the defenders to survive the repeated Zulu attacks.

so he slipped over the boxes and crept along the inner side of the wall towards a group of warriors. He cautiously raised himself up before them and aimed his rifle but one of them fired first and blew his hat off. Schiess quickly jumped onto the bags, his body illuminated by the glare from the blazing fire, and bayonetted the Zulu. He then shot another Zulu close by, and as a third warrior was coming to their aid, he met him with the point of his bayonet. The gallant corporal then returned to his post.

Dabulamanzi was directing his warriors from behind Witt's garden wall. As the battle went on he was becoming more and more anxious. He had disobeyed Cetshwayo's orders not to attack fortified places, and could only justify his actions by taking back a report of unqualified victory. But he had already launched his best attacks and the soldiers were still secure in their corner of the enclosure. Even if he did eventually succeed his losses were already heavy, and mounting. Being deprived of his fellow inDuna he was finding it increasingly difficult to stir up morale in such a large *impi*, and he could see signs that they were losing heart. They were used to fighting out in the open, and not against quick-firing rifles behind frustrating forti-

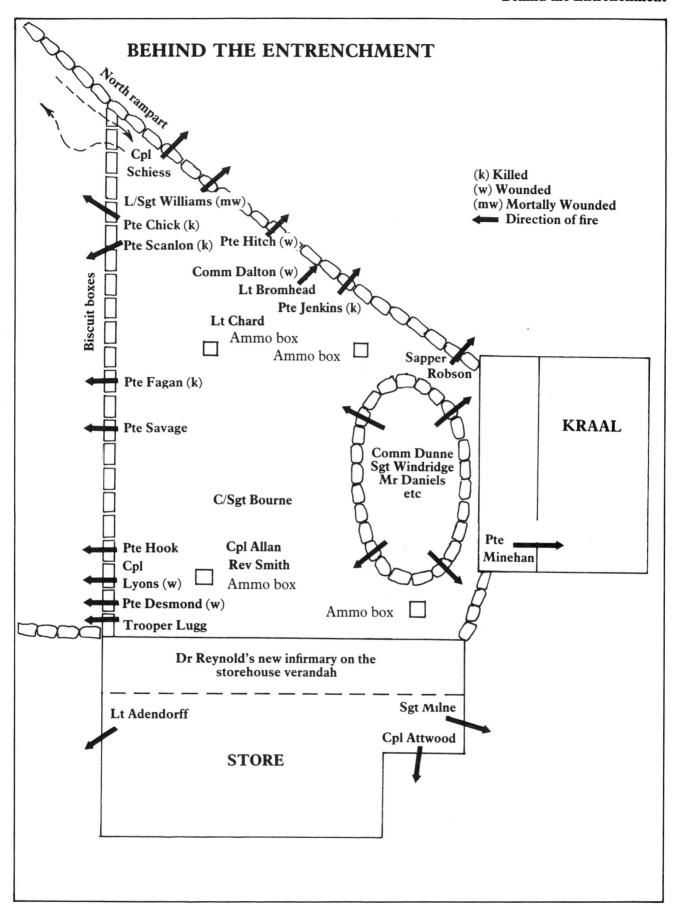

BEHIND THE ENTRENCHMENT

North rampart

Cpl Schiess

L/Sgt Williams (mw)

Pte Chick (k)

Pte Scanlon (k)   Pte Hitch (w)

Comm Dalton (w)

Lt Bromhead

Pte Jenkins (k)

Lt Chard

Ammo box

Ammo box

Sapper Robson

(k) Killed
(w) Wounded
(mw) Mortally Wounded
← Direction of fire

Biscuit boxes

Pte Fagan (k)

Pte Savage

C/Sgt Bourne

Comm Dunne
Sgt Windridge
Mr Daniels
etc

KRAAL

Pte Hook

Cpl Allan
Rev Smith
Ammo box

Cpl Lyons (w)

Pte Desmond (w)

Trooper Lugg

Ammo box

Pte Minehan

Dr Reynold's new infirmary on the storehouse verandah

Lt Adendorff

Sgt Milne

Cpl Attwood

STORE

77

Above: *This sketch drawn by Frank Bourne to illustrate his narrative for the Listener in 1936, differs slightly from Lt Chard's, but shows the scene at the post how he remembered it.*

fications. They had not eaten properly for days, and had travelled over sixteen miles on foot before the assault.

The three defenders outside the perimeter shivered in the cold night air. Pte Waters lay nursing his wound as Zulus moved about near him. He was trodden on several times, but the darkness hid his identity and they left him alone. Pte Beckett was still curled up in the drainage ditch, with his abdomen saturated in his own blood, and he had lost consciousness. Gunner Howard had also nearly been discovered several times. He had contemplated making a dash for the enclosure, but there were too many warriors about so he lay motionless, in fear of his life.

For the defenders thirst and fatigue had now become as much an enemy as the Zulus, especially among the wounded. The water cart was near the burning hospital where it was impossible to reach without putting more men in danger. Some men tried to get at the rum casket, but Sgt Milne warned

Right: *This is a preliminary sketch by Lady Butler of a soldier at Rorke's Drift in the low guard position. He appears in the finished painting farthest left of the defenders at the breastwork.*

Lieutenant Chard as he may have appeared at Rorke's Drift. He is wearing a scarlet single-breasted Engineer officer's jacket, with garter-blue facings. His buff cord riding breeches are tucked into brown leather boots. He is seen here firing a rifle, and he also carried a hand gun. He also used his sword to defend himself at close quarters.

Above: *Three warriors of King Mpande's army proudly display their exotic dress.*

Below: *The animal skin flying over this small kraal near Umlazi signifies that the inDuna is at home.*

Above: *Utimuni, Shaka's nephew, stands on parade. After taking part in a ceremonial war dance he will march past the king stooping in respect.*

Above: *This classic painting by C. E. Fripp, shows the survivors of the 24th Regiment rallying around the colours for a last stand at Isandhlwana. The massacre of nearly a whole infantry battalion shocked the nation and humiliated the British Government.*

Left: *'Saving The Colours', painted by Alphonse de Neuville, depicts Lieutenants Teignmouth Melville and Neville Coghill, 1st/24th Regt, during their heroic dash to try to save the Queen's colour of their battalion. They managed to reach the Buffalo River but were caught and killed by Zulus on the Natal side, at a place called Sotondose's Drift.*

Right: *The foreign service helmet worn by this sergeant has been dyed. He wears the undress serge frock with grass-green facings. The regimental badge is a brass sphinx and the '24' on the shoulder strap is of white metal. His accoutrements are part of the valise pattern equipment first used in 1871.*

'The Defence of Rorke's Drift, January 22nd 1879'
by Lady Elizabeth Butler. This stirring painting was
commissioned by Queen Victoria. Some of the
'principal heroes' were made available for the artist
to study, as they were asked to re-enact their part in
the action dressed in the uniforms they had worn on
the day. Certain individuals have been identified in
the painting. Lt Chard is in the centre, pointing, with
Lt Bromhead next to him. On Chard's left, Acting
Commissariat Officer Dalton flings his arm in the air
as he is hit by a rifle bullet. To his left, in the white
helmet, Surgeon-Major Reynolds treats a wounded
man. On the exteme right, his shoulder bandaged,
Pte Hitch brings up more ammunition. On the
extreme left are Ptes William and Robert Jones.
Behind them the Rev smith, his hand to his mouth,

shouts a warning. To his left, lying on the ground, is
Cpl Schiess of the Natal Native Contingent. Not all
the incidents shown in the picture happened at the
same time, but Lady Butler's intention was to include
portraits of the eleven men who were awarded the
Victoria Cross. This was the highest number ever
awarded for a single action.

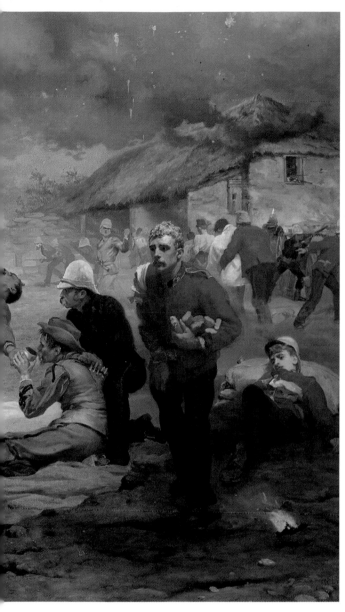

Right: *This warrior of the uDhloko regiment, following the usual practice on campaign, has jettisoned much of his ceremonial dress and retains only the otterskin headband and cowtail arm and leg decorations. Reflecting his married status he wears the headring and also a charm necklace made up of small wooden blocks and pouches of animal skin.*

Above: *The Union Jack that flew over the mission-station at Rorke's Drift during the Zulu attack.*

Left: *Lieutenant Gonville Bromhead VC, was in command of 'B' Company at Rorke's Drift. Generations of his family had served with the 24th Regiment, and he was with the South Wales Borderers when he died in 1891.*

Below: *Time and again the Zulu warriors leapt onto the barricade and tried to get at the defenders. But they were brought down by British bullets or were met with the point of a bayonet. This picture by W.H. Duggan shows the ferocity of an attack on the north perimeter.*

Above: *As Surgeon Reynolds attends to a wounded man, a soldier of the 24th Regiment is hit by a Zulu bullet and reels back from the barricade. The hospital water cart can be seen in the background close to the burning hospital.*

Right: *The British stand their ground as yet another wave of warriors assault the perimeter in their effort to wear the defenders down and break their spirit. The battle lasted for twelve hours and left dreadful memories in the minds of the survivors.*

Above: *The Dalton medals. The South Africa Medal is a replacement for the original, which was lost. Dalton's service record shows him to be entitled to the single bar 1877-78-79.*

Right: *The memorial at the grave of Colonel John Chard VC, 'The Hero Of Rorke's Drift', in the churchyard of St John the Baptist, Hatch Beauchamp near Taunton.*

Below: *The 'VC Case' in The South Wales Borderers Museum. Ten soldiers of the regiment were awarded the Victoria Cross for the Zulu campaign of 1879. Soldiers of the regiment have won twenty-three in all.*

them of his orders, and he jumped on the barrel threatening to shoot any man who touched it. Eventually, the cries for water became unbearable, so a handful of men jumped over the boxes and ran to fetch some water in. Pte Fagan was supporting himself on the boxes pleading for water, and Pte Savage heard him, so he crawled along to help him. But Fagan collapsed and later died.

As ten o'clock came and went, many men were beginning to consider their situation as hopeless, and they could see no chance of escape. But they still intended to fight to the end. They had been firing continually for five hours, changing shoulders when they became bruised and sore from the recoil of their rifles, until they both hurt so much that they had to hold the weapons at arm's length to fire. The rifle barrels became so hot that their fingers and palms became scorched, and they had to use a rag to hold them. Others picked up the weapons of their dead and wounded comrades and used them alternately. They had frantically to clear the barrels with a ramrod when they fouled up and jammed, and their hands became cut and splintered as they fumbled for cartridges in the ammunition boxes. The bayonets were effective, but they were not strong, and most of those that had not snapped from the rifles had bent during the struggle. Their clothes were ripped and begrimed, and their faces were dirty and splashed with blood. Some men could no longer speak from exhaustion and the smoke that parched their burning throats.

Chard and Bromhead joined the men in the redoubt to get a better view of the situation. The hospital fire blazed on, and although it had completely destroyed the medical supplies, it still enabled the defenders to keep the Zulus in view as they approached the barricade. Chaplain Smith was praying that the warriors would go away, and the men who could no longer fight encouraged those who could. Pte Hitch was moving along the barricade giving out cartridges when he began to feel faint and thirsty. He collapsed with his back against the boxes close to Pte Deacon. Deacon saw that Hitch was losing consciousness and asked him if he would prefer to be shot when it came to the end. Hitch declined the offer before he passed out, and he was taken to the shelter of the storehouse.

Towards midnight the attacks became less frequent, but the Zulus kept the soldiers on constant alert. Dabulamanzi was still trying to stir up aggression in his tired warriors, and the ground shook as they stamped their feet and clashed their shields in the darkness. On one side of the post the commands of the Zulu leaders would call out, and a cry of 'Usuthu!' would follow. The men defending that area would then strain their already weak and sore eyes, and prick their ears to detect an attack. But then the same thing would happen at a different point around the perimeter, and another section would be alerted. They could never be sure from where the next Zulu attack would come. Dark shadowy figures would then run up to the barricade, and as they became illuminated by the glare from the fire the defenders shot most of them down as they approached. The few who reached the wall clambered up the bodies of their dead and pounced on the defenders. But the shock of sharp steel always met them and they died.

The fire began to burn itself out, and as a pale light appeared from behind the Oscarberg, some men were daring to think that they might still be alive to see the dawning of a new day. The battleground became still, but now and again some rafters or timbers would collapse in the building, and as flames and sparks rose up from the embers new targets were illuminated and a few shots were exchanged. Then all became silent again, but for the cries of the wounded and dying. Those Zulus who had been too gravely wounded were put out of their misery by their fellow warriors with a sharp *assegai* thrust under the armpit. Brave and gallant men from totally different cultures, who had been brought together in conflict, had earned a deep respect for each other.

Towards morning the soldiers became suspicious of a longer than usual silence. But at last the dull light rose from behind the hills and glimmered across the sky, and the streak of dawn moved across the shattered post. And as the defenders looked out beyond the hundreds of black corpses were scattered all around, groups of dejected and spent warriors could be seen retiring over the rise from where they had appeared twelve hours earlier. They dragged many of their wounded and dead away on their shields, but some warriors could be heard groaning among the carnage.

CHAPTER SEVEN:
The Smoke Clears

'It seemed that out of battle I escaped . . .'
Wilfred Owen

The early light revealed a devastating scene of carnage. The defenders could hardly believe their eyes at the sight of what men are capable of doing to their fellow men under the dreadful banner of war. The burned-out hospital was still smouldering, and the charred remains of the men who had died in the building smelt awful. Around the hospital and all along the breastwork were piled hundreds of Zulus, many with horrible injuries. Their limbs were tied in knots, and broken and bent from the blasts of rifles. Some warriors had been pinned to the ground by the bayonets that had killed them. Trampled grain, pot-holed tins and used cartridge cases from the twenty-thousand rounds of ammunition that had been expended were strewn all around, and the fortifications were stained with blood.

A Zulu who had feigned death in the kraal got up and fired his rifle at the defenders as they began to move about the barricade. Then he fled towards the

As news of the epic defence of Rorke's Drift began to reach England, wildly inaccurate jingoistic sketches such as this view of the post began to appear in British newspapers during March 1879. The arrow points out the approach of the relief column.

Above: *Rorke's Drift today: The stone pillar in the foreground is a national monument erected on the site where the two wagons were incorporated in the line of defence.*

Below: *The area where the biscuit boxes met the north perimeter of mealie bags, which has been marked out by a line of stones. To the right a chapel stands on the sight of the original storehouse.*

river. His shot did no harm, and he had taken everyone so much by surprise that by the time a few shots were fired after him, it was too late and he got away.

Pte Waters had taken refuge in the cook house and was so relieved to see red coats moving about the post, that without thinking he came out and approached the wall. Several rifles were trained on him at once, but he managed to identify himself just in time. Gunner Howard had also surived his ordeal, and Chard's wagon driver came stumbling in.

Nobody believed that they had seen the last of the Zulus, and although many of the men could hardly move their aching limbs, Lt Chard kept them busy repairing the perimeter and preparing for any renewed attack. He also hoped that this would prevent them from dwelling on their uncertain situation. They put ropes through the loopholes in the blackened walls of the hospital and pulled them down. The thatch was stripped from the roof of the store and piled into the kraal. The bushes and trees were cut down as much as possible, with the dead horses being left tied to the stumps. Two men tied a piece of white material to a length of wood and got up onto the roof of the store to act as lookouts. They were to give warning of any Zulu advance by waving the flag.

Patrols were sent out, cautiously watching for any surprise attack. They collected all the Zulu rifles and ammunition they could find, and brought in hundreds of *assegais* that had been left around the defences. Many warriors were still alive, and shots rang out now and then as they tried to get away when they were discovered. As Trooper Lugg limped about among the dead, he saw a rifle on the ground, and was going to pick it up when a Zulu who had been lying close by rose up and jammed the barrel against his body. The trigger clicked, but the weapon misfired. Before the Zulu could recover, Lugg dropped on him and stabbed him with his hunting knife. Pte Hook was following the course of a dry stream as he was patrolling near the river carrying a pile of *assegais*. Suddenly, he came upon a Zulu lying still on the ground. The man was unarmed, and though Hook saw blood running from a wound in his leg he sus-pected a trap. As he passed him Hook watched for any others who might be about to ambush him, but the warrior on the ground suddenly sprang into action and grabbed hold of his rifle. As the Zulu tried to wrestle Hook to the ground, he dropped the pile of *assegais* he had been carrying and hit the Zulu in the chest, then

At the time of the centenary, parts of the perimeter were marked out and included these two wagons, which are identical to those of the period. The building stands on the site of the hospital.

stepped back as he loaded the rifle and shot the warrior through the head. After these incidents the men were allowed to leave the fort only in numbers.

There were twenty-seven casualties. Eleven soldiers of the 24th Regt had been killed, and a twelfth was added when Pte Beckett was found alive but mortally wounded. Dr Reynolds did all he could to save his life, but he had lost too much blood and he died later. The bodies of the dead defenders whom the Zulus had managed to get hold of had been treated horribly. The corpse of Joseph Williams was found badly mutilated, but he had sold his life dearly, for there were many Zulu bodies scattered about the area that he had defended. The bodies of Ptes Hayden and Adams had been badly burned, but it was still possible to tell that Hayden had been stabbed sixteen times, his stomach had been slit open twice, and part of his cheek had been cut off. Their corpses, along with those of Horrigan, Maxfield and the Xhosa native were removed from the ruins of the hospital and placed in the kraal. One man's head had been split open, and another man, who still had his rifle pointing over the parapet, had been hit between the eyes by a Zulu slug, which had taken the back of his head away but left his face perfect except for a little hole. Trooper Hunter had received six stab wounds, and one of the Zulus had

The remains of the hospital are still smouldering, and Zulu corpses litter the area, while the defenders wave their arms to welcome the mounted infantry as it approaches the post from the drift. This is Crealock's interpretation of the scene at Rorke's Drift when he returned on 23 January, with Lord Chelmsford and the remains of the column.

been shot and killed as he was cutting up the corpse of a dead man. His stiffened body was still leaning over his victim when he was found.

Dr Reynolds continued to attend to the wounded. He took thirty-nine pieces of bone from Hitch's shattered shoulder joint, and dressed the neck wound suffered by Cpl Lyons. The ball had passed down his body and struck his spine, where it lodged. There was little he could do for him under the circumstances, but try to nurse him back to strength. The bullet that hit Lance-Sgt Williams had passed through him but he was very ill. Pte Waters had a hole four inches deep in his shoulder. Dr Reynolds applied a temporary dressing, and intended to cut the bullet out later that day. Several other men had minor lacerations and less serious injuries.

Lts Chard and Bromhead assessed the situation. There were fewer than two boxes of ammunition left in reserve, which meant that each defender had about twenty cartridges. Some men had slumped down behind the barricade to rest their aching limbs, while others shivered with cold, and the effects of shock, after a hard-fought battle. They had no idea if or when another assault might begin, but even though the men had fought far beyond their expectations, and morale was still high, they knew that if the Zulus continued to attack they would eventually be worn down, and would lose the will to fight. When the work of repairing and securing the defences was done, they returned to their places at the perimeter, and waited in an almost unbearable state of uncertainty.

At about 07.00hrs the signalmen drew attention to the south-west, where a large body of Zulus had advanced over the rise and were waiting menacingly. And then the white flag was waved for a second time, as the lookouts brought attention to a line of men that was winding down through the Bashee Valley, coming towards the river and about an hour's march away. It was impossible to tell if they were British or Zulu. But if they were the latter, the defenders' fate was sealed. They had no real ideas what had become of the rest of the column and even had they survived they might well have assumed that Rorke's Drift had fallen, and had made their way direct to Helpmakaar.

A young kaffir then came running up to the barricade. Daniels could speak a little Bantu, so Chard asked him to interrogate the native. He was found to be friendly, so Chard sent him on to Helpmakaar with a note explaining the situation and requesting immediate reinforcement.

Eventually the defenders could see the approaching force more clearly through field glasses, and hopes were raised when they could see red tunics among them. But it was then suggested that these men could be Zulus dressed in the uniforms of the men who had fallen at Isandhlwana. The Zulus on the rise were gradually moving forward, but they also seemed to be equally unsure about the advancing force. The weary men in the fort watched anxiously, not knowing what to expect. Suddenly, there were hysterical shouts from the roof of the store, and the signallers began waving the flag frantically. A body of mounted men was approaching the river. They were British. The men were overcome with relief and some cried with joy. Wild cheers rang out and helmets were thrown into the air. On the rise, a Dabulamanzi turned his dejected warriors away, and they disappeared around the hill. Lord Chelmsford was returning with the portion of the column that he had taken out from the base camp at Isandhlwana on the previous day.

At 08.15hrs, Major Russell of the 12th Lancers brought an advance detachment of mounted troops up to the post. He was anxious to know if any of the men from the Isandhlwana base camp had managed to escape to Rorke's Drift. But Lt Chard informed him that very few survivors had passed the post on their way to Helpmakaar, and most of these had been colonial volunteers. They were stricken with grief at this reply. Lord Chelmsford and his staff arrived shortly afterwards. He was dejected and emotional, and thanked the defenders for what they had done. The main body of the column then began to arrive.

They had lost everything, including their pride, and they were weary and hungry. While the mission-station had been under attack they had spent a restless night among the death and destruction at Isandhlwana. Zulu campfires could be seen on the hills all around them, and as they looked towards Rorke's Drift, the light from the burning hospital illumi-nated the night sky. As they had approached the river they passed Dabulamanzi's *impi* as it was moving away from the battle at the Drift. A few stragglers at the rear of the columns had exchanged shouts, but apart from that they passed each other without incident.

The Commissariat provided them with bread, biscuits, and tins of corned beef, and there was reasonably fresh water. It was their first food for two days. Colour-Sgt Bourne then issued a welcome tot of rum. Many men moved about the post anxiously looking for their friends. Neither Sub-Lt Griffith nor Pip's master were among the survivors. Many men lost close friends, and some districts of South Wales would be devastated by the loss of several of their menfolk. The defenders had been continually on alert for eighteen hours, but they were far too unnerved and tense to sleep. As they wearily began to reflect on the events they were gradually coming to realise that they had taken part in an action that might very well be considered special. Every man was thankful that he had survived the terrible ordeal.

Lt Chard was without his tunic as he washed his powder-blackened face in a muddy puddle, along with Pte Bushe, who was covered in blood from his injury. Bushe offered to share his dirty towel with Chard, and the Lieutenant accepted thankfully. Chard then went to check his wrecked wagon. It was a mess but the Zulus had left an unbroken bottle of beer, so he and Bromhead celebrated together.

Pte Hook was sent back to his duty of making tea for the sick. However, a sergeant came up and told him that he was to drop everything and report to the officers at once. So Hook found himself standing before Lord Chelmsford in his shirt sleeves and with his braces dangling at his side, giving him his account of the action in the hospital. Capt William Penn-Symons, 24th Regt, wrote down everything that was reported.

Look-outs were posted and mounted patrols were sent out. The natives were ordered to collect stones from around the post so that a more permanent loop-holed fort could be constructed. The Zulu weapons and shields were thrown into a ditch and burned, and the kaffirs were also to dig two deep pits in front of the hospital so that the corpses could be buried. The natives disliked touching dead bodies, so it took the soldiers nearly two days to collect the 351 corpses from around the post and bury them. Recent events had turned the men bitter and some wounded Zulus were also thrown in. One pri-

The New Camp, Rorke's Drift. The confined, insanitary conditions at the mission-station affected the troops badly, and as the official lists record, many men died of disease or became seriously ill while they were stationed at Rorke's Drift. The situation was only improved when a more spacious camp was established a quarter of a mile away.

vate with a Zulu prisoner reported to the officers and he seems to have taken them literally when they told him to dispose of the captive. Lt Smith-Dorrien had escaped from Isandhlwana, and when he returned to Rorke's Drift he found two head-ringed Zulus hanging from the transport appliance that he had built. Many Zulus were found between the post and the place where the *impi* had recrossed the river, and scores of blood-stained shields were also found on the banks. Some warriors had crawled long distances from the battlefield to die in dignified solitude, and for months afterwards their stiffened corpses were found in the bush and in caves in the area. It is believed that, in all, over five-hundred Zulus had been killed.

On the 25th January Lance-Sgt Williams finally succumbed to his wounds and he was buried with the others. Seventeen of the defenders were officially recorded as killed in action. This number included the Xhosa Native and Cpl Anderson. Thirteen soldiers of the twenty-fourth were buried close together, and later a wall was built around their graveyard. A makeshift wooden cross was at first put up, but afterwards an obelisk-shaped stone monument was erected in the centre of the little cemetery. A bandsman named John Mellsop used pieces of broken bayonets to carve out the names and a picture of the fight.

For the gallant defence of Rorke's Drift eleven men were later awarded the Victoria Cross, more than for any other single action in British military history. Four men were awarded the Silver Cross for Distinguished Conduct in the Field. Chard and Bromhead received accelerated promotions to Brevet-Major, dated 23rd January 1879, and they both received the thanks of the House of Commons. Surgeon Reyonolds was promoted to Surgeon-Major dated 23rd January 1879, Sgt Milne was promoted to Colour-Sgt on his return to Canterbury, and Colour-Sgt Bourne was offered a Commission. Five other NCOs of 'B' Company were also promoted from 23rd January 1879, but they were all

The Smoke Clears

reduced later. Rev Smith was given a permanent commission as Chaplain to the Forces, and there were also a number of civilian presentations.

In the days that followed, as the men exchanged stories and details, they were able to piece together the events of the 22nd January. The defenders learned that when Major Spalding had arrived at Helpmakaar, he found that the officer in command there had held back the company of the 1st Bn, because he felt that he could not spare them until reinforcements had reached him. Spalding over-

Below: *The men who held Rorke's Drift. A truly historic picture of the survivors of 'B' Company, 2nd/24th Regt. Lt Bromhead is seated far right of the front row with Pip, the dog, who spent much of his time barking at the Zulus during the battle.*

Left: *Many men used their civilian skills when on Active service. Here a burial team builds the monument and engraves the stone with the names of the dead. Rorke's house can be seen in the distance.*

ruled him, and ordered a detachment of troops to follow him back to the mission-station. The Major rode on in front, and about three miles from Rorke's Drift he came upon some abandoned wagons, a number of which were still loaded. He then met several fugitives fleeing towards Helpmakaar, including Ptes Grant and Johnson, whom he ordered to return to Rorke's Drift with him. About a mile further on they met Lt Henderson and Bob Hall, who brought attention to a column of smoke rising from the hills in the direction of the Drift. Although the buildings were not visible, Major

Spalding accepted their report that the post had fallen into Zulu hands. They then saw a number of natives blocking the road ahead, so Spalding decided to turn back, and take the two companies of the 1st Bn to prepare to defend Helpmakaar. It was never ascertained if these were the red-coats that the men in the garrison had thought they had seen soon after the Zulu attack started.

Lord Chelmsford questioned Major Spalding's decision, and this became a point of controversy. But then some of the actions and decisions of senior officers at Isandhlwana could also be considered folly and insurbordinate.

Below the mountain at Isandhlwana, because the base camp was only a temporary one, they did not laager the wagons. This was a difficult manoeuvre to perform, and the Natal kaffir wagon drivers did not have the skill to manage it. The ground was considered too rocky to make an effective entrenchment, but there was a steep *donga* running across the face of the camp, and the slopes of Isandhlwana hill gave adequate protection at the rear. Look-outs were posted on high ground to the north, where the Nqutu plateau would hide any Zulu advance until it was very near the camp. Vedettes were also posted in other strategic places.

Lord Chelmsford had left nearly six-hundred regular soldiers in the camp, made up of five companies of the 1st Bn and most of 'G' Company of the 2nd Bn. There were two 7-pounder field guns, and when Colonel Durnford arrived with his detachment of troops at about 10.30hrs there were 1,800 men to guard the camp.

But Colonel Durnford did not stay. Although command of the camp had devolved on him, he moved out across a plain in front of the tents with a section of his men and the rocket battery, to pursue a Zulu *impi* which had been sighted in that direction. He had sent some of his Basutos out scouting earlier, and they came upon a party of Zulus herding cattle about four miles north of the camp. They chased them over the edge of a ridge, but suddenly found themselves staring open-mouthed into a ravine. Covering the slopes and sides as far as they could see were thousands of Zulu warriors squat-

By 22 January 1879 the British had established themselves at the foot of Isandhlwana. When Col Durnford went out on a sortie, the Zulus attacked the ill-prepared camp and annihilated the weakened force left to guard it.

ting in silence. They had located the main *impi*. As they quickly withdrew to warn the camp, 20,000 Zulus swarmed after them.

The British troops had already been called to arms and had turned out to meet them. Colonel Durnford had also been attacked, and was being driven back towards the camp. So Pulleine deployed his men in extended lines across the plain to try to give him support. Durnford's force then lined the *donga* to make a stand and the heavy volleys from the ranks of infantry temporarily checked the Zulu advance. But they began to run short of ammuni-

tion. The swift Zulu onslaught had taken the Quartermasters by surprise, and they found it impossible to open the heavily fastened boxes quickly enough to replenish the ranks. As the Zulus took advantage of the lull in fire and raced forward, the native contingent broke and fled, leaving wide gaps in the British lines. The Zulus moved in.

The British soldiers found themselves cut off, and when they realised that they were being overwhelmed they turned back to back for their last stand. Colonel Durnford and his men had been pushed back to the camp area, and were also

engaged in a desperate hand-to-hand fight. Many warriors died at bayonet point before the British soldiers were finally wiped out. Not one single red-coat escaped, because none of them tried to, and they fought bravely until they died where they stood.

The uNdi Corps and the uDhloko Regiment had formed part of the right horn which moved around

The Zulus swarm down from the Nqutu plateau, as a detachment of British soldiers try to extend the line in an effort to support Col Durnford's force who were falling back towards the camp.

to the west of Isandhlwana mountain to block the road back to Rorke's Drift. When the men who had managed to get out of the camp encountered them, they made across broken country towards the river, and for four miles they were closely pursued by the Zulu.

With the battle clearly lost, Lts Teignmouth Melville and Neville Coghill of the 1st Bn tried to save their Queen's Colour. They got across the river at Sotondose's Drift (now called Fugitive's Drift), but they were exhausted and the Zulus caught and killed them. Both colours of the 2nd Bn were left in the guard tent at the camp. About 450 men got out in all. Two weeks' supplies fell into the hands of the Zulus, along with two artillery guns, hundreds of rifles and large quantities of ammunition.

No one will ever know what acts of gallantry and devotion to duty were performed by the soldiers

Lts Melville and Coghill are attacked by Zulu warriors as they desperately try to reach the river with the colours of the 1st Battalion. A memorial on the bank of the river, at what is now called Fugitive's Drift, marks the spot where they fell.

Charles Fripp's heroic painting of the 24th Regiment's last stand at Isandhlwana, shows the British soldier gallantly standing fast against an attacking foe, which had great appeal to the Victorian public. Accounts by Zulus who had fought at Isandhlwana confirm that the red-coated soldiers died bravely at their posts. A bandboy, such as the one seen in the centre of the picture trying to bring attention to the oncoming warrior, refused an offer to leave the battlefield, while the Zulus were all around him, stabbing and gutting his comrades. He stayed behind to suffer a fate that was far from glorious.

who all perished in the camp area. But three men were rewarded for their gallantry. Pte Samuel Wassall, 80th (Staffordshire) Regiment, was awarded the Victoria Cross for saving a fellow soldier from the Buffalo river in the face of great danger and under a heavy enemy fire. At that time the award was not given to soldiers who did not survive. So Melville and Coghill received no more than a mention in a citation memorandum. But King Edward VII changed the ruling, and in 1907 they became the first men to be awarded the Victoria Cross posthumously when relatives received the medals on their behalf.

The dead on the battlefield at Isandhlwana were treated with disgusting savagery. They were disembowelled, and their entrails scattered amongst the debris. Some men were decapitated and their heads placed in a gruesome ring. But one sight more than any other sickened the men who visited the battlefield. The Zulus had seized five band-boys, and either tied them to wagons by their feet and slit their throats, or hung them on butcher's hooks by their chins, sliced them up, then cut their privates off and put them in their mouths. Because of this incident boys were never again taken on active service by the British Army.

This is how Lt Chard's official report was introduced, when it appeared in British newspapers during the second week in March 1879.

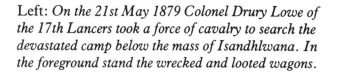

Left: *On the 21st May 1879 Colonel Drury Lowe of the 17th Lancers took a force of cavalry to search the devastated camp below the mass of Isandhlwana. In the foreground stand the wrecked and looted wagons.*

The Zulu War

Madeira, Monday

The following has been received here from Cape Town:–

Lord Chelmsford has issued the following general order:–

The Lieutenant-General commanding her Majesty's Forces in South Africa has much satisfaction in publishing for general information the subjoined official report of the gallant defence of Rorke's Drift Post, made on Jan. 22 and 23. The Lieutenant-General feels sure that the gallant conduct of the garrison will receive most ample recognition, and trusts the example set by a few brave men, and the success that attended their noble efforts, will be taken to heart by all under his command. The odds against them were nearly thirty to one; but taking advantage of the material which lay to hand, and hastily constructing with it such cover as was possible, this heroic little garrison was enabled to resist during the space of twelve hours the determined attacks made upon them, and, further, inflicting heavy loss on the enemy, the killed alone being more than three times their own number.

Left: *Five companies of the 2nd/24th Regt, who were still stationed at Rorke's Drift, accompanied Drury Lowe's squadrons. A lone sentry stands guard amongst the carnage where many of his regiment perished.*

CHAPTER EIGHT:
Revenge

'If you can keep your head when
All about you are losing theirs
And blaming it on you . . .'
Rudyard Kipling

The invasion of Zululand had suffered a serious reverse. The gallant defence of Rorke's Drift returned some order and morale to the troops, but the colony of Natal was thrown into panic. Every frontier town expected to be attacked at any moment and barricades went up as far south as Pietermaritzburg. On the day after the battle the people at Helpmakaar were brought to arms, when hundreds of black figures came streaming over the hills towards the outpost. But they turned out to be men of the Natal Native Contingent, which Lord Chelmsford had decided to disband. The Commander-in-Chief arrived in Pietermaritzburg on Sunday, 26th January, with re-invasion already in his mind. He sent a telegraph at once, which contained a short account of the recent events, and requested reinforcements, stressing the need for cavalry units.

In early February the British newspapers repor-

On July 4 1879 the British formed a military square near Ulundi and 20,000 Zulus moved towards it for their last great battle. A hail of bullets broke the attack, the warriors fled, and the 17th Lancers delivered the final blow.

'B' Company 2/24th Regt, Major Bromhead standing far left. They were presented with a scroll of honour by the Mayor of Durban, and seven men received the Victoria Cross, the largest number ever awarded to one regiment for a single action.

ted that the troops had crossed the frontier and all was well. Communication was slow in those days, and as the public waited for an expected report of a victory of some kind, more than a thousand white men had already died. A shock-wave was sent across the nation when news of the Isandhlwana disaster came to their breakfast tables. There was a public outcry, and both Lord Chelmsford and Prime Minister Disraeli came in for much criticism. The British public had felt that the conflict with Cetshwayo's warriors was inevitable, and had shown only passing interest in the South Africa situation. But the massacre of nearly a whole British infantry battalion by half-naked, primitively-armed natives made them take notice of the Zulu affair. The appearance of Lt Chard's official report helped to heal some wounded pride, and Disraeli focused extra attention on it as a diversion away from the dreadful disaster at Isandhlwana. But stories of outstanding bravery performed by the army were commonplace, and only an overwhelming victory would be acceptable. Both the public and the military wanted revenge and reinforcements were prepared at once. The government more than met Lord Chelmsford's requests.

Meanwhile, seven companies of the 2nd/24th Regt and the 5th Company, Royal Engineers, stayed at Rorke's Drift. They had to cram into the little fort while work progressed on a more spacious stronghold a quarter of a mile away. There was heavy rain every morning, which brought the stench of the dead corpses to the surface and attracted even more flies. Swarms of bacteria-carrying insects contaminated the food and water. The water was still khaki-coloured even after boiling. Conditions were dreadful, and sickness prevalent.

'B' Company were given the privilege of sleeping in the roof of the storehouse, with a tarpaulin thrown over the rafters for shelter. But the remainder had to sleep out in the open with only one blanket and a piece of canvas to cover them. Men on guard duty cut arm holes in sacks to wear over their tunics to keep warm, and everyone had to live in their damp and soiled clothes for a month. They were kept on constant alert, and there was increasing mis-

The front cover of The Illustrated London News *for 29 March 1879, shows an artist's impression of the scene at Helpmakaar when the colours of the 1st Battalion, 24th Regiment were recovered. In spite of* its tattered condition the colour stayed in service until 1933.

conduct. Surgeon-Major Reynolds and his men were kept much busier than they had been during the battle.

Eventually they received new blankets and supplies, and were subsequently transferred to the new fort. But it was too late for Pte John Williams (not the VC) who died of dysentery on 5th February in the post that he had so gallantly helped to defend. Two more men of 'B' Company had died of disease before the end of the year.

Major Chard had supervised the burial parties, which made him very vulnerable to disease. His infected injection also sapped his strength and he became seriously ill with fever. On the 17th February he was sent to Ladysmith and later the *Natal Colonist* reported that he had died. But he was nursed back to health by friends, and on the 29th April he reported for duty at Landman's Drift, where General Wood was organising a Flying-Column of over three thousand men in preparation for the re-invasion of Zululand.

Pte Hook had transferred to 'G' Company, and had been appointed servant to Major Wilsone-Black, who on the 4th February took a detachment of troops to Fugitive's Drift. They found the *assegai*-riddled bodies of Melville and Coghill, and after they had buried them, the Rev Smith read a short service over their graves. To everyone's relief the Queen's Colour was recovered from the river and was proudly carried back to Rorke's Drift, where it was received with scenes of emotion. Both colours of the 2nd Bn were lost.

Otto Witt arrived in England on 5th March 1879, and with him, Umkwelnantaba. Witt had no sooner stepped off the *Warwick Castle* at Plymouth than he was selling his story to the press. After taking the awe-struck youth on a tour of London, he travelled about the country giving talks on his experiences in South Africa. He made an attempt to sue the crown for £600 in compensation for the damage at Rorke's Drift, but he could not produce documents to prove that the property was legally his, and his claim was unsuccessful. He returned to Sweden before the end of the year.

Dabulamanzi and his warriors were considered cowards when they returned to Ulundi. The prince tried to play down his failure to take Rorke's Drift by stressing that he had been successful in burning the hospital. The criticism was unjustified for they had fought bravely, and it had been their bad tactics not lack of courage that lost them the battle. Dabul-

amanzi had followed Cetshawayo's instruction to try to conserve energy whilst on the move and advanced at a leisurely pace, giving the garrison time to prepare. His method of assault was to attack the ramparts in sections, instead of launching his whole force in one over-whelming rush.

Dabulamanzi was eager to regain some honour, and took the uDhloko south to join the regiments that were blockading Colonel Pearson's column near Eshowe. The uNdi Corps joined the regiments under Tsingiswayo and Usibebu, who were moving towards Khambula Hill to attack Wood's column. It was estimated that nearly two-thousand warriors had been killed at Isandhlwana–Rorke's Drift, and on the same day four hundred more had died when an *impi* was repulsed by Pearson's Column as it crossed the Nyezane river on its way to Eshowe. The British however had also suffered a setback on the 12th March, when a company of the 80th (Staffordshire) Regt was almost wiped out on the banks of the Intombi river to the north. But the decisive battle of the 1st invasion of Zululand in 1879 was at Khambula.

On the 28th March a British force under Lt-Col Sir Redvers Buller moved forward from the Khambula camp to storm an enemy stronghold on the summit of Hlobane mountain. While the skirmish was in progress, the main *impi* moving towards Khambula became aware of the fighting and detached a regiment to assist. The British were forced to retreat, and the conduct of Buller and four other men as they withdrew down the hill towards the base camp earned them the Victoria Cross. On the following day 25,000 warriors attacked Wood's laagered wagons on Khambula Hill. A murderous fire from the British weapons left 2,000 Zulus dead on the battlefield, and knocked the heart out of them. They streamed back to their domestic kraals, many having no more stomach to fight. Another severe blow to their morale followed on the 2nd April. A large Zulu *impi* under Dabulamanzi was defeated at Gingindhlovu as it tried to prevent Lord Chelmsford's force from reaching the mission-station near Eshowe to relieve Colonel Pearson. A

A large Zulu impi *surprised a detachment of the 80th Regiment on the banks of the Intombi River. Had it not been for Col-Sgt Anthony Booth, who rallied a few men and covered the retreat of fifty others, not one man would have escaped. Col-Sgt Booth was awarded the Victoria Cross.*

Left: *While reinforcements arrive from England, General Lord Chelmsford and his staff search the hills with field-glasses in preparation for the re-invasion.*

thousand more Zulu warriors died.

When reinforcements arrived from England, Lord Chelmsford formed a 2nd Division of 5,000 men, and on the 1st June he re-invaded Zululand. But on that day another tragedy occurred. The exiled Prince Louis Napoleon of France, who had been allowed to go to South Africa as a volunteer, was out with a patrol when it was attacked by a Zulu scouting party, and he was killed. The senior officer on the patrol was severely criticised for his conduct, and the incident certainly caused more anxiety in England than the Isandhlwana affair had done.

The Flying Column met the 2nd Division on the 17th June, and the combined force was in sight of Ulundi by the end of the month. With defeat staring him in the face Cetshwayo tried to negotiate a cease-fire. He sent representatives with peace offerings, but all his efforts were ignored. A decisive battle in the open would have to be fought. On the 4th July, Major Chard, Surgeon-Major Reynolds, Commissary Dunne, and Rev Smith were part of the huge square of British troops as it moved towards Ulundi. All the main Zulu regiments, including the three that had fought at Rorke's Drift, attacked. The total

Below: *A long column of British infantry and Colonial mounted troops move through hostile country towards the Zulu capital. The Flying Column met the 2nd Division on 17 June, and the combined force was ready for the final breaking of the Zulus.*

Above: *As Ulundi burned Cetshwayo fled, and it took a carefully planned military operation to track him down. He was escorted back to Wolseley's camp by The King's Dragoon Guards and the 3/60th Rifles.*

Below: *After capturing Cetshwayo the British were uncertain what to do with him. He was exiled at Cape Town for over two years, and then he found himself on board HMS* Natal *en-route for England.*

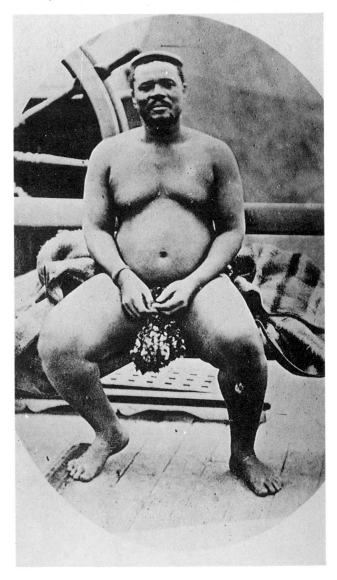

Zulu strength was about twenty-thousand warriors. The Zulus were shot down in their hundreds before they could get anywhere near the British lines, and they were finally routed and hunted down by imperial lancers. The most powerful native military machine that the African Continent had ever seen was no more.

The war was brought to a close when Cetshwayo ka Mpande was captured on the 28th August, and made a prisoner of Sir Garnet Wolseley who had replaced Lord Chelmsford. After being kept a prisoner in Cape Town castle, he was taken to London in 1882 where the man once known as an 'ignorant and bloodthirsty despot', and whose warriors had killed nearly two and a half thousand imperial and colonial troops was admired by the British public.

He was restored as king of the Zulus in 1883, but Zululand had been divided into thirteen small kingdoms and he had little overall authority. He was attacked by his old rival Usibebu and had to seek asylum on British territory. On the 8th February 1884 he was found dead in a kraal near Eshowe, and it is believed that he was poisoned. His son Dinizulu succeeded him and Zululand, torn by civil war and with a more uncertain and fragile future than it had ever known, was annexed to the British crown three years later.

Back in southern Africa, the mayor of Durban presented each survivor of 'B' Company with a scroll of honour – 'Out of gratitude for their courage, loyalty and duty, in the face of the darkest cloud of invasion that had ever lowered over the wild frontier of British Dominion in South Africa.' The Mayor of London set up 'The Mansion House Fund' to give financial help to the widows and children of the men who had died at Isandhlwana and Rorke's Drift. Queen Victoria contributed £100, and after three months the sum had reached £6,600. Government compensation amounted to a grey shirt and a pair of trousers for each man, and they were allowed to retain their rifles. Lady Butler, who

was well known for her military paintings, was commissioned by the Queen to paint a scene of the action, and many of the defenders were invited to

On his arrival in London, Cetshwayo was taken on tours of the capital in smart suits, and the British public were enthralled by him. He was invited to an audience with Queen Victoria, who presented him with a silver goblet.

CETEWAYO'S COMING!

WHAT 'LL THEY DO WITH HIM? "NO REASONABLE OFFER REFUSED."

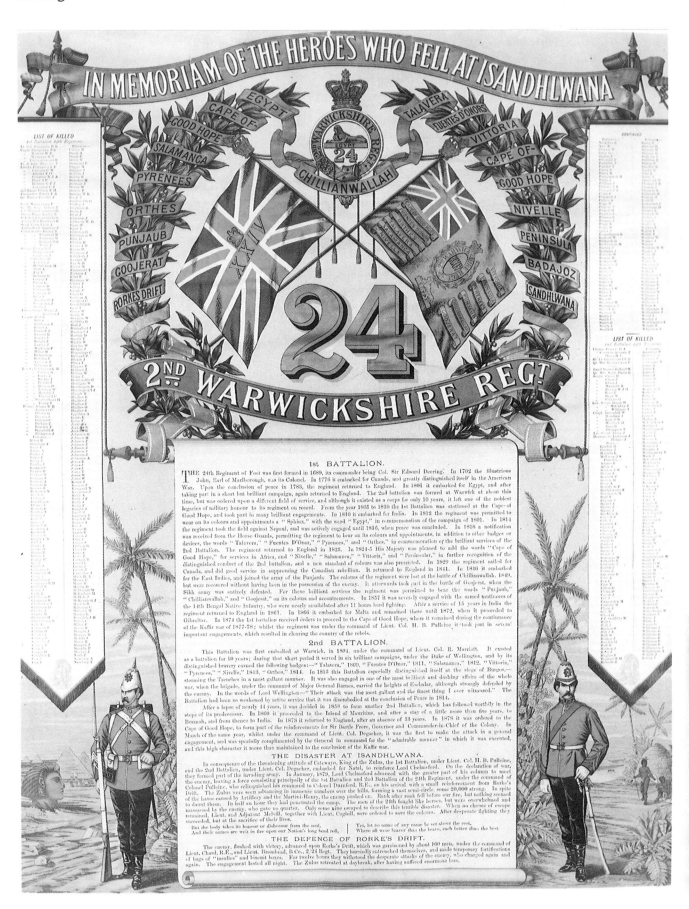

IN MEMORIAM OF THE HEROES WHO FELL AT ISANDHLWANA

24 2ND WARWICKSHIRE REGT

1st BATTALION.

THE 24th Regiment of Foot was first formed in 1689, its commander being Col. Sir Edward Deering. In 1702 the illustrious John, Earl of Marlborough, was its Colonel. In 1776 it embarked for Canada, and greatly distinguished itself in the American War. Upon the conclusion of peace in 1783, the regiment returned to England. In 1801 it embarked for Egypt, and after taking part in a short but brilliant campaign, again returned to England. The 2nd battalion was formed at Warwick at about this time, but was ordered upon a different field of service, and although it existed as a corps for only 10 years, it left one of the noblest legacies of military honour to its regiment on record. From the year 1805 to 1816 the 1st Battalion was stationed at the Cape of Good Hope, and took part in many brilliant engagements. In 1810 it embarked for India. In 1812 the regiment was permitted to wear on its colours and appointments a "Sphinx," with the word "Egypt," in commemoration of the campaign of 1801. In 1814 the regiment took the field against Nepaul, and was actively engaged until 1816, when peace was concluded. In 1818 a notification was received from the Horse Guards, permitting the regiment to bear on its colours and appointments, in addition to other badges or devices, the words "Talavera," "Fuentes D'Onor," "Pyrenees," and "Orthes," in commemoration of the brilliant services of the 2nd Battalion. The regiment returned to England in 1823. In 1824-5 His Majesty was pleased to add the words "Cape of Good Hope," for services in Africa, and "Nivelle," "Salamanca," "Vittoria," and "Peninsular," in further recognition of the distinguished conduct of the 2nd battalion, and a new standard of colours was also presented. In 1829 the regiment sailed for Canada, and did good service in suppressing the Canadian rebellion. It returned to England in 1841. In 1846 it embarked for the East Indies, and joined the army of the Punjaub. The colours of the regiment were lost at the battle of Chillianwallah, 1849, but were recovered without having been in the possession of the enemy. It afterwards took part in the battle of Goojerat, when the Sikh army was entirely defeated. For these brilliant services the regiment was permitted to bear the words "Punjaub," "Chillianwallah," and "Goojerat," on its colours and accoutrements. In 1857 it was severely engaged with the armed mutineers of the 14th Bengal Native Infantry, who were nearly annihilated after 11 hours hard fighting. After a service of 15 years in India the regiment returned to England in 1861. In 1866 it embarked for Malta and remained there until 1872, when it proceeded to Gibraltar. In 1874 the 1st battalion received orders to proceed to the Cape of Good Hope, where it remained during the continuance of the Kaffir war of 1877-78; whilst the regiment was under the command of Lieut. Col. H. B. Pulleine, it took part in several important engagements, which resulted in clearing the country of the rebels.

2nd BATTALION.

This Battalion was first embodied at Warwick, in 1804, under the command of Lieut. Col. R. Marriott. It existed as a battalion for 10 years; during that short period it served in six brilliant campaigns, under the Duke of Wellington, and by its distinguished bravery earned the following badges:—"Talavera," 1809, "Fuentes D'Onor," 1811, "Salamanca," 1812, "Vittoria," "Pyrenees," "Nivelle," 1813, "Orthes," 1814. In 1813 this Battalion especially distinguished itself at the siege of Burgos,—storming the Trenches in a most gallant manner. It was also engaged in one of the most brilliant and dashing affairs of the whole war, when the brigade, under the command of Major General Barnes, carried the heights of Eschalar, although strongly defended by the enemy. In the words of Lord Wellington—"Their attack was the most gallant and the finest thing I ever witnessed." The Battalion had been so weakened by active service that it was disembodied at the conclusion of Peace in 1814.

After a lapse of nearly 44 years, it was decided in 1858 to form another 2nd Battalion, which has followed worthily in the steps of its predecessor. In 1860 it proceeded to the Island of Mauritius, and after a stay of a little more than five years, to Burmah, and from thence to India. In 1873 it returned to England, after an absence of 13 years. In 1878 it was ordered to the Cape of Good Hope, to form part of the reinforcements for Sir Bartle Frere, Governor and Commander-in-Chief of the Colony. In March of the same year, whilst under the command of Lieut. Col. Degacher, it was the first to make the attack in a general engagement, and was specially complimented by the General in command for the "admirable manner" in which it was executed, and this high character it more than maintained to the conclusion of the Kaffir war.

THE DISASTER AT ISANDHLWANA.

In consequence of the threatening attitude of Cetewayo, King of the Zulus, the 1st Battalion, under Lieut. Col. H. B. Pulleine, and the 2nd Battalion, under Lieut. Col. Degacher, embarked for Natal, to reinforce Lord Chelmsford. On the declaration of war, they formed part of the invading army. In January, 1879, Lord Chelmsford advanced with the greater part of his column to meet the enemy, leaving a force consisting principally of the 1st Battalion and 2nd Battalion of the 24th Regiment, under the command of Colonel Pulleine, who relinquished his command to Colonel Durnford, R.E., on his arrival with a small reinforcement from Rorke's Drift. The Zulus were seen advancing in immense numbers over the hills, forming a vast semi-circle, some 20,000 strong. In spite of the havoc caused by Artillery and the Martini-Henry, the enemy pushed on. Rank after rank fell before our fire, but nothing seemed to daunt them. In half an hour they had penetrated the camp. The men of the 24th fought like heroes, but were overwhelmed and massacred by the enemy, who gave no quarter. Only some nine escaped to describe this terrible disaster. When no chance of escape remained, Lieut. and Adjutant Melvill, together with Lieut. Coghill, were ordered to save the colours. After desperate fighting they succeeded, but at the sacrifice of their lives.

But their body takes its honour or dishonour from the soul, | Yet, let no name of any name be set above the rest,
And their names are writ in fire upon our Nation's long head roll, | Where all were braver than the brave, each better than the best.

THE DEFENCE OF RORKE'S DRIFT.

The enemy, flushed with victory, advanced upon Rorke's Drift, which was garrisoned by about 100 men, under the command of Lieut. Chard, R.E., and Lieut. Bromhead, B Co., 2/24 Regt. They hurriedly entrenched themselves, and made temporary fortifications of bags of "mealies" and biscuit boxes. For twelve hours they withstood the desperate attacks of the enemy, who charged again and again. The engagement lasted all night. The Zulus retreated at daybreak, after having suffered enormous loss.

Left: *A commemorative scroll bearing the long list of names of soldiers from the 1st and 2nd Battalions, 24th (2nd Warwickshire) Regiment, who lost their lives on the field of honour at Isandhlwana.*

pose for it.

On the 2nd October *The Eagle* docked at Spithead and the 1st Bn, 24th Regt, brought their colour home. Surgeon-Major Reynolds and Gunner Arthur Howard were also aboard, as was Major Chard, who was given a hero's welcome. A message from the Queen was awaiting him, inviting him to Balmoral. While he was there he gave her a verbal account of the defence, and she asked him to prepare for her an extended written version of his original report. The Queen liked his modest manner, and it was the first of many visits. Major Bromhead was also invited but he missed the engagement.

While the 1st Bn was stationed at Gosport in 1880, Queen Victoria requested to see the colour that had been recovered from the Buffalo river. It was taken to Osborne House on the Isle of Wight, where she placed a silver wreath of immortelles about the crown, in memory of the two men who tried to save it, and of the noble defence of Rorke's Drift. Both the colour and the wreath were laid up in the Regimental Chapel at Brecon Cathedral in

When Queen Victoria inspected the colour of the 1st Battalion she placed a small wreath of silver immortelles about the crown. The wreath is now kept in a case at Brecon Cathedral.

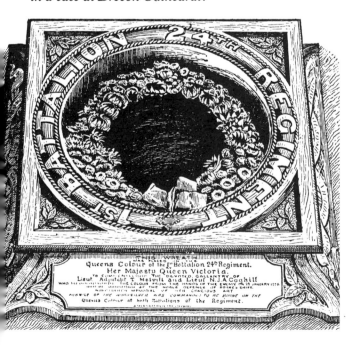

1933, where they are still on display.

The last nine survivors of the Rorke's Drift garrison sent a wreath to the funeral of John Fielding in 1932. Their names were: Thomas Buckley, George Deacon, Caleb Woods, John Jobbins (died 1934), Alfred Saxty (died 1936), Henry Martin (died 1937), William Cooper and George Orchard (both died after 1937) and Frank Bourne. A tenth name – Peter Caine – also appeared on the wreath, but he was at the general depot from October 1878 until April 1879, and therefore could not have been at the defence. At least four men of the garrison are known to have suffered mental illness, and many struggled with great hardship in later life.

In 1965 an American, Cy Endfield, directed the film 'Zulu', which did much to bring the defence of Rorke's Drift to the attention of the general public. William Jones's daughter, Elizabeth, who was in her eighties, travelled around cinemas in Manchester and Yorkshire to open the film. Donald Morris – another American – published 'The Washing of the Spears', which many Zulu War enthusiasts consider the most notable book on the subject. A steady flow of books and pamphlets concerning the war came out at the time of the centenary.

On Sunday, 21st January 1979, to celebrate the centenary of the battle, several corps of the Royal Engineers assembled at the grave of John Chard, with some of his family descendants. The Chief Royal Engineer laid a wreath on behalf of the Corps, and after the ceremony Chard's great-nephew, presented the Corps with a marble bust of Chard and the sword that he had carried during the defence. The curator of Taunton Museum had prepared a display of items connected with Rorke's Drift, and among the relics was a sword of honour that had been presented to Chard by the people of Plymouth. On the same day The Royal Corps of Transport at Aldershot (into which part of the Army Service Corps has amalgamated) arranged a wreath-laying ceremony at the grave of James Dalton in South Africa.

The 24th Regt became The South Wales Borderers in 1881. It amalgamated with The Welsh Regt (41st Foot) in 1969, to become The Royal Regt of Wales 24th/41st Foot. They organised a concert and commemorative service at Brecon in January 1979, and sixty descendants of the Victoria Cross winners attended. Ann Jones (Miss United Kingdom), whose great-grandfather Evan Jones had been one of the defenders, took part in the celebra-

While the defence of Rorke's Drift was taking place the soldiers in the garrison at Helpmakaar manned the ramparts confused and restless. They saw themselves as the only obstacle to a Zulu invasion of Natal.

tions with the 1st Bn which was serving in Armagh. A wreath was layed on the memorials at Isandhlwana and Rorke's Drift on behalf of the Regiment, at about the same time as the commemorative service was taking place in Brecon. And a pilgrimage to South Africa was also arranged. On the 24th May 1979 the Colonel of the Regiment personally laid wreaths on both memorials.

There is a Zulu War room at the Regimental Museum in Brecon, and among the exhibits is a Bible that Harry Hook had picked up on the battlefield at Isandhlwana, and the Zulu slug that wounded Cpl Lyons. After it was extracted he had it mounted on a chain, and it was presented to the museum after his death on the 1st May 1903. There is a display case devoted to Rorke's Drift at The Royal Corps of Transport Museum at Aldershot, and there are items of interest at The National Army Museum and The Imperial War Museum in London.

The defence of Rorke's Drift had no significant effect on the outcome of the war. Some aspects of the Anglo-Zulu War are shrouded in controversy to this day, and the political and personal motives of prominent individuals connected with the conflict are questionable. But no such issues surround the ordinary men who took part in the events at Rorke's Drift. The Zulu warriors were there to gain military honour by repulsing an invader. They followed the fighting traditions of their forefathers, and beat a drum of resistance that is still being heard in southern Africa today. And the British soldiers – well, 'Theirs not to reason why': They were guardians of the empire – a job for which they received a shilling a day in wages. On the 22nd January 1879, while men in Britain were farming the land, or working factory machinery to earn their living – these men fought the Zulu!

CHAPTER NINE:
Notes and Tributes

*'Great Occasions do not make heroes or cowards;
they simply unveil them to the eyes of men.'*
Bishop Westcott

When I first began this work my intention was to get as close to the facts as I possibly could, and the notes in this chapter are intended simply to express my own opinions and explain my conclusions of what happened at Rorke's Drift, not to criticise previous writers on the subject, although it has been necessary to quote some works in order to show why I needed to explain some of my points in the first place.

I always find it helpful to discover which aspects of a subject interests people the most, so while researching the book I occasionally brought up the subject of the Zulu War in conversations, of course highlighting the events at Rorke's Drift. On more than one occasion I was asked what happened to the men when they returned to civilian life. I had a basic knowledge of the lives of the Victoria Cross winners, but I had to often admit that I didn't know a great amount about any of them.

I was aware that William Jones had lived in desti-

Frank Bourne, Alfred Saxty, William Cooper, John Jobbins and Caleb Woods were the original survivors who took part in this re-enactment of the defence of Rorke's Drift for Military Tattoo held at Gateshead in July 1934.

tution for most of his life outside the army, and it had added a kind of personal touch when I had learned that he was buried in the cemetery where many of my own paternal ancestors are laid to rest. So I decided that a chapter of quite detailed biographies about the men who played the most prominent part in the action would add extra interest to the reader, especially if like myself, the soldier had a connection with their own region. The story of Pte Jones's struggle had greatly saddened me, and the tragic circumstances of the death of Pte Robert Jones, who was the second man I chose to research, had me considering whether or not I should drop the biographies idea. But I continued, eventually with much enthusiasm, and the result, I hope, will help to increase our knowledge of Britain's recognised heroes.

In a Britain where people are no longer used to hearing the call to arms, and are less willing to accept discipline than they were in Victorian times, it was proved by the operations in the South Atlantic in 1982 that the modern British soldier is still capable of going out to fight a war with the same comradeship and determination as his predecessor did over a hundred years before. The men I have chosen to record represent my tribute to all those who fought at Rorke's Drift, at the same time remembering the Zulu warriors who fought equally well, but whose names have long been forgotten.

GEORGE SMITH was born at Docking, Norfolk, on 8th January 1845. He was at college in Canterbury before going to South Africa as a Lay Missionary in 1870. He was ordained Deacon in 1871, and Priest in 1872. He was appointed to the Estcourt and Weston Missions in Natal, where he earned the reputation of a hard-working man.

For his part in the defence of Rorke's Drift his behaviour won him the praise of several men when they mentioned him in their reports about the action. He was then commissioned as Chaplain To The Forces on 1st January 1880, and he received the Zulu War medal with clasp.

After a period at home, he was in north-east Africa from 1882 until 1887. He was present at the battle of Tel-el-Kebir, Egypt, under Lord Wolseley, on 13th September 1882, for which he received the Queen's Medal for Egypt and the Khedives Bronze Star. He was present at the battle against the Dervishes at El Teb, Sudan, in 1884, and at Ginnis during the Nile Expedition, for which he was awar-

The Rev George 'Daddy' Smith. Following the defense of Rorke's Drift he was appointed Chaplain to the Forces and went on to serve in Egypt and the Sudan.

ded a clasp. His great bushy beard earned him the nickname 'Daddy' Smith.

He was Chaplain at various stations in Britain and abroad between 1887 and his retirement in 1905. This included a spell at Fulwood Barracks near Preston from 1899 until 1903, and it was here that he eventually settled. He took a room at Sumner's Hotel, Fulwood, where he lived a quiet batchelor's life both as Chaplain, and in retirement.

He became ill with bronchial trouble, and after being confined to his room for six months, he died some time during the night of 26th/27th November 1918. His funeral was a small military parade, and among the floral tributes was one from the officers of the 24th Regt, 'In Memory Of Rorke's Drift'. He was buried in Preston Cemetery, and a stone monument was erected to the memory of one of the heroes of Rorkes Drift, 'who was a brave and modest Christian gentleman'.

On his retirement, the Rev Smith settled in Preston and was buried in the Church of England plot of the town's New Hall Lane cemetery.

WALTER ALPHONSUS DUNNE was born on 10th February 1853, in Cork, and **LOUIS ALEXANDER BYRNE** was also born in Ireland in 1857. His father Richard became a prominent ship-owner and merchant after the family had moved to Wales. Dunne served with the Commissariat Department in Dublin from 1873 until 1877, before being posted to South Africa.

For their conduct at Rorke's Drift, Walter Dunne and Louis Byrne were mentioned in despatches. Byrne's name appears on the monument at Rorke's Drift, and his brother Alfred collected his effects. Dunne took part in the re-invasion as a Deputy Commissary.

He was again involved in a siege during the Transvaal war of 1880-81, and like Chaplain Smith, he was present at the battle of Tel-el-Kebir in 1882, and took part in the campaign against the Dervishes. He completed most of his service on the African

Below: Walter Dunne was the senior Commissariat Officer at Rorke's Drift. He and his fellow officers played a vital part in the organisation and construction of the barricade. He served the British Army for 35 distinguished years.

Above: Louis Byrne was twenty-two years old when he was killed in action at Rorke's Drift. For some reason he was buried just outside the little cemetery, but his name appears on the monument.

Continent and was transferred to the Army Service Corps as a Lieutenant-Colonel in 1888. He was appointed CB in 1896, and was promoted to Colonel in 1897. After thirty-five distinguished years, he retired from the service in Gibraltar in February 1908. He died at The English Nursing Home in Rome on 2nd July 1908.

JAMES LANGLEY DALTON was born in the parish of St Andrews, London. He left his job as a stationer's lad to enlist into the 85th Regt, at Victoria, London, on 20th November 1849. He gave his age as 17 years 11 months, but he was probably younger.

He served his first six months in Ireland, and was then in England, before being posted to Mauritius in 1853. Dalton was a good soldier, and he left the island three years later as a Sergeant. He then went to the Cape to take part in the 8th Frontier War. He was back in England when he was transferred to the Commissariat Staff Corps in 1862, becoming a Colour-Sergeant in June of the following year. He attended the School of Musketry at Hythe in Kent, and was stationed in Aldershot until 1867, becoming a clerk and Master Sergeant. His final tour of overseas duty was in Canada from 1868 until 1871, and while he was there he was transferred to the Army Service Corps, eventually becoming a 1st Class SSGT. He took his discharge in London on 20th November 1871, and was awarded the Long Service Good Conduct Medal.

Below: *James Dalton's excellent initiative and gallantry at Rorke's Drift earned him the praise of several fellow defenders in their subsequent reports on the action.*

Above: *The memorial at the grave of James Langley Dalton VC, at the Russell Road cemetery, Port Elizabeth. In recent years the cemetery has been plagued by vandals.*

He went to South Africa, and volunteered for the appointment of Acting Assistant Commissary on 13th December 1877, when troops were being prepared for the 9th Frontier War. For his conduct at Rorke's Drift, he was mentioned in despatches, and was awarded the Victoria Cross. He was on sick leave for six months after the defence. He then became senior Commissariat Officer at Fort Napier, where he received his medal from General Gifford at a special parade in November 1879. He was given a permanent commission as Sub-Assistant Commissary, and was promoted to Assistant Commissary three weeks later. He was also awarded the South Africa Medal of 1877, with bars for service in 1878 and 1879. He sailed for England in February 1880. It is believed that he served as a volunteer in Egypt, before returning to South Africa in 1884 to try his hand at gold mining in the Transvaal.

He went to stay with his old friend, ex-Sgt John Sherwood Williams, at the Grosvenor Hotel, Port Elizabeth, just before Christmas 1886. After spending the 7th January 1887 in bed, he died suddenly during the night. He was given a quiet civilian burial in the Russell Road Roman Catholic Cemetery, and a memorial was erected in memory of a defender of Rorke's Drift, by Sgt Williams and friends of Natal.

His medals came up for auction at Spink & Son, on 26th September 1986. They had been part of the estate of the late David Spink, who had bought the Victoria Cross in 1949. The Royal Corps of Transport Medal Trust purchased the medal set for £62,000.

FRANCIS ATTWOOD was awarded the silver medal for Distinguished Conduct, and was promoted to Sergeant. He received the medal at the same parade as Dalton in November 1879.

On his return to England, Francis Attwood married, and served with the Commissariat and Transport Corps at Plymouth. He died suddenly at his home there, on 20th February 1884, aged 38. His medals are on display at The Royal Corps of Transport Museum.

Right: *The Distinguished Conduct Medal and South Africa Medal awarded to Cpl Attwood, now in the Royal Corps of Transport Museum.*
Below: *Cpl Francis Attwood, DCM, was posted in the storehouse during the attack, where he shot down several Zulus who were trying to fire the roof.*

JAMES HENRY REYNOLDS was born on 3rd February 1844, at the inland sea port of Dun Laoghaire, County Dublin, which at the time was called Kingstown. He was the son of Laurence Reynolds JP, of Dalyston House, Granard, County Longford. He was educated at Castle Knock and Trinity College, Dublin, where he graduated BA MB ChB in 1867.

On 31st March 1868 he entered the Medical Staff Corps as an Assistant Surgeon, and joined the 36th (Hereford) Regt as Medical Officer on 24th March 1869. For his efficient service during an outbreak of cholera in the regiment while it was in India, he received a commendation from the Commander-in-Chief, General Lord Sandhurst, and was promoted to Surgeon in 1873.

He served throughout the Zulu War, and for his conduct at Rorke's Drift, he was mentioned in despatches, and was awarded the Victoria Cross. He received his medal from Lord Wolseley during a special parade at St Paul's, Zululand, on 16th July

James Reynolds was promoted to Surgeon-Major after the defence. He died in London in 1932 and was buried in St Mary's cemetery, where several VC recipients are laid to rest.

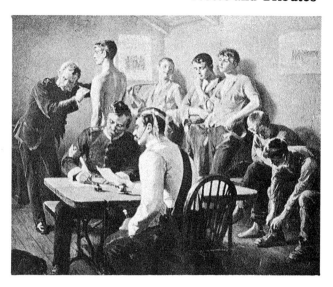

Late Victorian medical attention 1884-98. A typical scene of the day. A corporal of the Medical Staff Corps looks on as the army doctor examines soldiers.

1879. He was given special promotion to Surgeon-Major, dated 23rd January 1879, and was elected honorary Fellow of the Royal College of Physicians of Ireland; and made honorary Doctor of Law, Dublin. He was awarded a gold medal by the British Medical Association in July 1879.

He married his wife Elizabeth in 1880. He was a keen all-round sportsman, and was a member of the Army and Navy Club from 1890 until his death. He was promoted to Lieutenant-Colonel in 1887, and to Brigade-Surgeon Lieutenant-Colonel in 1892. He retired in 1896, and became senior medical officer at the Royal Army Clothing Factory at Pimlico in London. On 9th November 1929, he and John Williams VC were among the guests of honour at a VCs' dinner given by the Prince of Wales in the House of Lords.

He died at the Empire Nursing Home, Victoria, London, on 4th March 1932, and is buried in the north-east corner of Kensal Green Roman Catholic Cemetery, Harrow Road, London. Grave number is 504. A black stone cross marks the spot.

On the day after the battle Doctor Reynolds stated: 'I am glad to say that the men of AHC behaved splendidly.' For his conduct at Rorke's Drift, 2nd Cpl Michael McMahon AHC was mentioned in despatches, and on the 15th January 1880 he was recommended for the Distinguished Conduct Medal. But this was cancelled two weeks later for going absent without leave and stealing certain items.

GONVILLE BROMHEAD was born at Versailles in France, on 29th August 1845. He was the third son of Edmund de Gonville Bromhead, 3rd Baronet. He was a landowner, who had been a Lieutenant at Waterloo, and had retired from the army as a Major. The family home was at Thurlby Hall, Newark-on-Trent, Lincolnshire, and he was educated at Magnus Grammar School there. He enjoyed sports, and was a good left-hand medium bowler in their successful cricket eleven.

He entered the 24th Regt as an Ensign by purchase, on 20th April 1867. He was tutored at Croydon, where he was popular among his fellow soldiers, and was always ready to offer help to new recruits. While he was there he was the champion at boxing, wrestling and singlestick. He was 5 ft 10 inches tall, and carried a strong broad frame. He was promoted by selection to Lieutenant, on 28th October 1871.

He served in the 9th Frontier War, and for his conduct at Rorke's Drift he was mentioned in despatches and was awarded the Victoria Cross. He was also promoted to Captain, and Brevet-Major dated 23rd January 1879. Just before the re-invasion he moved to Utrecht in the Transvaal, where he received his medal from Lord Wolseley on 22nd August 1879. He also received a South Africa medal with clasp (1877-78-79). He was then posted to Gibraltar.

On 25th June 1880, at a special banquet at Lincoln Masonic Hall, he was presented with an illuminated address and a jewelled dress sword on behalf of the people of Lincoln. In his acceptance speech he mentioned Major Chard, Surgeon-Major Reynolds, Mr Dalton, Mr Dunne, and Rev Smith. The tenants of Thurlby Hall gave him a revolver and Queen Victoria presented him with a picture of herself.

He was posted to the East Indies until March 1881 and on his return home, in 1882, he spent two months at the Hythe School of Musketry, where he gained a First Class Extra certificate. He then joined the South Wales Borderers at Secunderabad in India. He was promoted to Major on 4th April 1883, and served in the Burmese Expedition 1886-88. (Medal with clasps 'Burma 1885-87 & Burma 1887-89'). He then moved back to the East Indies.

He never married, and he died of enteric (typhoid) fever, at Camp Dabhaura, Allahabad, India, on 9th February 1891. His awards and mementos were left to his brother Charles, and his

Major Gonville Bromhead was the only officer of the 24th Regt present at the battle for Rorke's Drift. Upon his return to England he finally attended upon Queen Victoria when this photograph was taken.

Victoria Cross was presented to the Regimental Museum in 1973. His name is inscribed on the colour-pole of the 24th Regiment, and his portrait and uniform can be seen on display in the old Magnus Grammar School building, which is now Newark's Appletongate Museum.

Right: *After the Zulu War, Gonville Bromhead served in Gibraltar, the East Indies and England before being posted to India. Following further service in Burma and the East Indies, he died in India in 1891.*

Below: *A contemporary view of the old Magnus Grammar School at Newark. It was here that Bromhead was educated and the building now houses the Appletongate Museum which contains his uniform.*

THE NATAL MOUNTED POLICE.

The first man was enrolled into the police on 12th March 1874. **SYDNEY H. HUNTER** was born in September 1856, and **HENRY LUGG** at Okehampton in Devon in 1859. Lugg had come out from England with Edward and Henry Camp whose sister, Mary, Lugg was courting. They all joined the police at Pietermaritzburg, on 22nd May 1878. **ROBERT S. GREEN** had also enrolled in the capital on 31st August 1877. His father worked in Cape Town, and his brother Harold was also in the police.

Hunter's name appears on the monument at Rorke's Drift, and Green was discharged on 30th April 1881. Harry Lugg was sent to Greys Hospital in Pietermaritzburg with an attack of rheumatic fever, and was discharged as physically infirm for further service on 28th February 1879. Later he became District Adjutant to the Natal Volunteers and magistrate of Umsinga.

Right: *The information shown on this death certificate is all that is known about Sydney Hunter, the mounted policeman killed at Rorke's Drift.*

Above: *The Natal Mounted Police on their way to the front. Under Major John Dartnell, a veteran of the Indian Mutiny, they were a well-trained unit.*

Right: *This section taken from the enlistment register of the Natal Mounted Police at the time of the Zulu War, gives details about R. Green and his brother.*

NAME (in full).			Sydney Hunt...
1	2	3	4
BIRTH-PLACE.	NAMES OF PARENTS.	AGE.	Married or Unmarried, Widower or Widow.
notknown	notknown	22½	Unmarried

23

Name	Date and place of enlistment	...
Green Robt.	P.M.Burg 31. Aug. 1877	
Green Harold	P.M. Burg. 14th March 1878	

EATH NOTICE.

|9.i

	RESIDENCE.				OCCUPATION
	Hilpmakaar				*mounted Policem*

house, died.	7 NAMES OF CHILDREN.	If minors, when born.	8 Whether left any will.	9 PROPERTY LEFT. (Kind and Value.)
			none	*Saddlery Ketg,* *about £ 10*
	J. M. MacLaren (signature)			

Relatives   *Remarks*

African Glass Works.
Cape Town

discharged 20 apl 1881.

as Robt Green
sup 23

Discharged 28th April 1884

P. M. Burg, 2nd August, 1884.

To

Colonel Mitchel.
Colonial Secretary
P. M. Burg.

Honored Sir

I venture to address your Honor once
more for the purpose of getting your valuable
assistance in obtaining some employment for me
in the Government service as you will see by the
attached letter from Mr. Hunter, Genl. Manager, N.G.Ry
that there is not the slightest chance to get employed
on the Railway at the present time.
I would regard it as an act of great favor, if you
would kindly recommend me to the Superintendent
of the Govt. Prisons to enable me to get employed
as turnkey or anything else in that branch of the
service. in fact any situation in any other Dept. of
the Govt. service would suite me, no matter how
small the salary will be.
Trusting you will be good enough to give this
application your favorable consideration

I remain
Honored Sir
very respectfully
Your obedient servant
F. C. Schiess
G. Post Master
P. M. Burg.

CORPORAL SCHIESS preferred to be called Friedrich, but his real names were Ferdnand Christian.

He was born at Bergedorf, Berne, in Switzerland, on 7th April 1856. He was brought up in an orphanage, and at the age of fifteen he served on the side of France in the Franco-Prussian War. He then went to South Africa.

For his conduct at Rorke's Drift he was mentioned in despatches, and became the first man serving with South African forces, under British command, to be awarded the Victoria Cross. Wearing the green uniform of Lonsdale's Horse, he received the medal from Lord Wolseley, at a parade of the troops in the market square in Pietermaritzburg, on 3rd February 1880. Schiess was a shy man and he soon took the medal off. But he enjoyed the rest of the day being driven round the town in an open carriage.

At that time he was employed in the telegraph office at Durban. But by 1884 he had fallen on hard times, and was desperately applying for government work in Pietermaritzburg. But he was unsuccessful. He was offered a passage to England aboard the troop-ship *Serapis*, the cost of his rations being paid for by a public fund. But he was too ill to survive such a trip, and he died on 14th December 1884. He was buried at sea off the coast of Angola, West Africa.

Schiess could speak and write good English, and it was only discovered that he was a Swiss national after his death. Even though he was destitute he did not part with his Victoria Cross. It was brought to England, and after spending some years locked away in a drawer at the War Office, it is now in the display at The National Army Museum, London.

A strange note appears at the back of a page in Capt Penn-Symons's report at Brecon. It states: 'I saw Corp. Schiess in Nov. 1891, in Allahabad, India. He had been working in a jeweller's shop, and was just going to Australia. Being afraid to lose his Victoria Cross, he has sent it on ahead by registered post to his destination.'

Left: *This application for employment was written by Corporal Schiess shortly before his death. The reply was: 'Inform applicant that there is very little chance for him.' One of the heroes who had saved South Africa from: '. . . the darkest cloud of invasion', was unable to gain employment there. He died in utter destitution at the age of 28.*

Above: *Although Corporal Schiess became destitute he retained possession of his Victoria Cross, and when he died on board the* Serapis *the medal was found on his body. It was shipped to England and ended up at the War Office. It has now found a permanent home in the National Army Museum.*

JOHN ROUSE MERRIOTT CHARD was born at Boxhill, near Plymouth, on 21st December 1847. He was the second son of William Chard, who came from Pathe, Othery, in Somerset. He was educated at Plymouth New Grammar School, at Cheltenham College, and passed out of the Royal Military Academy at Woolwich as a Lieutenant in the Royal Engineers on 15th July 1868.

He served for two years at Chatham, three years in Bermuda, and one year in Malta. Then after three more years in southern England, he boarded the *Teuton* at Plymouth on 2nd December 1878 to sail to the Cape. He arrived in Durban on 4th January 1879.

For his conduct at Rorke's Drift he was awarded the Victoria Cross, and was promoted Captain, and Brevet-Major, dated 23rd January 1879. He received the medal from Lord Wolseley, at a parade of the troops at St Paul's, Zululand, on 16th July 1879.

He returned to a hero's welcome. The people of Plymouth presented him with a sword of honour and a gold chronometer watch. And he received an illuminated address from the St George's Lodge of Freemasons in Exeter. John Chard was an unassuming man and a likeable soldier. But he seems to have been a person who took life as it came, with no particular ambition. However, Queen Victoria was fond of him, and he was invited to an audience with her on several occasions.

He served at Devonport, in Cyprus and in India, with postings at home depots in Chatham, Preston and Cardiff in between. He was made substantive Major in 1886, and was promoted to Lieutenant-Colonel on 8th January 1893, while he was in Singapore. On 8th January 1896, he was promoted to Colonel, and appointed commanding Royal Engineer at the sub-district of Perth, Scotland.

He was attacked by cancer of the tongue, and was too ill to go to Balmoral on the Queen's invitation in November 1896. He missed attending the Queen's jubilee celebrations in 1897. But on 11th July he received a Jubilee Medal from her, and a signed portrait. He went to Edinburgh three times for operations to remove his tongue, and although he was still able to speak, his condition became worse, and he was placed on sick leave from 8th August 1897. He suffered much distress towards the end, and he died at his younger brother Charles's rectory of St John the Baptist, in Hatch Beauchamp, near Taunton, on the evening of 1st November 1897. Being such a travelled man he had never married.

Lt John Chard VC was promoted Brevet-Major and returned to a hero's welcome in England. He received several presentations, including some from Queen Victoria, who invited him to an audience with her on several occasions. He was a handsome and modest man. He suffered a painful death when he was fifty, struck down by cancer of the tongue.

He was buried in the churchyard there with military honours. The Duke of Connaught, who had been with him as a young officer at Woolwich, sent a letter of sympathy, as did Lord Chelmsford. Queen Victoria had shown much concern about him, and had enquired about his condition throughout his illness. She sent a laurel wreath to his funeral with the inscription: 'A mark of admiration and regard for a brave soldier, from his sovereign.' This tribute – and an anonymous wreath bearing the inscription: 'In remembrance of Rorke's Drift, 22nd January 1879 – That day he did his duty' were

Above: *Sir Garnet Wolseley decorates Major Chard at St Paul's, Zululand, on 16 July 1879, when a number of awards were presented, including the VC to Surgeon-Major Reynolds. Fate seems to have placed Chard in command at Rorke's Drift, and by 3 o'clock on 22 January 1879 he was destined to become a national hero.*

placed on the coffin. There were wreaths from Sir Bartle-Frere's widow, Colonel Bourne and the officers of the South Wales Borderers; and Colonel Walter Dunne, A.A.G. York. A marble cross is the memorial to the hero of Rorke's Drift.

A memorial window was placed in Hatch Beauchamp church; there is a memorial to him in Rochester Cathedral; and he is the subject of a bronze bust in the Shire Hall at Taunton – which is a replica of one in The Royal Engineers' Museum, Chatham. His name is inscribed on the colour-pole of the 24th Regt, and on the Roll of Honour, Big

Above: *'In Memoriam – Colonel J.R.M. Chard VC, RE, died 1st Nov. 1879'. The window in Hatch Beauchamp Church is one of the memorials that have been erected in honour of his name.*

Classical, Cheltenham College. There is still a John Chard decoration awarded to the South African Defence Force.

The whereabouts of his original Victoria Cross are not known, but his family has a replica.

FRANK BOURNE was born in the village of Balcombe, near Crawley in Sussex, on 27th April 1854. He was the youngest of eight sons in a farming family. He enlisted against his father's wishes, at Reigate, on 18th December 1872. He was 5 feet 6 inches tall, with a dark complexion, grey eyes and brown hair.

He was promoted to Corporal on 11th April 1875 and, shortly after arriving in South Africa, he was promoted three times in as many weeks – finally becoming Colour-Sergeant on 27th April 1878. He served in the Frontier War, and for his conduct at Rorke's Drift he was mentioned in despatches, and in July 1879, he was awarded the Distinguished Conduct Medal, with an annuity of ten pounds. He was also offered a commission, but he did not, at that time, have the finance needed to follow the life of an officer.

He married his wife Eliza in 1882, and had five children. He served in Gibraltar, India and Burma, eventually becoming a Honorary Lieutenant and Quartermaster in 1890. He was then appointed Adjutant at the Hythe School of Musketry until his retirement in 1907. He worked for the Society of Miniature Rifle Clubs in London, and was Adjutant at the Dublin school of Musketry during the Great War. He was promoted to Lieutenant-Colonel, and was awarded the OBE for his services.

The Northern Command Military Tattoo, which was held in Gateshead in 1934, included a sketch acting out the defence. Lt-Col Bourne appeared in the arena with Sgt Saxty and Ptes William Cooper, John Jobbins and Caleb Woods, who were also survivors of the battle. The verse taken from Macauley's *Lays of Ancient Rome*, which introduces the fourth chapter of this book, was used to present the programme of the tattoo. And Bourne remembered it. On 20th December 1936, he spoke on BBC radio about his experiences in South Africa, and recited this verse to end the programme. He replied personally to the hundreds of letters he received afterwards.

The anniversary of the battle was always celebrated by a family dinner at his home, and for the rest of his life he was proud of the way the men of 'B' Company had behaved on that fateful day. He died on 8th May 1945, possibly the last survivor of the Rorke's Drift garrison, and is buried at Elmers End, Kent.

Right: *Col-Sgt Frank Bourne DCM, was the senior NCO during the defence of Rorke's Drift. He rose to the rank of Lieutenant-Colonel and was awarded the OBE during his long and distinguished career. When he died in Beckenham at the grand old age of 91, he was the last known survivor of the Rorke's Drift garrison.*

Below: *Although no official Rorke's Drift commemoration society came into being, many of the surviving defenders kept in touch. This is the front cover of the programme for the Gateshead Military Tattoo in 1934, where five survivors appeared in the arena to act out the progressive stages of the battle.*

ALFRED HENRY HOOK, or 'Harry' as he preferred to be called, was born at Alney, Churcham, near Gloucester, on 6th August 1850. His father was a farmer. He served in the Monmouth Militia for five years, whilst living in Drybridge Street, Monmouth. He is believed to have married and had a daughter before enlisting at Monmouth on 13th March 1877.

He went with his Battalion to South Africa, and took part in the Frontier War. For his conduct at Rorke's Drift he was mentioned in despatches, and was awarded the Victoria Cross. He was stationed at Rorke's Drift throughout the Zulu War, and at a special parade there on 3rd August, he became one of the very few people to be decorated with the Victoria Cross at the place where he had earned it. Lord Wolseley conducted the ceremony. He also received a Medal for South Africa (clasp 1877-8-9), and a number of Good Conduct and Marksmanship badges. He was then posted to Gibraltar.

He bought himself out of the army for eighteen pounds, on 25th June 1880. When he got home he

Left: *Alfred Henry Hook of the 24th Regt was presented with his VC at Rorke's Drift in August 1879. A year later he bought himself out of the army and moved to London.*

Below: *Seven members of the 24th Regt, all holders of the VC, gather for a reunion. Of these, six fought in the Zulu War of 1879. Top row, left to right – Robert Jones, 'Harry' Hook, William Jones. Front row – David Bell (awarded VC in 1867), Colonel Edward Browne, Frederick Hitch and John Williams (Fielding).*

VICTORIA CROSS HEROES PRESENT AT THE CEREMONY.

found that his wife (who may have been only his common-law wife) had sold his property and had remarried because she thought that he had been killed. He moved to Sydenham Hill, London, and at Christmas 1881 he began working for the British museum, eventually becoming a cloakroom attendant in the reading room. He married his wife Ada at Islington in 1897, and lived in Pimlico. He served for twenty years as a Sergeant in the 1st Volunteer Bn of the Royal Fusiliers, and was a well respected member of The Loyal St James Lodge of Oddfellows.

He began to suffer ill-health, and retired on the last day of 1904. He returned to his native county to see if the air would help to combat his condition, and he was welcomed as a popular hero. His Victoria Cross annuity was due to increase to fifty pounds on 1st April 1905, but he did not live to benefit. He died of pulmonary tuberculosis on the morning of 12th March 1905, at 2 Osborne Villas, Roseberry Avenue, Gloucester, leaving his wife and two young daughters. A print of the famous painting 'The Defence of Rorke's Drift' by Alphonse De Neuville, which is reproduced on the cover of this book, was hanging by his head. He had been known as a quiet man who would only talk about the defence in private conversation.

His funeral was a striking spectacle. John Fielding VC sent a message of sympathy, and Fred Hitch attended with his son who, as a Corporal in the South Wales Borderers, was one of the bearers. Twenty-three regiments were represented in all. He was buried with full military honours at Churcham. Eighteen months later a marble cross was unveiled over his grave. 'Erected by admiring civilians and local Regiments, in memory of his heroic share in the defence of Rorke's Drift, Natal, 1879.' His Victoria Cross is now with the Regimental Museum, and there is also a memorial in Brecon Cathedral.

Left: *Henry Hook in the uniform of a sergeant in the 1st Volunteer Bn, the Royal Fusiliers with whom he served as a weapons instructor.*

Below: *Henry Hook's funeral cortège, escorted by representatives from twenty-three regiments, moves through Gloucester on the 18 March 1905.*

Sgt Hook's coffin is carried past the guard of honour by the door of Churcham church on the outskirts of Gloucester.

On 22 September 1906, Col Curll of the South Wales Borderers prepares to unveil the memorial over Henry Hook's grave.

FREDERICK HITCH was born in New Southgate, which until 1881 was a borough of Edmonton, Middlesex. He had been a building labourer, and when he attested at Westminster Police Court on 7th March 1877, he could not sign his name on the papers, and his monument records the 2nd November 1856 as the date of his birth. He was 5 feet 9 inches tall, with a fresh complexion, hazel eyes and brown hair.

He took part in the Frontier War, and for his conduct at Rorke's Drift he was awarded the Victoria Cross. After the defence he travelled by ambulance wagon to Durban, and from there was invalided home aboard the *Tamar*. Queen Victoria decorated him personally at Netley Military Hospital, Southampton, on 12th August 1879. A medical board found that his arm had been permanently disabled, and he was invalided from the army on 25th August 1879. He received a medal for South Africa (clasp 1877-8-9).

He went to live in Southgate, where he married his wife Emma in July 1880, and began working for the Corps of Commissionaires, at the Imperial Institute. Cecil Rhodes visited him to congratulate him on his bravery. While he was working at the Royal United Services Institute, Whitehall in 1901, a thief cut his medal from his coat. A replacement was ordered by King Edward VII, which was presented to him in 1908. Some years later one of his sons had to bid £85 at a public auction to buy back the original medal that had been stolen.

He owned a horse-cab and two horses, but when the age of the automobile began to make its mark, he went to work as a taxi-driver for the General Motor Cab Company. After his wife died he lived quietly for the last seven years of his life, in lodgings at 62 Cranbrook Road, Chiswick. Whilst on strike from his job, he died suddenly of pleuro-pneumonia and heart-failure, on the evening of 6th January 1913. He was aged 56 years, and left six grown-up children.

John Fielding VC and Frank Bourne DCM attended his funeral, along with more than a thousand London cabbies. He was buried with full military honours in Chiswick Old Cemetery. A memorial was erected by voluntary subscription, to commemorate his heroic action at Rorke's Drift Among the subscribers was a relative of Col Chard. His Victoria Cross was sold in 1929 and is now with the Regimental museum.

Left: *Pte Frederick Hitch VC, a twenty-two year old North Londoner, was dangerously wounded at Rorke's Drift, and was invalided to Netley Military Hospital, where Queen Victoria presented him with the Victoria Cross.*

Below: *Fred Hitch with his Martini-Henry rifle. His shattered shoulder joint ended his army career, and he returned to London. He worked as a member of the Corps of Commissionaires until acquiring his own horse-cab. He was employed as a London cab-driver when he died suddenly in 1913.*

RETREAT TO HELPMAKAAR. In his 1905 report Pte Hook says: 'Lt Chard rushed up from the river, and saw Lt Bromhead. Orders were given to strike camp and make ready to go, and we actually loaded up two wagons. Then Mr Dalton came up . . .'

Rev Smith states that: 'A praiseworthy effort was made to remove the worst cases in hospital to a place of safety. Two wagons were brought up after some delay, and the patients were being brought out, when it was found that the Zulus were too close . . .'

These statements contradict Chard. In both of his reports he says that the men had already started the barricade when he arrived from the river. Both Bourne and Dunne mention the wagons being brought up to be included in the barricade, but make no reference to their being used in an attempt to evacuate the wounded. In my opinion none was made.

I believe that, when the wagons were being brought up to the barricade, it coincided with the time when the ambulatory patients were leaving the hospital to take their places at the wall. And Rev Smith, who was still on the Oscarberg when the decisions were made, confused this with an effort to remove the sick. And Hook, who would have been occupied with his work within the hospital, mistook the utilisation of the wagons for an attempt to retreat. He makes no mention of an attempt to retreat in his 1891 report, but he is likely to have read Rev Smith's report in *The Historical Records of the Twenty-Fourth Regiment*, and this may have jogged his memory that he had noticed the wagons being brought up, and had simply drawn the same conclusion as Smith.

The outposts of Helpmakaar were situated ten miles from the border with Zululand on the road from Pietermaritzburg to the Buffalo River at Rorke's Drift. It was little more than a clutter of makeshift buildings and corrugated sheds when Lord Chelmsford established his headquarters here, and two companies of the 1st/24th Regiment were posted to guard the supply depot. Luckily, the regimental colour of the 1st Battalion was also left behind at Helpmakaar.

LT ADENDORFF is normally ascribed to be the man who informed Lt Chard about the advancing *impi*. In his official account Chard reported that Lt Adendorff: 'who afterwards remained to assist in the defence', informed him 'of the disaster befallen at the Isandula [sic] camp, and that the Zulus were advancing upon Rorke's Drift.' In the same report he also states that when he got to the store he: 'found that a note had been received from the third column, stating that the enemy was advancing in force against our post.'

However, in a longer account he wrote for Queen Victoria a year later – having had time to think – he makes no mention that Adendorff had informed him of the *impi*, but confirms the reference to the note from the third column and its details. There is evidence that Adendorff left the camp at Isandhlwana very early on, and therefore would not have known about the *impi*.

This means that either Bromhead passed the information to Chard by way of his message, or that Chard was unaware of the danger until he got to the store. The reports suggest that Bromhead sent for Chard as soon as Pte Evans brought the news of the disaster, which was before the note from the third column had arrived. Rev Smith states that Bromhead sent for Chard 'to come up and direct the preparations for defence.' If this was so, Bromhead would also have explained to Chard why it was necessary to do so. But as I have said previously, Rev Smith was still on the Oscarberg with Mr Witt when the reports came in, and in both of his accounts Chard says that the messenger arrived: 'asking me to come up at once', with no warning of the *impi*. Which brings me to the conclusion that Chard had no knowledge of the danger until he got to the mission-station.

There has also been doubt that Lt Adendorff took part in the defence. The suspicion arises from the fact that he was arrested in Pietermaritzburg to face a charge of desertion, and also because he was not known to have been positively recalled during the fighting. But the charge of desertion in the face of the enemy is more likely to have been from the camp at Isandhlwana. No trial is known to have taken place.

In his account to Queen Victoria, Chard makes a reference to Adendorff's being in the store. Pte Hook says that the Lieutenant stayed behind. And a Natal Carbineer called J.P. Symons, who was with the column when it relieved the garrison on the morning of 23rd January, makes a reference in his account to having been told of a German who had been posted in the store. This could also have been Adendorff. Both Chard and Symons state that the man to whom they refer, was responsible for shooting a Zulu who was trying to set light to the roof of the store. This would account for his not being remembered much during the battle. Cpl Attwood, who received a DCM, was also posted in the store and he is not mentioned in any of the reports that I have read.

The Carbineer who was with Adendorff when he arrived at the drift (said to have been a Sgt Vane), is quite positively recorded as riding on to Helpmakaar. Several other fugitives are named by the defenders as having retreated to Helpmakaar, but there is no account stating definitely that Adendorff decamped. His name also appears on a roll of defenders that was put together on 3rd February 1879.

I find it impossible to accept that Lt James Adendorff left Rorke's Drift before the Zulu attack and I believe it would be doing him an injustice if I did not include him in the narrative.

THE EXPERIENCES OF COMBAT and how the men at Rorke's Drift felt, are based on a study of the statements made by the defenders, and the stories told to me by my late grandfather, George Hallam, who was with the Lancashire Fusiliers in the trenches at Ypres during the Great War; and my uncle, James Bancroft, who was with the Highland Light Infantry (City of Glasgow Regt) during several campaigns in the Second World War. Same feelings – whoever the enemy!

'AS BLACK AS HELL AND AS THICK AS GRASS', is a favourite quote from the action, so it is important to ascertain who said it.

Donald Morris states in 'The Washing of the Spears', that it was Pte John Wall, 24th Regt, who used the words to warn the post as he returned from the Oscarberg with the two clerics. But neither Rev Smith nor Rev Witt mention either Wall or the quote in their accounts, and he did not return with Dr Reynolds, if he ever did go up the Oscarberg to begin with.

In his book 'Rorke's Drift', Michael Glover states that it was Pte Hitch who said it, as he slid off the roof of the storehouse. But Hitch says nothing of this in his accounts and I cannot find any evidence to connect Hitch with the quote at all.

Trooper Lugg states in his account that: 'A man named Hall of the RMB rode out to see if he could see anything of them, and on going out about 1,000 yards, he could see them just a mile off, as he described it, "as black as hell and as thick as grass".' This report was written soon after the event.

In a letter to the *Natal Witness*, Robert J. Hall confirms that he was asked to reconnoitre over the hill, and on seeing the Zulus galloped back to the house (where Lugg was posted), remarking: 'The Zulus are upon us.' It is not unlikely to suppose that Hall forgot his exact words spoken in a situation of great excitement, with thousands of Zulu warriors on his heels, when writing about it nearly thirty years later.

Trooper Henry Lugg, seated second from the right on the front row, remained in South Africa in a civilian capacity after the Zulu War. Alphonse de Neuville used Lugg's letters as basic information for his painting, which is reproduced on the cover of this book.

WILLIAM WILSON ALLAN was born in February 1844 at St Andrews, Newcastle-upon-Tyne. He enlisted at York on 27th October 1859, and joined the 24th Regt at Aldershot. He was 5 feet 4 inches tall. During his early career he served on Mauritius, and was confined in cells on several occasions. He re-engaged in 1873 and was posted to the Regimental Depot in 1874, eventually becoming a Corporal on 6th July 1877, and being appointed assistant schoolmaster. He returned to his battalion just in time to go to the Cape.

He took part in the Frontier War, being promoted to Lance-Sergeant in May 1878, but on 21st October 1878, he was reverted back to Corporal. He was also awarded a Good Shooting and Distance Judging Prize in the same year. For his conduct at Rorke's Drift he was awarded the Victoria Cross. He was invalided to Netley, but he was serving at Brecon again by November. The Zulu bullet had left his arm partly disabled.

He received his medal from Queen Victoria, in the lobby at Windsor Castle, on 9th December 1879.

For his conduct at Rorke's Drift, Pte William Roy, a red-haired Scotsman from Edinburgh, was mentioned in despatches, and was presented with the Distinguished Conduct Medal at the same ceremony. But a disease had affected his vision and he had been discharged from the army two days previously. Both men also received the Medal for South Africa (clasp 1877-8-9).

Cpl Allan became provisional Sergeant at Colchester on 11th June 1880, and then in 1886 he was appointed Sergeant, Instructor of Musketry, to 'C' Company, 4th Volunteer Bn, South Wales Borderers at Monmouth, where he became a popular and respected man. His eighth child, Jessie, was born there in the same year but she died before she was two.

In February 1890 an influenza epidemic hit the town and Sgt Allan was a victim. He died on the morning of 12th March 1890, at 85 Monnow Road, Monmouth, leaving his wife, Sara-Ann, and seven children, none of whom had reached their teens. The Mayor of Monmouth set up an appeal to help them. Sgt Allan was buried with full military honours in Monmouth cemetery and the occasion created great interest in the town. A stone cross was later placed over his grave by the Volunteer Bn of the South Wales Borderers. His Victoria Cross was sold in June 1906, and is now in the possession of the Regimental museum.

Corporal William Wilson Allan VC was a small man with a tough 'Geordie' character. He received a wound at Rorke's Drift which left his arm partly disabled, but he was serving the regiment again before the end of the year. He was a good marksman, and used his skill to gain an appointment as an Instructor of Musketry in Monmouth. He succumbed to a serious bout of influenza at the age of 46, leaving seven young children.

ALFRED SAXTY was born at Buckland Dinham, near Frome in Somerset, in 1857. He enlisted at Newport on 11th September 1876. He was 5 feet 7 inches tall, with a fresh complexion, blue eyes and light-brown hair.

He was mentioned in despatches for his conduct in the Frontier War, and was promoted from Corporal to Sergeant after the defence of Rorke's Drift, but he was reverted back to Corporal later. He was promoted and demoted several times during his army career. He moved to Gibraltar and then served in India. He married in Madras in December 1885, and his first child was born there. Then after his wife died he re-engaged into the Bedfordshire Regt on the first day of 1888, to complete twenty-one years. He married his second wife, Mary, at Secunderabad, where his second son was born in 1890. His third son was born at Rangoon, which is where he had moved to after transferring into the 2nd Royal Inniskillin Fusiliers, on 30th November 1891. He was discharged at his own request, at Thayetmayo, Burma, on 28th February 1895, and settled in Rangoon. Some time later he returned to Britain.

He was admitted as an in-pensioner at the Royal Military Hospital, Chelsea, on 12th June 1930, and then made his home with friends in Blewitt Street, Newport. Early in 1936 he suffered a stroke and was moved to Woolaston House Infirmary Newport, as a private patient. He died there on 11th July 1936, of myorcarditis and senility, and was buried in the Roman Catholic section of Newport cemetery, with full military honours. Lt-Col Bourne and five other survivors of the Rorke's Drift garrison sent a wreath, although two of the names – Owen and Thomas – may not have actually taken part in the defence. Pte John Lawton, aged eighty-six, who was with Lord Chelmsford's relief column, insisted on walking with the cortège as a mark of respect.

RICHARD SCOLLIN

THE DESCRIPTION OF THE EVENTS WITHIN THE HOSPITAL is based on the points below. The figures tally if it is accepted that Pte Waters was counted as one of the sick, and there is much evidence to suggest this.

Before the news of the Isandhlwana disaster reached Rorke's Drift there were thirty-six patients in the hospital. When Lt Purvis left there were thirty-five, but thirty-six men including Waters.

Pte W. Jones stated in his account that there were twenty-three sick men in the hospital during the struggle and three of these were left behind when he got out. The only three men whom he could have witnessed were Sgt Maxfield and Ptes Beckett and Waters. Thus Pte Waters was counted as a patient in his number of the sick.

In the London Gazette VC citations it states that John Williams and two patients got out of the first hole. In Pte Hook's 1891 account, he says that he retired to a room where there was a number of sick – 'for a few moments I was the only fighting man there. A wounded man of the 24th came to me from another room with a bullet wound in the arm. I tied it up. Then John Williams came in . . .' This was undoubtedly Pvt Waters, who was the only man to receive such a wound in the vicinity of the hospital. In an interview on his return to England, Pte Waters stated: 'I saw Pte Horrigan killed.' For Waters to have witnessed Pte Horrigan's plight he must have been in the vicinity of the first escape hole, and Horrigan must have been one of the two patients who escaped with John Williams. In his account, Rev Smith states that Pte Jenkins was seized and dragged away as he ventured through an escape hole. But Lt Chard makes a reference to Pte Jenkins' fighting close to him. It seems certain that Rev Smith meant Horrigan, both men being from the 1st Bn.

In his 1905 account Hook states: 'In the room where I now was, there were nine sick men, and I

'Lest We Forget': Pte Joseph Williams and Pte William Horrigan hold back the Zulu horde with rifle fire, in a desperate attempt to give John Williams time to cut a hole in the partition. They fought hard, but both men were soon to die at the hands of frenzied warriors. Their names are among those recorded on the monument at Rorke's Drift. Of the two defenders and four patients who were trapped in this room when the Zulus attacked the hospital only John Williams survived.

was alone to look after them for some time. Suddenly in the thick smoke I saw John Williams . . .' Pte Waters was thus one of these nine, as he was already in the room before Williams and his surviving patient entered. This also confirms the VC citation that Hook and Williams had rescued eight patients. Ten patients got through the second escape hole and in his interview Pte Waters said that he and Pte Beckett had not got through the third hole.

Finally, the VC citations state that the Joneses got six patients out through the window, Sgt Maxfield being left behind, and a number of accounts refer to Trooper Hunter being killed as he struggled to get to the entrenchment. Reports state that five corpses had burned in the hospital – Adams, Hayden, Horrigan, Maxfield and the native. And a medical report states that seven patients had been killed during the struggle to escape from the building – add Beckett and Hunter.

JOHN FIELDING was born in Merthyr Road, Abergavenny, on 24th May 1857. He was one of eight children. The family moved to Cwmbran when John was five. He went to work in the Patent Nut and Bolt Factory in 1865, but after being in the Monmouthshire Militia, he enlisted at Monmouth on 22nd May 1877. His father disapproved, so he used the name Williams so as not be traced.

He went with his Battalion to South Africa and took part in the Frontier War. For his conduct at Rorke's Drift he was mentioned in despatches, and was awarded the Victoria Cross. He moved to Gibraltar where he received the medal from Major-General Anderson on the Almeda Parade Ground,

on 1st March 1880. He also received a medal for South Africa (clasp 1877-8-9). The action is said to have turned his hair white overnight.

He was posted to India, and returned home from Secunderabad in October 1883. He was transferred to the army reserve, becoming a sergeant in the 3rd Volunteer Bn, South Wales Borderers. He was discharged from this unit on 22nd May 1893, and was attached to the civilian staff at Brecon until his retirement on 20th May 1920. His eldest son, Tom, had been killed whilst serving with the South Wales Borderers in the Great War.

On 26th June 1920, he attended a garden party for holders of the VC, given by King George V and Queen Mary at Buckingham Palace. He also attended the VC dinner in 1929 with Reynolds.

After his wife Elizabeth died, he went to live with his daughter at 28 Cocker Avenue, Cwmbran. On 24th November 1932, he took his daily walk to the house of his other daughter at Tycoch. Whilst there he became ill and died of heart failure on the following morning. He left four grown-up children.

His impressive funeral cortège was half-a-mile long, and there was a place of honour in the procession for survivors of the Zulu War. Among them

Left: *John Fielding VC enlisted under the name of Williams because he did not want to be traced. He served with The South Wales Borderers until 1920. As a result of the horrific experience he went through in the hospital at Rorke's Drift his hair went white while he was still a young man.*

was John Jobbins who lived in the nearby village of Pontnewynydd. Relatives of Fred Hitch and Harry Hook sent floral tributes, as did Colonel Bourne and the survivors of the Rorke's Drift garrison. He was buried with full military honours in St Michael's Roman Catholic Churchyard, Llantarnum. Later the South Wales Borderers erected a gravestone to his memory and a residential home for the mentally handicapped in Llantarnum was named after him. His Victoria Cross is with the Regimental Museum.

Pte Joseph Williams had worked at the Cordes Dos Works in Newport, prior to enlisting at Monmouth on the day after John Williams, and they were posted to the battalion together. He is mentioned in the citations for the VC awards to Hook and Williams, and his name appears on the monument at Rorke's Drift. It is almost certain that he would have received the VC himself if he had survived, and it is perhaps an injustice that he was overlooked when the rules for the award were changed in 1907.

Below: *On 26 June 1920 John Fielding was among the 324 holders of the Victoria Cross who marched to Buckingham Palace to attend the first reunion garden party as guests of King George V and Queen Mary. Here, members of the royal family and the military look on as a veteran is presented to the Queen.*

Pte William Jones VC was discharged in 1880 with chronic rheumatism. He appeared at 'Hamilton's Pansterorama' in Rochdale Civic Hall during the 1880s, and in 1887/88 he toured with Buffalo Bill Cody. But by 1893 he was destitute and was forced to sell his Victoria Cross.

WILLIAM JONES was born in 1839, probably in Evesham, Worcestershire, but possibly in Bristol. His father, James, was in the building trade and he worked in the footwear business before enlisting in Birmingham on 21st December 1858. He was 5 feet 5 inches tall and had a sallow complexion, with brown eyes and hair.

He served on Mauritius, where he was promoted to Corporal in 1859, but he was reduced to Private on 4th September 1860. He then went to Burma where he re-engaged at Rangoon on 10th January 1868. He sailed with his battalion to South Africa and his wife, Elizabeth, went with him. While he was serving in the Frontier War she became ill in childbirth, and he obtained leave to look after her. He worked at repairing footwear to pay for a few comforts for her before she died. He returned to his regiment immediately after her burial.

For his conduct at Rorke's Drift he was mentioned in despatches, and was awarded the Victoria Cross. He was found to be suffering from chronic rheumatism in September 1879, and was invalided to England. He was invited to Windsor Castle, and on 13th January 1880, Queen Victoria decorated

him in the lobby there. He was discharged from Netley on 2nd February 1880, as unfit for further service and he went to live in Birmingham.

He re-married, and with the five children he had from his first marriage, he moved to Rutland Street, Chorlton-on-Medlock, Manchester. He toured with Buffalo Bill's Wild West Show in the 1880s and occasionally appeared on the theatre stage in Rochdale to recite an account of the defence. Sadly, he eventually hit on hard times and he was forced to pawn his VC for five pounds in 1893 to feed his family, and then he had to sell the pawn ticket. He began to suffer ill health towards the end of his life. His mind would wander and he began to have nightmares that the Zulus were going to attack. He sometimes took his grand-daughter from her bed and would leave the house in the middle of the night with her in his arms. In 1912 an impoverished old man with a white goatee beard was found wandering the streets, and had to be collected from Bridge Street Workhouse.

He died at the house of his daughter, 6 Brampton Street, Ardwick, on the evening of 15th April 1913,

The resting place of a Rorke's Drift hero in a Manchester cemetery. The 'VC' engraving was added in 1983 but the plot has since grown over.

leaving his wife, Elizabeth, and seven children. A large crowd witnessed his funeral cortège as it made its way to Philips Park cemetery, Bradford, Manchester, where he was buried with full military honours. The helmet that he wore during the defence had been placed on the coffin. His family were poor at that time and he was put in a public grave, with no mention of his Victoria Cross. But this was put right in 1983, and in 1985 a plaque was put on the wall of the cemetery church to commemorate his burial. His VC turned up in Preston in the 1930s and his family tried to buy it back. It is now with the Regimental museum.

ROBERT JONES, a Welsh country boy, was born at Clytha, near Raglan in Monmouthshire, on 19th August 1857. He was a farm labourer like his father, who was displeased when, on 10th January 1876, he enlisted at Monmouth. He was 5 feet 7½ inches tall, with a fresh complexion, grey eyes and brown hair.

He served in the Frontier War, and for his conduct at Rorke's Drift he was mentioned in despatches, and was awarded the Victoria Cross. He received the medal from Lord Wolseley at Utrecht on 11th September 1879. His service in South Africa left him with one bullet and four assegai wounds. He also received a medal for South Africa (clasp 1877-78-79).

He moved to Gibraltar and then served at Secunderabad, India, 1880-81, before returning to the depot at Brecon. He married at Llantilio in January 1885. He had been transferred to the army reserve in 1883, and after being recalled, he was discharged from the army reserve on 26th January 1888.

He went with his family to live at Peterchurch, near Hereford, where he worked as a labourer for a retired Major. He owned a piece of land in the nearby village of St Margaret's. He had been wounded close to his eyes and this sometimes caused him to have pains in the head. In August 1898 he collapsed at work and was never the same person again. On the morning of 6th September 1898 his wife, Elizabeth, noticed him acting wildly before going to work. When he got there he borrowed the Major's gun and two cartridges and walked off into the garden. He was never seen alive again. Next day a jury decided that he had been temporarily insane, and returned a verdict of suicide while of unsound mind.

He was a good father to his five children and he had been a talented amateur poet. He was given a

Pte Robert Jones VC never really escaped from Rorke's Drift and died in tragic circumstances. On 6 September 1898, aged 41, he placed the muzzle of a loaded rifle in his mouth and pulled the trigger.

modest military funeral, and some members of his old regiment brought a beautiful wreath. A fine marble headstone marks the place where he was buried in St Peter's churchyard. His Victoria Cross is the only one of 'B' Company that is still in the hands of a private collector.

JOHN CANTWELL was born in Dublin in 1845. He enlisted into the 9th (Norfolk) Regt in November 1868, and was transferred to the Royal Artillery in 1872. He joined the 5th Brigade in July 1877 and arrived at the Cape with it in January 1878. He was promoted to Bombardier Wheeler in July 1878, but he was reverted to Gunner on the day before the defence. For his conduct at Rorke's Drift he was awarded the Distinguished Conduct Medal in February 1880. He was discharged from Woolwich on 19th July 1889 as medically unfit and went to live in Natal. The whereabouts of his medal is not known.

APPENDIX A

Decorations Awarded to the Defenders of Rorke's Drift

VICTORIA CROSS

Royal Engineers
Lt John Rouse Merriott Chard

24th (2nd Warwickshire) Regt
Lt Gonville Bromhead
1240 Cpl William Wilson Allan
1362 Pte Frederick Hitch
1373 Pte Alfred Henry Hook
716 Pte Robert Jones
593 Pte William Jones
1393 Pte John Williams

Army Hospital Corps
Surgeon James Henry Reynolds BA MB ChB (Dublin)

Commissariat and Transport Department
Assistant Commissariat Officer James Langley Dalton

Natal Native Contingent
Cpl Ferdnand Christian Schiess

DISTINGUISHED CONDUCT MEDAL

24th (2nd Warwickshire) Regt
2459 Colour-Sgt Frank Bourne
1542 Pte William Roy

Royal Horse Artillery
2076 Gunner John Cantwell

Army Service Corps
24692 2nd Cpl Francis Attwood

APPENDIX B

Casualties at Rorke's Drift

According to the official figures there were twenty-five casualties. But the medical report of twenty-seven is more likely. And many men had slight wounds that were not officially reported.

1st Battalion, 24th Regiment

1861	Pte William Horrigan	killed in action
841	Pte James Jenkins	killed in action
625	Pte Edward Nicholson	killed in action
135	Pte William Beckett	died of wounds
568	Pte Patrick Desmond	slightly wounded
447	Pte John Waters	severely wounded

2nd Battalion, 24th Regiment

623	Sgt Robert Maxfield	killed in action
987	Pte John Adams	killed in action
1335	Pte James Chick	killed in action
801	Pte Thomas Cole	killed in action
969	Pte John Fagan	killed in action
1769	Pte Garrett Hayden	killed in action
1051	Pte John Scanlon	killed in action
1398	Pte Joseph Williams	killed in action
1328	Lance-Sgt Thomas Williams	died of wounds
1240	Cpl William Allan	severely wounded
1112	Cpl John Lyons	dangerously wounded
1362	Pte Frederick Hitch	dangerously wounded
716	Pte Robert Jones	slightly wounded
1812	Pte William Tasker	slightly wounded

Commissariat and Transport Department

Acting Storekeeper Louis Byrne	killed in action
Commissariat Officer James Dalton	severely wounded

Natal Mounted Police

Trooper Sydney Hunter	killed in action

Natal Native Contingent

Cpl Michael Anderson	killed in action
Pte Xhosa native	killed in action
Cpl Carl Scammel	dangerously wounded
Cpl Friedrich Schiess	slightly wounded

BIBLIOGRAPHY OF RESEARCH AND REFERENCE MATERIAL

ATTWOOD, Sgt F: Letter from Rorke's Drift dated 25th January 1879. Royal Corps of Transport Museum.

BOURNE, Lt-Col F: Article in 'The Listener' for 30th December 1936, taken from his radio broadcast ten days earlier.

CHARD, Lt J R M: Official report dated 25th January 1879. Published in newspapers in March 1879, and in The Royal Engineers' Journal for August 1879. An account submitted to Queen Victoria on 21st February 1880. The Silver Wreath.

CLARKE, Lt-Col W J; NMP: 'My Career in South Africa'. The Killie Campbell Library.

DUNNE, Lt-Col W A: 'Reminiscences of Campaigning in South Africa. 1877-81'. The Army Service Corps Journal (The Waggoner), for February 1892. Royal Corps of Transport Museum.

EMERY, F: 'The Red Soldier', London 1977.

FYNN, H F: 'My Recollections of a Famous Campaign'. The Natal Witness, 22nd January 1913.

HALL, R: Letter to The Natal Witness c 1906. Killie Campbell.

HALLAM-PARR, Cpt H: 'A Sketch of the Kaffir and Zulu Wars'.

HAMILTON-BROWNE, Col G: 'A Lost Legionary in South Africa'.

HARFORD, Col H: 'Zulu War Journal' of Col Henry Harford CB. Edited by Daphne Child. Pietermaritzburg, 1978.

HITCH, Pte F: Interview at Netley Hospital, published in 'The Cambrian' newspaper, Swansea, 13th June 1879.
    An Original account held by the South Wales Borderers Museum.

HOLME, N: 'The Silver Wreath. Being the 24th Regiment at Isandhlwana and Rorke's Drift, 1879'. London 1979.

HOOK, Pte A H: 'How They Held Rorke's Drift'. Published in The Royal Magazine for February 1905.
    His account in the Strand Magazine, 1891.

HOWARD, A: Letter in the Daily Telegraph, 25th March, 1879. J. M. – Natal Volunteer: 'Reminiscences of the Zulu War'. The Natal Witness – Killie Campbell Library.

JOBBINS, J: Letter from Rorke's Drift, published in the Hereford Times, 29th March 1879. The Red Soldier.

JONES, Pte R: His account in the Strand Magazine, 1891.

JONES, W: Account in his obituary in the Manchester Evening News, 16th April 1913.
    His account in the Strand Magazine, 1891.

LABAND, J: 'Fight Us in the Open', Pietermaritzburg, 1985.

LONDON GAZETTE for 1879: Including VC citations dated 2nd May; 17th June; 17th November; and 29th November.

LUGG, H: Letter in the North Devon Herald Supplement, 24th April 1879.

LUGG, H C: 'A Natal Family Looks Back', Durban, 1970.

LUMMIS, Canon W: 'Padre George Smith of Rorke's Drift', Norwich, 1978.

LYONS, Cpl J: Interview at Netley, published in 'The Cambrian' newspaper, Swansea, 13th June 1879.

MASON, C: Letter from Rorke's Drift to his family in London. Dated 8th February 1879. National Army Museum.

MITFORD, B: 'Through the Zulu Country', London, 1883.

MORRIS, D: 'The Washing of the Spears', New York, 1965.

NORRIS-NEWMAN, C: 'In Zululand with the British throughout the Zulu War of 1879', London, 1880.

ORCHARD, G E: Letter from Rorke's Drift dated 29th January 1879, to his brother in Bedminster, Bristol, published in the Bristol Observer, 29th March, 1879.

PATON, G; GLENNIE, F; PENN-SYMONS, W: 'Historical Records of the 24th Regiment', London, 1892.

PENN-SYMONS, Capt W: Report written in 1879. The South Wales Borderers Museum, Brecon.

REYNOLDS, Surgeon-Major J H: Report to the Army Hospital's Dept. 1878-79. The Royal Army Medical Corps Journal.

SAVAGE, Pte E: Interview on his return to Brecon, 16th July 1879. Published in The Manchester Weekly Post, 19th July 1879.

SMITH, Rev G: Report dated 3rd February 1879. The Royal Army Chaplain's Department Journal for July 1936.

SMITH, Sgt G: Letter from Rorke's Drift dated 24th January 1879. Brecon County Times – The Red Soldier.

SMITH-DORRIEN, Gen H: 'Memories of Forty-Eight Years' Service', London, 1925.

SYMONS, J P: 'Reminiscences of the Zulu War', by a Natal Carbineer. Natal Witness – Killie Campbell Library.

WAR OFFICE PAPERS: Including 'The Narrative of the Field Operations connected with the Zulu War of 1879'. Published by the Intelligence Branch in 1881, and reprinted in 1907.

WATERS, Pte J: Interview at Netley Hospital, published in 'The Cambrian' newspaper, Swansea, 13th June 1879.

WILLIAMS, W A: 'The VC's of Wales and the Welsh Regiments', Wrexham, 1984.

WITT, Rev O: Statement given at Bramhall Hall in Cheshire in 1879.

Index

AFRICAN BANTU

BRITAIN

BRITISH AND COLONIAL FORCES

Index

ACKNOWLEDGEMENTS

The Public Records Office, Kew.
The British Library Newspaper Library, Colindale.
The Killie Campbell Africana Library, Durban.
The Natal Archives Depot, Pietermaritzburg.
The Natal Midlands Branch of the Geneological Society of South Africa, Pietermaritzburg.
The National Army Museum, Chelsea.
The Imperial War Museum, London.
The South Wales Borderers Regimental Museum, Brecon.
The Royal Engineers Museum, Chatham.
The Royal Corps of Transport Regimental Museum, Aldershot.
The Royal Army Medical Corps Historical Museum, Aldershot.
The British Broadcasting Corporation.
The Staff of Manchester Central Library, Eccles Public Library, and various other libraries
in Britain and South Africa.

Picture research was through Military Archive & Research Services, Braceborough, Lincolnshire.
The publishers and researchers would like to thank the following individuals and organisations
who kindly furnished illustrations for this book.

Reproduced by gracious permission of Her Majesty the Queen – Copyright reserved: p48, 84-85, 129b,
130, 136, 144, 149, 153, 154t.
J Bancroft: p39, 44, 53, 58-59, 61, 78t, 126, 132-133, 134, 139, 154b.
BBC Hulton Picture Library: p11, 13, 50-51, 80, 90-91, 98-99b, 102-103, 112-113, 156-157.
The Buffs and Canterbury Royal Museums: p21t.
H E R Bunting: p142, 143.
Gateshead Central Library: p122-123, 138.
Canon W Lummis: p125.
Killie Campbell Africana Library: p6-7, 12, 24-25b, 27, 31b, 36-37, 38, 52, 81, 92, 93, 97, 98-99t, 110,
146, 148.
Lancashire Library Services: p124.
J Maber Collection: p16.
Military Archive & Research Services: p8, 9, 22-23, 29, 32, 35, 66, 67, 72-73, 88tl, 103, 111, 114-115,
117, 119, 120-121, 131, 132, 137r.
National Army Museum: p2-3, 10, 17, 18-19, 21b, 24-25t, 26-27, 28, 30, 31t, 33, 34, 45, 46, 56, 82,
100-101, 104-105, 106-107, 108-109, 114, 116, 118, 127b, 135, 137.
The Royal Army Medical Corps Historical Museum: p87t, 129t.
The Sherwood Foresters Museum: p23, 94-95.
The South Wales Borderers & Monmouthshire Regimental Museum: p86, 87b, 88b, 140, 141, 145, 152,
155.
Spinks & Company: p88tr.
The Regimental Museum of the Royal Corps of Transport: p127t, 128.
C Wilkinson-Latham: p76, 78b.